Praise for 1

"'Mr Recruitment International' is how I think of Greg Savage. We have both been in the business most of our working lives, but I can truly say I have never met a person more passionate and genuinely in love with recruitment than Greg. His natural, infectious enthusiasm is captured perfectly in his book and, after reading it, you will want to follow the 'Pied Piper'."

Geoff Morgan AM, CEO, Suite Black Pty Ltd, Co-founder of Morgan & Banks and Talent2

"I loved this book. I think it's not only a great read for anyone remotely connected to recruitment or talent management, but it could also be regarded as a 'bible' for how to succeed in business. I, for one, will make this compulsory reading in my own organisation – it is exciting and inspirational."

Geoff Slade, Chairman, Slade Group and Past President RCSA

"Greg has found an artful way of blending his legacy, his passion for the recruitment sector and his commitment to remaining relevant in this book. He has chosen to share some deeply personal stories which provide the reader with a great insight into what made him the highly regarded leader he has become in our industry. He falsely claims in this book that he was a good, not a great recruiter, but I beg to disagree. The best recruiters I have met are those who bring their whole selves to work every day, and Greg has been bringing his whole self to our industry for the past four decades, and we thank him for sharing this rollercoaster ride with us in *The Savage Truth*."

Sinead Hourigan, QLD Director, Robert Walters and President at RCSA ANZ

"Informative and inspiring, a thoroughly entertaining read of an extraordinary life in recruitment from one who got it right."

Robert van Stokrom, CEO, DFP Recruitment, Past President and Fellow RCSA (life)

"What a great read... It's an honest, enlightening and entertaining account, full of wit and wisdom on how you rise to the top in a tough and competitive industry. It's packed with so many lessons and nuggets of gold on what to do and, importantly, what *not* to do as you navigate the ladder of success.

Failure is something most people hide from, but Greg reveals what it takes to rise and rise up again to a new level of success. It's inspiring, motivational and a must-read for anyone wondering what it takes to achieve success in business today."

Nigel Harse, FRCSA, Staffing Industry Metrics

"If you're a cricketer, you can read the biographies of legends of the game. If you're a budding chef, you can read the secrets hidden in recipes of masters of the past. Now recruiters have our own reference in this book of stories and secrets for leadership in business and the staffing industry."

Mark Smith, Group Managing Director, people2people

"To have such knowledge and commentary all captured in one document is very special. This book is a great read, written from the heart, with plenty of practical tips for those new to the industry, and a gentle nudge for those who have been around a while. I am confident you, like me, will be marking the pages you want to go back to again and again."

Julie Mills, Managing Director, APSCo Australia

"Without a doubt, every recruiter in the world should read this book, and take the lessons – of which there are many – and implement those lessons into their recruitment/search business.

The real genius of the book lies in the fact that Greg's brutal, honest and amusing stories about some of the mistakes he has made make it a must-read for anyone looking to grow their business."

Terry Edwards, Renegade Recruiter, makemoreplacements.com

"This book is long overdue. Greg is widely recognised as one of the recruitment industry's true global thought leaders. His book does not disappoint; it provides insight, guidance and practical advice to anyone who is leading a recruitment business, gained from Greg's wealth of experience as CEO, chair and non-executive director of multiple recruitment organisations.

I would recommend this book to anyone who wants to grow and develop their recruitment business. It's a must-read!"

Kevin Green, Former CEO of the Recruitment and Employment Confederation and best-selling author of *Competitive People Strategy*

Dedication

Forty years in a profession as quirky as recruitment brings you into contact with myriad great people. I thank them all for contributing to my exhilarating recruiting life.

But I dedicate this book to three wonderful people we have lost along the way.

Kristen Florance (Hambly), my PA, as a shy 19-year-old in her first job, supported, helped and saved me countless times for 12 years. She followed me without hesitation when we started Recruitment Solutions, despite the personal risk. She put up with my moods, tantrums, outrageous demands and put me in my place when required. After starting her family, she stayed connected to mine by partnering my wife in competition tennis for over a decade. I gave the speech at her 21st birthday, her wedding, her 50th birthday and, heartbreakingly, at her funeral. Kristin was a strong, warm, kind, sporting, humorous and exceptional woman. The most loving mother, the most loyal friend, who I will never forget.

Duncan Cunningham worked with me for 10 years at Aquent, opened the Hong Kong office, and then bravely moved to China to start our businesses there. A gentle, optimistic and kind man, a whisky-drinker, a song-singer and the most loyal of colleagues. He called me 'Mr Savage' all those years, not sarcastically, and not in deference either, but it was just his way of showing respect and familiarity at the same time. He left us suddenly, shockingly, and far too young. I think about him often.

Maria Mexis was one of the five people who sat at the desk the day people2people opened in 2005, and she was exactly the person you wanted on your team in trying times. A natural recruiter with a powerful work ethic, she was tenacious, loyal, passionate, incredibly resilient and a top producer, and so much loved by the people2people family. Also sadly lost to us at a tragically young age.

To these three, their families and friends, who live every day with the loss, I dedicate this book.

After all, what is a career, indeed a life, if not for the people who were with you on the journey?

The
Savage
Truth

Lessons in leadership, business and
life from 40 years in recruitment

GREG SAVAGE

First published in 2020 by Major Street Publishing Pty Ltd
PO Box 106, Highett, Vic. 3190 E: info@majorstreet.com.au
W: majorstreet.com.au M: +61 421 707 983

Quantity sales. Special discounts are available on quantity purchases by corporations, associations and others. For details, contact Lesley Williams using the contact details above.

Individual sales. Major Street publications are available through most bookstores. They can also be ordered directly from Major Street's online bookstore at www.majorstreet.com.au.

Orders for university textbook/course adoption use. For orders of this nature, please contact Lesley Williams using the contact details above.

The moral rights of the author have been asserted.

A catalogue record for this book is available from the National Library of Australia.

NATIONAL LIBRARY OF AUSTRALIA

ISBN: 978-0-6485159-7-5

Cover design by Simone Geary
Internal design by Production Works
Printed in Australia by Ovato, an Accredited ISO AS/NZS 14001:2004
Environmental Management System Printer.

10 9 8 7 6 5 4 3 2 1

About the author

GREG SAVAGE started his career in Executive Search in Australia, before he went on to manage the London office of the United Kingdom's largest accounting recruiter for two years. In the early eighties, he returned to Australia to run the Sydney office of Accountancy Placements (now the Hays Group), where he was invited to join the board of directors at age 27.

With two others, Greg founded Recruitment Solutions in 1987, and rapidly built the start-up across Australia and New Zealand, culminating in its successful listing on the Australian Stock Exchange, with Greg as both Executive Director and COO.

In April 2001, Greg joined Aquent and, as International CEO, assumed responsibility for all Aquent businesses outside of North America, which then comprised more than 25 offices in 17 countries across Europe, Asia and ANZ.

In 2010, Greg acquired the Permanent and Search business of Aquent in a management buyout and founded Firebrand Talent Search. He quickly created a global brand for this specialist digital and marketing recruiter, and successfully sold the business, in seven countries, in January 2013.

In recognition of his contribution to the Australian recruitment industry, Greg was made an Honorary Life Member of the Recruitment and Consulting Services Association (RCSA) in 2004.

In 2011, he was awarded a special commendation by the RCSA for "Outstanding Contribution to the Recruitment Industry", was named the most influential Australian business person on Twitter in 2016, and the most influential recruiter in Australia in the past 60 years in 2015.

In 2018, Greg was inducted into the Recruiter International Hall of Fame.

In November 2018, he was named one of LinkedIn's 'Top Voices'. An early adopter of social media for recruiting, Greg's industry blog, The Savage Truth, is a must-read in the recruitment industry.

Greg now acts as a non-executive director for 14 recruitment and HR tech companies in Australia, Singapore and New Zealand and provides consulting, advisory and training services to recruitment, professional services and social media companies across the world.

Contents

Foreword

PEOPLE LISTEN to Greg Savage. We listen because he is authentic. We listen because he is a storyteller. We listen because his truth is the truth we need.

I remember it vividly. I was hosting an RCSA leadership event in Auckland for recruitment professionals in 2017. Greg offered to drop in to watch, listen and contribute to the development of our future leaders. I had not asked, nobody had asked, it was just a quiet, unassuming offer from the most in-demand recruitment speaker on the planet! I had, of course, heard Greg present before but, on this day, it was different. Greg had a new story to tell, a personal story, a story of reflection, a story of life, a story of meaning. Greg's willingness to share, in this way, genuinely moved me and I am personally more giving as a result. But, that's what Greg Savage does, he changes you.

The Savage Truth opens the door on a businessman, an influencer and a leader but, most importantly, it tells the story of a man who has a gift for sharing. In the world of business and recruitment, we all want to know more about what has made Greg so successful, and in this book we are provided with the answers. From his formative years growing up in South Africa, and the development of his business acumen in London, right through to the development of global-brand Savage, we learn what it takes to take the lead.

However, this is not just a biography. *The Savage Truth* is a playbook for managers, leaders, business owners and we who aspire to be successful. The inherent value of this book is found in its ability to provide practical, workable, guidance on how to take the complex and make it simple, relatable and executable. And, let's face it, that is what Greg Savage does. That is his true gift.

Read this book. Read it again and never put it away. *The Savage Truth* is the truth we need.

Charles Cameron, Chief Executive Officer,
RCSA Australia & New Zealand

PART I
A recruitment journey — from Africa to the world

According to the greatest recruitment cliché of all, most recruiters 'fall into' the industry. It's a career that few seek, and even fewer stay working in long term.

The second biggest recruiting cliché is that the industry has low barriers to entry which, while mostly accurate, fails to highlight the fact that it has even *lower barriers to exit!* And exit recruiters do, in their thousands – sometimes willingly, but often in shock with just a few minutes warning, ruing unmet 'targets'.

So, I guess it's fair to say that my 40-year recruitment career is rare. Rarer still is the quirky fact that I have only *ever* worked in recruitment: placing people, managing recruiters, owning recruitment businesses, and now advising and investing in them.

That is more than unusual. It's unheard of.

Fresh out of university in 1980, I embarked on a career that is now into its fifth decade, encompassing dozens of countries, surviving multiple recessions, riding mindboggling technology disruption, and enduring significant life changes.

Often people ask what it is about my background that has equipped me for such longevity (and reasonable success from time to time) in a business that few would describe as 'cushy'. Was I born to do this? Is it just in the DNA? Or was it a cocktail of upbringing and education that perfectly prepared me for the business few survive in for more than a handful of years?

Thus, in this first part of *The Savage Truth* I tell my story, starting at the beginning. This requires me to face the unfamiliar task of introspection, to try to find clues to what attracted me to recruitment, and drove me to love it as I do.

It all began in South Africa…

CHAPTER 1

Gazing at Mandela

I WAS born in Cape Town into a happy family, in a deeply unhappy country under the yoke of apartheid. Our family home in Camps Bay was situated just a brisk walk around the beach road to a view of Robben Island, prison to Nelson Mandela for 18 years.

However, such was the information control of the white-only government at that time, it wasn't until I reached university at age 18 that I first heard the name Nelson Mandela and, even then, it was only ever uttered in hushed tones. Under the bizarre restrictions of the time, Mandela was a 'banned person', 'banning' being a repressive extrajudicial measure used by the racist South African apartheid regime (1948–1994) against its political opponents.

The University of Cape Town (UCT), a beacon of relative liberal thinking in a country deep in a state of repressive racist laws, opened my worldview to a more inquiring, liberal narrative than I had yet experienced beyond the talk around my family table. This fortunate mix of family values and outspoken anti-apartheid ethos at UCT balanced the pervasive influence of state-controlled propaganda and the almost total absence of public debate about the inhuman status quo that existed at that time.

Stable, comfortable… and unfettered

I was lucky enough to have a very stable upbringing; middle class, not extravagant in any way. However, we wanted for little, especially in comparison to the vast majority of South Africans at that time.

Children were brought up differently then. Parental supervision was scant, a fraction of what it is today. I roamed our suburb freely, from what seems like the moment I was first able to walk.

We wandered down to the beach to surf and catch fish off the rocks, clambered up the slopes of Table Mountain, which loomed above our suburb, and went into the glen adjacent to our house to throw stones at other local boys. We lit fires, gathered pine nuts for our afternoon feast and hung around the 'cafe' (corner store) swapping soccer cards and borrowing a few cents off each other for chewing gum. I remember breaking into the scout hall where I had my first cigarette in the cellar.

We played cricket on the street until dark – the rule was that if you hit a parked car on the full, you were 'out'. When a moving vehicle rounded Willesden Road, it was the wicket-keeper's job to grab the stumps, an apple crate, and set it up again when the danger had passed. We also spent hour after hour in the backyard playing soccer, with a complex set of rules about which trees were actual players and which were the corner flags.

We had no TV. (The rest of Africa did, but the rest of Africa was not run by a white minority anxious to control all thought; Rhodesia aside, of course.) And there certainly wasn't any internet.

With both parents out at work, we were rich in time and poor on supervision. This taught us to be resilient, to build independence and a sense of savvy that enabled us to work things out and amuse ourselves.

We learned how to manage friendships and friction in equal measure. Indeed, for me, there was no intervention from my parents, not unless there was a crisis. More often than not, they wouldn't even know where we were most of the day. So, you fought your own battles and dealt with things alone.

Don't get me wrong; my parents were hugely involved and very supportive in our lives. Both were mentors and confidantes when required. However, they didn't hover. So, you stood up for yourself and you made it work. I do believe this must have shaped my personality somewhat – it's a clue to the resilience I have had to show during the last 40 years or so.

Family support on the big things was strong, but no one was going to fight your petty battles and, if you got roughed up a little on the street or in the park, it didn't occur to you to tell your parents because you deserved it, right?

I think those years defined for me what I now consider 'weak' behaviour.

Crying in a sad movie is not weak. (I do it all the time.) Compassion when another person is down, or hits misfortune, is not weak. Feeling guilty and on the verge of tears because you broke up with your girlfriend and you know she is hurting, is not weak (I'm proud of son number one on that score, actually). Nerves and self-doubt on big occasions is not weak. Saying sorry for a mistake is not weak. Admitting you are wrong is not weak. Suffering mental health issues is not weak.

Blaming everyone else for your shortcomings is weak. (Son number two learned my views on that when it was always due to an umpiring mistake that he was out, never his actual batting. That's fixed, by the way.) Giving up without giving 100% of what you have is weak. Undermining and gossiping out of jealousy is weak.

So while this lack of direct or constant parental supervision helped shape me, without a doubt one of the greatest influences in my life was (and still is) my father Ron. I am certain my siblings would agree, he shaped a lot of how we think and behave.

Major Ron Savage

Born in the East End of London, my father left school at the tender age of 15 and not many years later was sent to Asia with the British Army.

After the disastrous defeat and surrender of the British forces in Singapore in 1942, my father – along with more than 15,000 British and Australian prisoners – was captured by the Japanese and held as a prisoner of war in horrific conditions at the infamous

Changi POW camp. Then began three years of privation and the most horrendous torture and brutality. Changi was notorious for its harsh treatment of the men who were imprisoned there – of whom only a fraction survived. Few of my father's friends and fellow soldiers emerged alive at the end of the war.

Ron was severely injured in the defence of Singapore and, with his leg practically hanging by a thread, he was shipped off to the British Military Hospital, Singapore. On 14 February 1942, the 18th division of the Japanese Imperial Army rushed into the wards and operating theatres and bayonetted a total of 250 patients and staff.

Luckily for Ron, before they could repeat such brutality throughout his ward, an officer ordered them to assemble in the hospital grounds. Ron was subjected to the taunts of soldiers, who amused themselves by pulling on his traction ropes, but he survived.

He went on to spend six months recovering on a stretcher in a Changi hut, his injured mates on either side; Roy Cross to the left and Tubby Allen to the right. It was in that relentless hell-hole that the trio began to fantasise about what they would do 'when the war was over'.

Roy was of the view that Africa was the future. His father had a business in South Africa, and he suggested that Ron should join him after the war and start a new life in sunnier southern climes. Tubby believed Asia was a better bet, particularly Malaya, where he saw a post-war rubber boom. He wanted Ron to join him in Perak and start a rubber plantation.

They talked and talked. But as Ron revealed to me later, they never really believed they would outlive Changi, their discussions simply providing a much-needed distraction, rather than concrete plans. Incredibly, all three survived the war.

The story behind how my father then went on to live in South Africa is fascinating and has become a strong part of our family folklore. However, it has also always lingered at the back of my mind as a life lesson, particularly when I am faced with having to make decisions.

In 1945, Ron returned to London and his East End neighbourhood. German bombing in the Blitz had flattened it, the country was in ruins – and under rationing – and the future looked bleak at best.

While considering his options, a telegram arrived from Roy Cross.

"Come to Johannesburg. Job waiting."

A week later, Tubby was also in touch.

"Got job in Malaya. Spot here for you. Come at once."

Ron knew Europe was not for him. He was a proud Englishman – he'd literally given blood for the cause – but he knew the time had come for a new life elsewhere.

With two firm job offers, albeit scant on detail, it was time for him to decide. It's poignant to remember that this was a time of no internet, no comfort of jumping online for a bit of background research – it was merely a matter of trusting your gut and going with it.

After talking with his parents and friends, Ron decided he would take himself to the pub for one last think. Blitz bombing had devastated the area around Forest Gate where he grew up, so he caught a bus into the West End. A few mates joined him and the conversation raged. South Africa or Malaya? Which job should he take?

In the end, it was agreed that the toss of a coin would determine his fate. And so it was – on that night, at the pub, the decision would be made.

The coin came down. Heads. South Africa.

Ron left the pub, returned home and began to pack.

I have to say I am glad he did. A year later he met my mum in Johannesburg, and together they moved to Cape Town, where my three siblings and I were born and grew up.

Naturally, a story like this would stand tall in any family history, but for me it goes far beyond that. It's influenced the way I think. My mantra is to be brave, act and always work hard to ensure the decision you make turns out to be the right one.

This is not to say that I don't think through important decisions, or that I don't have moments of crippling doubt. I do, and I do move with caution. But often you have to leap, and certainly with businesses I have started, the offices I have opened and people I have hired… I haven't always been 100% sure, but have gone ahead and done it anyway.

For the most part, it has worked out just fine.

Ron didn't really have a plan. But he had a cast-iron character, and he had energy and drive. He was a do-er. And I would like to think that I am just a little like him.

Boarding at Bishops

One of the most significant decisions my parents made was to send me to Bishops (Diocesan College) in Cape Town. It's been one of the greatest influences on my character, and indeed my career in recruitment.

Bishops is one of the most highly regarded schools in the country and is based on the British public school system. It is 170 years old and is steeped in sporting and academic tradition, producing countless sporting, political, business and cultural icons across three centuries of South African history. However, it was undoubtedly a major impost on my parents. It's an expensive school – certainly one of the costliest in South Africa.

My father, the shoe rep, sent all four of us to private schools. There's no doubt that it would have been far more comfortable for my parents to choose not to pay for our education. While I didn't see it at the time, the sacrifices they made to fund our schooling were huge. I do remember sensing a whole new chapter begin as I was dropped at the school just a few days after I turned 13.

I was not wrong. Although highly regarded, Bishops in the 1970s was old-school in every way you might imagine. (If you're a parent reading this, you will likely cringe as I recall the horrors of initiation for the new boys…) For instance, there was 'running the gauntlet', which required us newcomers to push a tin of shoe polish down the dormitory, with our noses, while the older boys beat us with pillows and wet towels or, if they chose, cricket bats and hockey sticks.

I can still picture being forced to stand on a massive metal clothes locker with a blanket over the top of it, singing 'Winchester Cathedral' to the tune of 'Georgie Girl'. (Try it.) If you faltered, the 'rug was pulled' – literally, sending you cascading to the ground from a height of over a metre, much to the joy of a pack of jeering older, intimidating boys.

There was no staff intervention. It was a 'Lord of the Flies' environment in many respects, and the older boys held power exclusively. To this day, I ponder the truth that often the boys most bullied as newcomers became the even bigger bullies themselves as the wheel turned and the next victims came through.

Of course, in many respects the mental and verbal barbs far outweighed the physical. I thankfully suffered the least of it, but I do remember the very first night at boarding school when the main body of students arrived (we new boys got there a day early for orientation). We lay quivering in our beds, listening to the racket of the older boys settling in.

I can't begin to describe how eerie it is to hear the sound of your name spilling into the dark over and over...

"Savage, Savage, Savage..."

The older boys had surveyed the nametags on the new boys' lockers and, of course, had quickly latched on to a 'scum' of a new boy with the audacity to have a name as bold as 'Savage'. There was no question – it had to be beaten out of him.

So, my first year at Bishops was tough. You find in those situations that some do rise to the top, or at least survive, while others don't.

I won't lie. Some boys left. We had at least two attempted suicides that I can recall over the years (although, tragically, that number is far lower than my sons have experienced among their cohort in this more enlightened era, so it's hard to reconcile).

Boarding at Bishops was hardcore, especially at 'White House', as the punishments meted out by my fellow students were added to by the staff. There was zero tolerance for non-compliance, and nowhere to hide if you wanted to take a shortcut.

Cold showers and beatings were imposed for minor indiscretions. I held the house record while I was there: 44 strokes in my first year, all administered by the austere Mr Hunt. I often wonder if my tally has since been surpassed.

Detentions, gardening duty or a run around the Rondebosch Common were often prescribed for a little bit of toughening up. *"Fifty push-ups right now, Savage", "You are gated for the weekend", "Report to Mr Hunt in the morning..."*

Yet, here is the weird thing. I loved my five years at Bishops, although perhaps not so much the first year.

After two years there I had the opportunity to transfer to be a day boy. My family only lived 30 minutes away. The day boy life was a doddle in comparison to boarding, plus you got to go home to Mum every night. However, I turned it down – even though I loved my Mum. I had my 'family' at school by then. I was a boarder!

I don't condone the rituals of initiation and fagging that took place at Bishops. Indeed, only a few years later the school rightfully stamped it all out. Frankly, if you asked me would I have sent my own darling boys to the Bishops that I knew, my answer would be a resounding *"no"*. There's far too much risk that they could have ended up in the 'sink', rather than the 'swim', group.

Despite all that, I thrived at Bishops and I am grateful that I went there. We learned to cope, learned to deal with conflict and stress, learned the hard way that the world is simply not always 'fair', and not least we learned collaboration and teamwork. It instilled in me a need to do a job well because at Bishops that was the only way anything was done.

I developed a sense of loyalty to my team, house and school which, while it may have bordered on the fanatical at times, bred values of commitment and loyalty that I think have stuck with me to this day. Giving up was not an option, and you were never offered the easy way out. The expectation was to do the hard work, bring your talent, and together the two would prevail. So I learned to be organised and to get things done.

Leadership skills were also honed at Bishops for those who grabbed opportunities. At the age of 15, I led a group of five across the Cederberg mountains, with a map, water and carrying our food. We saw no one for an entire week while we navigated our way through the harsh South African bush. While there are no lions in that part of the Cape Province, there are certainly baboons, leopards, snakes, scorpions and cliffs.

So much more than soccer

Bishops made progress in social awareness too. This was the apartheid era. If you never lived through that, it's hard to describe how pervasive and insidious it actually was. Races were kept apart in every single way. I went to primary school on a 'whites only' bus. It was marked clearly on the front, next to the destination.

That was just the surface of the racist mindset that controlled every aspect of your life, and not for the better if you were not 'white'. Yet, Bishops was teaching tolerance and generosity and our responsibility to the underprivileged, who in apartheid South Africa were mostly black.

The laws of the land meant much was forbidden. Bishops was a rugby school through and through and has produced dozens of Springboks. Three Bishops old boys played in the 2003 Rugby World Cup. (One for Australia, one for England and one for South Africa. At Bishops we share the love.) I also remember our renegade, ragtag and highly unofficial soccer team organising matches with teams from the townships segregated for blacks.

We travelled into those townships where we played and were greeted with friendship and warmth. We had tea and scones with the black and 'coloured' players and families afterward.

It seems such a banal story to tell today, but at that time our actions were bordering on treason. These matches opened my eyes to a world most white South Africans either ignored or were ignorant of. It was Bishops that promoted such open-minded thinking, through the Social Responsibility Society, of which I was a member.

Lessons – and friends – for life

Indeed, Bishops had so much to offer if you grabbed the opportunities. Team sport, especially in my case, helped shape my work ethic, and my sense of team, but it was theatre and debating that sparked my enjoyment and confidence in public speaking.

I have a strong memory of an evening in the Founders House dining room, where a debate was in progress. I was the last speaker for the affirmative team. As I ran out of my formal argument, I began to ad lib – cracking jokes, gently mocking the other side's argument. The room broke into waves of raucous laughter which spurred me on like an adrenaline shot. It was then that the audience began to literally cross the floor, to show support for the affirmative.

It was a powerful moment, still etched in my memory 45 years later – the notion of people literally moving, changing sides, shifting their opinion because of the power of words. I harnessed those lessons as I neared the end of my time at Bishops, and countless times since then.

In my Bishops school leaving report dated December 1975, my Housemaster described me as: *"…a forceful influence in the House, possessing considerable leadership potential. He is imaginative, quick witted and clearheaded."* These sound like excellent recruiter attributes to me!

The headmaster, the terrifying Mr Mallet, wrote: *"He has displayed obvious qualities of leadership, always used for the good of others, and I have rarely come across a young man more devoted to the task of serving his house and school to the best of his ability."*

I was no superstar at school. Solid all-rounder would be my moniker. Yet, were these comments made about a 17-year-old a glimpse into how I ended up recruiting and leading for so long?

There were consequences for failure and a lack of effort. If there are three things I can say I gained during those years, which have impacted my business career, they are resilience, loyalty and optimism.

Also, of course, many friendships formed during those years at Bishops and most remain strong to this day. It was only in 2014 that I went back to South Africa, just to reunite with our house rugby team at our 40-year reunion! White House won the inter-house series in 1974, 7–6 in the final, with a try to win it in the last minute *(thank you for coming, School House!)*.

Thirteen of those 15 guys turned up. Most no longer lived in South Africa, so travelled a long way to be there, as had I. The banter and camaraderie clicked in after just a few minutes back together, despite some of us not seeing each other for 40 years. The bonds of teenage boarders are very tight indeed.

So, overall, Bishops was a liberal school in the context of South Africa at that time, and along with my parents' example it helped shape my views on fairness, discrimination and equality.

Loving university life

In 1976, after Bishops, I went to the University of Cape Town to do a degree in Social Science.

I studied hard enough to get a good degree, but I was also eagerly embracing rugby, parties, drinking, the beach, and Friday trips out to the Stellenbosch wineries, where Lanzerac was a favourite. Drinking and driving was the norm back then, it wasn't even something that was raised as an issue – I shudder to think about it now.

I also began to be more engaged in the South African political situation and took an active interest in political change and an alternative to apartheid. The Progressive Federal Party was the anti-apartheid party (within the framework of a whites only voting system!) led by Helen Suzman and Colin Eglin, who were icons at that time, offering the only white voices of resistance to the apartheid system.

I treasure to this day a letter from Eglin thanking me for my efforts in fighting apartheid. On 'Parliament of the Republic of South Africa' letterhead he wrote: *"The contribution you, and others like you, around the country have made... enabled the Progressive Federal party to emerge as the official opposition... the voters of South Africa will be presented with a clear alternative to the discriminatory race policies of the Nationalist government."*

He invited me and three other 'Young Progs' to lunch at the Parliament House Dining Room, which on reflection is extraordinary. Maybe he invited the wrong guy because to be fair my memory of my efforts is mainly putting up posters and ferrying elderly supporters to the polling booths on election day.

Learning on the job and making a (not so) tough decision

One of the most important experiences I had at university was my part-time job selling Cool & Light, an alternative to the drink Kool-Aid. My job was to travel from corner shop to corner shop, cold-selling to store owners, directly in the face of my dominant competitor.

It was a tough gig that took me to the 'coloured' suburbs of Kuils River, Bonteheuwel, Manenberg, Athlone and many others scattered across the Cape Flats. All South Africans lived under the confines of the 'Group Areas Act' at that time. These three Acts of Parliament, enacted under the apartheid government, assigned racial groups to different residential areas in a system of urban apartheid or 'separate development' as the silky euphemism had it.

It was a strange vibe for this young, white kid to enter areas usually sectioned off for 'another race' who were required, by law, to live separately. While I was mindful of the need to be careful, I never faced hostility. My biggest fear, in fact, was cold-selling, turning up unannounced to pitch my less favourable goods.

While it's hard to say that my three-month job prepared me for a life in recruitment, it did burnish resilience and the courage to ask for the sale, and taught me the fortitude to bounce back after many no's. Every time I hesitated in fear outside a shop, I gathered my resolve. "Ten seconds of courage, Greg." Once you were in, and it started, well… there was no backing out, was there? In fact, in a moment, you were in the middle of it – and it became exhilarating, not scary.

I was not a great salesman at 18, but it was a tough gig and I did persevere, and I'm proud of that.

When I turned 20, I was called up to compulsory military service, just as all other young white men were in South Africa at that time. My Dad, though, stepped in. Having witnessed the horrors of war, he didn't want me (or my brother) to endure the same fate as so many of his friends, particularly as it would have been in the service of the apartheid regime.

The likelihood of active 'enemy' engagement was also very real, as the South African Defence Force was fighting multiple border wars against terrorists/freedom fighters (pick your language) in Angola, Rhodesia and Mozambique. Many of my friends saw active service, and some never returned.

While I was adamant I would do my duty (as I saw it at that time), he suggested an alternative, and a deal was struck. I was to defer going into the army and go to Australia for just one year to visit my sister who was living in Adelaide with her Kiwi husband.

Soon enough, as Dad had clearly always known, Australia became home, and the prospect of the army was no more. I mean, picture the choice: freedom, equality, sun, beach, beer, beautiful girls, university life, playing rugby, or spend two years fighting a border war in Africa for a cause you despised.

It wasn't a hard choice. Thanks once again, Dad.

Lessons learned from Major Ron (aka Dad)

My father spoke very little about what happened to him as a prisoner of war in Changi, but we were always acutely aware that he was a man who had endured an enormous amount of suffering during that time.

He did end up a Major by rank, but he was a true leader to me not because of any status or title, but because of the example he set. He lived by his values. Rather than dictating his beliefs to others, he displayed them through the actions he took and the choices he made. He was always the life and soul of the party, could dance the jitterbug, play the ukulele and tell a joke as well as any man alive, and he never wasted a minute, never showed bitterness, and was the kind of person who got things done.

He was also a very loving father, before his time in many respects – he was wholly demonstrative in his love for his children. Yet he was strict, and he demanded compliance and respect. If you broke the rules, you wore the consequences.

I have no doubt I have inherited some of that. Not so much in the way I have brought up my kids – which, while firm, can hardly be described as overly strict – but certainly in my management style, particularly as a younger man.

Fine-tuning the learning

Indeed, sometimes the lessons learned from Dad needed a little tinkering.

The combination of my father's influence and my boarding school education meant my early management style was too black and white – lacking in empathy, certainly too demanding. I don't think I truly understood the nuances of people management in those early days of my management career. Thankfully, experience and maturity have softened me and the edges have smoothed over time, and I'm now a far better people manager.

Having said that, most of what I learned from Dad has stood strong. As anyone who has worked with me will confirm, I am a firm believer that it's always better if we do what we say we are going to do. I can't abide a management environment where big claims are made, big promises are voiced, and yet there's no follow-through by either management or staff.

I also don't think it's ever been an enjoyable experience for anyone to fall short of expectations in my businesses. Not so much concerning the outcome, which can falter for one reason or another, but absolutely in terms of effort. My view, gained in part from Dad, has always been that if you can control the controllable and you don't, there will be consequences. (I can almost sense, as I write, a generation of recruiters who have worked for me during the last 40 years nodding ruefully as they read that last sentence.)

I thank my father and my schooling because both taught me that high performance is a result of accountability and consequence. I learned that good people want to work in an environment with high-performance expectations and that working under pressure, as long there is support and resources, is always healthy.

Leadership through influence

Dad worked as a shoe rep, and he then went on to start his own business, representing European fashion shoe manufacturers in South Africa. While we were never wealthy, with hindsight I can see that he was clearly a man who made the very best of what he was, and made sure his family benefited in multiple ways as a result.

It is an example I've always held at the back of my mind. I find myself often telling my sons, in particular, that their father is much smarter than they might think he is. As was mine. I admit, more often than not, it falls on deaf ears.

I was no different; so much of what my father told me, advised me or even hinted at, I ignored, for no other reason than youthful arrogance. However, as I got older I began to realise how often he had been right and, in turn, how often I'd been wrong.

Mark Twain is credited as having remarked: *"When I was a boy of fourteen, my father was so ignorant I could hardly stand to have the old man around. But when I got to be twenty-one, I was astonished at how much the old man had learned in seven years."*

How true that rings. Still barely a week goes by that I don't wish I could ask his opinion, sound him out, even now. He has been gone 30 years. Although, in a way, his continuing influence on my behaviour means I don't have to, and this became very apparent to me recently when my siblings and I were facing the problematic conversation on how to transition my elderly mother from living independently to some kind of supported care.

Anyone who has dealt with this will know what a challenging time it is – dealing with emotions, dealing with pride and of course dealing with the financial decisions that need to be made at such a time. I remember talking to my brother and saying, *"Chris, this is how we should handle it, and this is why."* He asked why I appeared so confident, and my response was, *"Because if Dad were here, he would say, 'good decision boys, well done'."*

That moment brought home to me the influence that my father still has on my life: how we were making decisions based on his values and his leadership.

That episode reinforced what I have come to learn about leadership – because leadership is not so much about what you say or what you do. Leadership is how you influence people's behaviour and attitudes. Incredibly, Dad was still influencing our decisions some 30 years after his passing.

My father was a man who took calculated risks, and I believe so too am I, most likely because of his influence. Certainly, as you'll learn from reading this book, if you look at my work history it is littered with risks I've taken. Some have been failures while others have paid off in spades. The wins have outweighed the losses, as they also did for my Dad.

The sacrifices both he and my mother made equipped me well for a lifetime in what I believe can be a challenging career.

CHAPTER 2

Greg the recruiter

Calling Australia home

I WAS now in Australia, sleeping in my sister's spare room in Adelaide and studying a Diploma of Applied Psychology at Flinders University – and loving it. I was feeling very foreign in this new land, and totally unaware that a 40-year recruiting career would be born in this new city.

During my early days in Australia I worked in various jobs to support my studies. At the Arkaba Hotel on Glen Osmond Road I found my 'working home' for a year. I discovered Cold Chisel, Icehouse, The Angels, Skyhooks, Rose Tattoo, Australian Crawl and Mental as Anything, and honed my unwavering love for Australian rock music. Cheap wine and a three-day growth indeed!

As an aside, I can't tell you how cool it's been for me, in my fifties and now in my early sixties, to be able to take my son to these bands, then later to hear their vintage rock bursting from the walls of his room. (Along with some other music that frankly I cannot recognise, but hey, you can't win them all.)

Working three nights a week from 8pm to 3am with inebriated Adelaide youth was quite an experience. It taught me to think on my feet, deal with people behaving badly and, of course, give the right change to guys with huge muscles and tats.

I'd played rugby as a schoolboy at Bishops. I'd played for the University of Cape Town and also played three seasons at Villagers, the oldest rugby club in South Africa. So, once in Australia, I joined Burnside Rugby Club, where I played three years at prop and hooker in the First Grade, and even played three games for South Australia in the State team before I was found out and dropped like a hot potato, never to be seen again at that level.

Rugby Union is the only game they play in heaven. Trust me on that. It even provides some valuable life lessons, as I talk about at the end of this chapter.

In every club I have played with, the welcome has been overwhelming. Not because they valued my skill, because there was little of that. Mutual love of rugby is what opens the door. The Burnside club was no different. In fact, they were magnificent. They embraced me with open arms. I still go back to Burnside every few years, sit on the sidelines with my aging contemporaries, Coopers Ale in hand, and remind everyone how good we were 'in our day'.

More casual jobs

While I was still at university and working at the Arkaba, Burnside even lined me up with another job – at R.M. Williams, an iconic Australian brand, to be a storeman and packer in the warehouse. I was in charge of making sure that whips, boots, saddles and other farming paraphernalia were correctly sent off on time to the remote stations in the Northern Territory.

It was surprisingly hard work, bending, lifting and binding. It certainly teaches you the value of a dollar when you work eight hours, on your feet, on the move, with only a few short breaks.

The supervisor gave me a reference when I left R.M. Williams, which ended with the prophetic words: *"I have been particularly impressed by the way he has been able to produce the desired results under pressure."* I am pretty sure he was not predicting a career in recruitment for me, and nor was I at that stage, but that temperament sure came in handy later on!

One of my toughest jobs was cleaning the toilets at a Coolangatta caravan park, not for money, but in exchange for a free caravan and three days off a week, and the chance to explore the Gold Coast. At 20, fit and with an apparently alluring South African accent, it was a deal worth doing on the Gold Coast in the 70s, let me assure you.

However, all too soon reality loomed. It was late 1979. I'd been living in Australia for a year and had completed my Diploma of Applied Psychology at Flinders University. My parents were in South Africa, my sister needed her spare room back and money was tight.

The questions burned. What was I going to be? What about a career?

I had no idea.

The rookie recruiter

Adelaide is a hot place in January. While I lived there, the mercury topped 40 degrees one summer for ten days in a row.

I'd been enjoying the South Australian summer: on the beach, in the beer gardens and joining the Burnside Rugby Club in their pre-season training. However, now the need for a proper job loomed. But what exactly was a 'proper job'?

I had to my name a degree with honours in psychology and a vague ambition to pursue a future in what was then called 'Personnel Management'. The term 'Human Resources' had not yet been coined. I applied for jobs all over Australia, from junior training assistant to trainee personnel manager roles, and even social worker positions. I knew I was about people and interaction, but had no idea where I fitted.

I'd never heard of the recruitment agency concept. Then I had my lucky break. My sister introduced me to a friend whose father was the owner of the South Australian office of John P. Young & Associates, at that time one of the leading executive search firms in Australia.

It's hard to imagine the recruiting landscape 40 years ago. As I remember it, there were a few high-end search firms like John P. Young & Associates, PA Consulting and several others. Alongside these was a range of clerical recruiters, high among which stood Centacom – started by John Plummer, and later to be bought by Adecco in one of Australia's largest ever recruiter acquisitions at the time.

However, none of this I knew, as I arrived – 21 and fresh-faced – at the door of John P. Young & Associates on Greenhill Road, Wayville, Adelaide, ready to meet owner Jim Raggatt. Jim was a kindly man with a twinkling eye and a sardonic sense of humour. Having given me the courtesy of a proper interview, he began to wind up our meeting with some critical yet telling words.

"Greg, I'm sorry, but none of our clients would ever hire you. You have no experience or qualifications that they would value. However, you do seem like a likely lad, so we will give you a job here."

And so, on the 23rd of January 1980, I became an executive search consultant. My salary was $10,000 per annum. Thus the journey began!

While Jim was right in that I had few skills to offer, what I did have was fearlessness, good language skills and a commitment to work hard. However, it was still to be seen just how long this young 21-year-old rookie would last in recruitment.

John P. Young & Associates operated out of a converted Federation house, each consultant with their own office. There were six of us, the closest in age to me was in his early forties. We were all men. There was a typing team of three friendly ladies, without whose say little was done.

I was shown to my new office. I remember it had a picture of Don Bradman walking out to bat – a reassuring sight for a sports-lover like me.

There it was – my desk. It had three items essential for the work of a recruiter at that time: a telephone, pad of paper... and an ashtray.

In the drawer was a Yellow Pages, and against the wall a vast filing cabinet containing the records of thousands of pre-interviewed candidates. This was recruiting 1980s style.

I was lucky enough to be paired with Harold, a good man in his mid-60s working as an executive recruiter after a successful career in commerce. He was sharp, kind and taught me the ropes, cautioned me when necessary and refined my edges. I was grateful for the mentoring and counselling Harold gave me. As I learned and at times fumbled, Harold made sure my confidence stayed intact.

One time, a 40-year-old engineering manager I was interviewing (remember, I had zero experience of interviewing or engineering) saw through my greenness and demanded to see someone who was not a 'whippersnapper'. It was harsh, probably fair, but very humiliating.

Harold stepped in and calmed him down. I will never forget what he said to me after the man had left. *"Everyone starts somewhere, Greg. Every day you add a string to your bow and one day you will be the one offering the advice."* Prescient indeed.

Soon I was in the thick of it.

At John P. Young we sold retainers (where the fee is not contingent, but paid in stages). We received one third up front, one third on shortlist and one third on a candidate's acceptance of an offer.

We also sold 'client-paid advertising', which was way before its time in those days; the clients agreed to pay for a display advertisement, often in the *Adelaide Advertiser*, or perhaps the *Financial Review*. The budget could at times be as much as $3,000, a considerable amount when you consider that my starting salary was $10,000 per annum.

However, I learned right off the bat that we only worked with clients who showed commitment and valued our work, something now embedded into my DNA.

Next – rookie trainer... and beyond!

We also ran training and management programs. It horrifies me now to think that I was actually thrown into these as trainer towards the end of my first year. Sure, I had sat in many courses run by senior staff and to a degree was, of course, eased into it, but it was daunting to be running 'management supervision' training for people far more experienced than myself.

The new Director of John P. Young & Associates, Peter Middleton, showed tremendous faith in me and had me running the 12-session Professional Personal Development course for young executives. Then I moved into sales training. A daunting highlight was several trips to Darwin in the Northern Territory, to run a three-day Management Supervision workshop. I was without a doubt the youngest person in that room, I had never managed anyone, yet I was the 'teacher'. Learning to think on my feet, to 'read' the room and to deflect hard questions by getting the attendees to answer them, were skills quickly learned and still practised to this day.

One time I took three days off and drove back from Darwin to Adelaide, over 3,000 kilometres through tropical wetlands and then sweltering desert. In a bar in Katherine, I ran into a guy from the Burnside Rugby Club and with three miners and a German backpacker we sang and drank our way deep into the small hours.

I was an executive recruiter and a management trainer, but I was so young, only a few years out of boarding school in Africa, and everything was an adventure. I lapped it up.

I am hugely grateful for the way both Jim and Peter pushed me forward into work that few people ten years older than me would have been asked to tackle. It taught me to think on my feet and was tremendously powerful for my confidence and ability to shape ideas. It's also highly likely to have been the embryonic stage of my speaking career in recruitment.

By now I had started to handle executive search assignments, recruiting for accountants, engineers and senior managers.

You may be wondering, was I a good recruiter? Well, I worked at a desk for two and a half years in Adelaide, and I was getting there. I learned the craft quickly and became verbally adept – getting better at influencing others as time passed. And, in time, as you'll read in the following chapters, I became a good recruiter, but not a great one.

The greatest recruiters have deep empathy and never-ending love for the match, and the reward that it brings for both candidate and client. As you'll also read, I couldn't sustain such a never-ending love. My real passion for seeing other recruiters succeed emerged as I went on to build teams.

Even so, those early years provided me with myriad lessons and gave me skills and a view of recruitment that underpins my view of the recruiting world. My time at John P. Young taught me to sell and believe in retainers, exclusivity and partnerships, and so I have always fought the transactional multi-listed job order scenario of today, which I talk more about later in this book.

My early years allowed me to see that what we do has value, and that has stuck with me. (It makes me shudder how many recruiters concede so readily when it comes to fees, and I also talk more about this throughout the book.) I learned not to cut prices and commoditise what we do, but to see the value we bring to clients and candidates.

This served me well as I started looking further afield.

Lessons learned from rugby

In the 70s and 80s, rugby was still an amateur game and we all played it for love. After playing in South Africa and then Burnside in South Australia, I played for Barnet and Belsize Park Rugby Clubs during my time in London (plus a stint playing for London House in Mecklenburgh Square, where the guy in charge gave me free board as long as I turned out for the team). I then played for Chatswood in the Sydney suburban competition. I only retired in my thirties when on Saturday mornings I was still sore from the previous week, and also because the other guys in the team were 15 years younger than me and wanted to go clubbing after the game!

I have no doubt that rugby has been hugely instrumental in shaping my world view. It hurts, for a start – and no one cares. You suck it up, dust yourself off, get on with it, and sort out your own retribution if required. Few games are more competitive. None leaves you as few places to hide.

Truthfully, I lacked the talent and the courage to be a good rugby player, but I loved it, so had to work very hard to play at a certain level. As a result, it became part of my mindset that work comes before reward. Bizarrely for a chunky forward, I was a more than handy goalkicker, a huge responsibility that often leaves you lining up a winning (or losing) kick in the last minute of a fierce battle. I spent countless hours perfecting the nuance of timing, run up, follow through and balance – mostly done after training was finished and the other guys were lining up the cold ones at the bar, while I kicked goals, in the semi-dark, in the rain.

If you want to shoulder that responsibility, take the load and enjoy the feeling of winning a game from 50 metres into the wind – you have got to put in the work! The parallels to recruiting (and indeed leadership) are clear. If you want to be a great recruiter, you have to make sacrifices, do extra, hone the craft, be better.

Rugby was at that time (and maybe still is) a game that the vast majority played very hard, but very fairly, and I have approached business that way all my life. You tackle very hard, but you don't tackle high or late.

Above all, rugby is about the team. I know it sounds clichéd and all sports claim something similar, but in rugby it is true. For the wing to score that flashy try, some grunt in the forwards suffered intense pain, or did something stunningly courageous, which no one saw.

Rugby provides many parallels with business and life. I had no idea at the time, of course. I was there for the laughs, the adrenaline, the fitness, the beer and the groupies (although there were never actually any groupies). That's what I thought the game was about then. Instead, there was so much more, and I am grateful for the game and for the many men I played with and against.

They say recruitment is character building. Try rugby! Particularly when you are hurting… and losing.

CHAPTER 3

London calling

AFTER TWO and half years of productive and happy work at John P. Young, I decided it was time to travel and see more of the world.

I played my last game for Burnside Rugby Club against our perennial rivals Old Collegians. It was a rather ignominious occasion, in that it was the one and only time in a 30-year rugby career I was sent from the field! We did win, however, so I took solace in that.

I took a flight to Perth and then got on a boat to Singapore, and from there flew to London. I joined up with old schoolmates and together in a yellow campervan we travelled the length and breadth of Europe.

In December 1982, I arrived back in London, broke, to the reality of sleeping on the floor of my mate's flat in Brixton.

Chalk Farm Rugby Club was my priority in the first week, and I made my debut that Saturday. By Monday, though, things were different. I was down to my last £5. I remember sending a telegram to my brother asking him to send me some money. A return to the world of work was needed.

From executive search to the recruiting jungle

I scoured the papers for jobs in the recruitment industry (no job boards in those days) and saw a recruitment consultant job for Accountancy Personnel, based in Harrow. I'd never heard of either, but applied for it nevertheless and was invited to attend an interview in Moorgate.

The morning of the interview I walked into the city. I had no smart shoes at the time, but my plan was to find a shoe shop and get a pair in time for the interview. Thus, I headed into town in my running shoes and suit.

My plan failed. The shops were closed and there I was with little choice but head to the interview. I went to my meeting with Dennis Waxman, MD of Accountancy Personnel, looking pretty good… from the ankles up.

Dennis proved to be a fearsome boss, and he was no doubt very instrumental in the success of 'AP' which went on to be acquired by Hays and was the platform for the extraordinary success of that business. However, Dennis also oozed charm when it was required. We had a delightful chat and as he warmed to me he remarked on how I'd enjoy life with Accountancy Personnel as there were *"lots of colonials"* working there (bar brawls have erupted for less!).

I got the job – but not in Harrow. I was to be based in Oxford Circus as a permanent recruitment consultant at 14 Great Castle Street, W1. I still have my offer letter: a starting salary of £4,000 per annum payable every four weeks in arrears.

So, on Friday the 10th of December 1982, my next foray into recruitment began. The Accountancy Personnel office was on the first floor above a trendy wine bar. It comprised two small rooms: one for the permanent division and the other for the temp team.

I was in the permanent team: an Australian, a Welshman, a Scot, two Englishwomen and a South African. We sat around one large table. Candidates were interviewed at a desk behind a shoulder-high screen, every word audible to everybody.

There could be no more significant contrast than this. From my own office at the executive search firm in sleepy Adelaide, to this high-paced broking house environment that was Accountancy Personnel circa 1982.

Our mortal enemies sat on the other side of a wooden door. No, not Michael Page or Reed. It was our own Temporary Division. They were buddies by night, whom we drank with enthusiastically, yet enemies in daylight whom we would try to outdo in nefarious skulduggery. When I think about the sophistication of the double-dealing that went on in this extraordinarily competitive environment, it makes me smile when I see consultants today trying to clumsily 'bottom-drawer' temp jobs when they should be permanent, or vice versa.

The temporary team was run by Nick Cox, who turned out to be a good mate despite being an Arsenal supporter. In fact, at the time of writing this book, he still works at Accountancy Personnel (now Hays).

It's extraordinary to think that we drank beers at the George Hotel in 1983, after a hard day placing accountants, and now we are still in this incredible industry all these years on. I salute all those 'lifers' in this industry who have survived and thrived in this most gruelling of professions.

It was certainly gruelling in 1983. We had no internet, no fax, no social platforms, no job boards, and certainly no mobile phones. Contact was made by letter or home phone.

Jobs were always 'phoned-in' and, as we had no receptionist, the consultant who picked up the phone took the job. The lure of opportunity provided colossal motivation to answer those phones, because if you took the job you were likely to fill it.

You took the call, you took the job, you had the first opportunity to present candidates to that client there and then. The requirements to think fast, to know your candidates and to influence the client were imperative.

The house rules were that once you had put in your two, three or four candidates and tied up interview times (remember, candidates hadn't even been informed at this point), then the next consultant would take over the phone call. It would be passed around the table, until in many cases the client had up to 12 interviews lined up with candidates.

As soon as the phone was put down, it was time to start calling candidates. Urgency was key, as the chance a client would cancel

– having realised he or she had too many interviews – was high. Candidates were out on multiple interviews too, so it was the quick and the dead.

Remember, candidates had no mobile phones. So the smart recruiter circa 1983 had all of their best candidates call them every day – sometimes twice a day. We would have secured interviews for them, sometimes for that very night. We had to talk! So taking a lunch hour was risky because what if your hot candidate called while you were out?

It sounds breakneck, sloppy and aggressive. It was probably all of those things, but it was also extraordinarily efficient. The team made dozens of placements, many in the same week. The company was thriving, opening offices across the country.

I loved the cut and thrust of it, but I started poorly. I had made no placements in my first month, which was a dangerous predicament for anyone, particularly as the last Friday of the month drew closer. 'End of month Friday' was infamous for 'freeing up the careers' of non-performing recruiters at AP at this time.

However, I was given a second month, maybe because my senior manager, Eileen Clarke, was a fellow South African and took pity on me. I made one placement in that month. I was hardly setting the world of recruitment on fire and when the Director came around for his Friday evaluation, I was more than nervous.

Yet, I survived and in the next month I billed £9,000, which was a lot of money when you think placement fees back then were under £1,000.

I was off and running. It was fast, noisy and competitive, but also collegial and hilarious.

We interviewed people at our desks. Every office in central London was taking dozens of orders, and once they had set up their interviews on the phone, the jobs were 'written up' and circulated from office to office by motorbike. There were huge politics at play regarding in which order that bike visited those seven or eight central London offices. You didn't want to be last. By then your colleagues in other offices would have flooded the client with candidates.

There were few rules; anyone could call any client at any time with any candidate they had secured. A good recruiter would often place three or four people a week, numbers most accounting recruiters today would scarcely believe.

We were actively discouraged from visiting clients. It was seen as way too time-consuming and unnecessary, because making the match and setting up interviews was where the value lay.

Does this sound like throwing mud against the wall? Definitely. Yet, so much mud stuck that it's hard to disagree that at that time, in that place, it was a money-making machine.

Blundering at high speed

In those days, yes, the process of recruitment was undefined and certainly fast. You merely referred candidates to jobs you thought would suit them, based on the interview you had conducted.

At the time it was routine to refer candidates to roles without their specific permission on that role or that client. It was all too fast. It was standard recruiting practice in accounting in London at that time.

As a result, we often placed people on the day they came in to see us. Most clients would interview candidates based on our 'telephone sell' of their background. A résumé was not even necessarily needed.

However, often the only way to secure an interview for your candidates was to send the client résumés. It was, as described above, a bun-fight to get your candidates included on the client's shortlist. It was a case of the quick and the dead because, of course, you were competing against many other recruitment firms, but you were also in earnest competition to get résumés to the client before other offices of your company, and even colleagues in your own office, did!

Nevertheless, all this is no excuse for what I did on this occasion. There is no easy way to say this, so here goes:

I sent the résumé of a qualified accountant, a delightful young woman, *to her employer!*

There it is. I did the unthinkable. I was moving so fast that I quickly matched a job description with a candidate and put the two together. It was a good match, too. Of course it was. It was *her own job!* (They were advertising for another person to perform a similar role, not replacing her.)

Did I realise my blunder? No.

I found out when the client called me. *"Did you send me the résumé of Mary Candidate?"* he asked in a monotone. *"Oh yes sir, I certainly did,"* I gushed, still unaware of the horror about to unfold. *"Well, this is to inform you that I am her boss and until now I was unaware she was looking for a new job. Thank you for this information."*

"Click."

The horror – the shame – the guilt…

I phoned my candidate, many times. She never took my calls – never called back. I never spoke to her again.

Where are you now, Mary?

I don't know what happened to her or what the consequences were. Labour law was not nearly as supportive of the employee in those days, and she could easily have lost her job. At the very least, I put her in an awful position.

However, in the long run, the whole diabolical episode did me much good. For a start, it brought me down a peg or two, made me realise that there was a significant flaw in the way we were doing things. I was only in my early 20s, after all, and we were being told, *"This is how it's done."*

It also taught me the importance of diligence, and it reminded me of our duty to candidates and how attention to detail counts. I never made a mistake like that again.

Overall, I loved my baptism of fire into the world of a hard-core recruiter. I learned a lot. I blundered a lot. I had a lot of fun and held no conscious aspirations for management. I never thought much about it. I was still only 25 and was living day to day.

However, at that juncture, just as I was sure I was about to be fired – management was thrust upon me. (The next chapter tells all.)

Lessons learned from the 'dark ages' of recruitment

If you're on the younger side of me, no doubt you giggled at the recruiting world I've described in this chapter. Prehistoric? Hilarious, you say? Maybe. But what can we learn from that era? What skills, honed in a different time, still resonate?

Quite a few, actually. Pay heed. Here begins the lesson from the 'dark ages'.

Qualifying a job order

No one sent you a job description in those days. There was no one-line email from a disengaged client saying, *"Send me someone like you did last time."* (And trust me, many recruiters act on this type of 'brief' right now, scurrying around like headless chooks, busily working hard for the pleasure of *not* being paid!)

No, 'dark ages' recruiters took briefs over the phone; alternatively, face to face. So, the good recruiters became mega-skilled at qualifying those job orders; working with the client to create *a fillable brief*. They asked the hard questions. They gave advice and finessed the details for the benefit of all parties. They sold exclusivity and retainers. These are skills lost on most recruiters today, who hardly speak to their clients at all, and try to fill orders by keyword matching candidates' résumés against emailed briefs. Madness!

Telephone influence

Listen up! The telephone is the *most powerful social tool you have*. So many modern recruiters ignore this weapon of mass placements. The beauty of the telephone is that it allows you to influence crucial decisions.

Dark ages recruiters were masters of telephone influence. It was a beautiful thing to listen to. I mean it – gorgeous. I am not talking about hard sell. Quite the reverse – I am talking about charm, about reason, about subtlety, about seeking to understand, about listening as an art, about common sense. Few things are more exhilarating than being in a room full of sophisticated recruiters making things happen on the phone.

Nowadays? Seriously? It's like being in a public library. Or a typing pool from the 50s. I have to get up and leave.

Telephone screening

Dark ages recruiters knew that an hour in an interview with an inappropriate candidate was a *dead hour* for everyone. However, they also knew that a great candidate might *not* shine through a résumé. So, they phone screened – powerfully, efficiently and with deadly effect – homing in on great candidates, and gently screening out the less appropriate with empathy and guidance. Now? It's almost as if speaking to the candidate is a dirty thing to do. This is both sad and costly.

Selling candidates

Oh, but now it gets sexy. One of my best party tricks as a young manager in the dark ages was to pick up the résumé of a good candidate that a recruiter was struggling to place, and phone a client to '*sell them in*'.

Yes, I would research the candidate first, and yes, it's best if it's *your* candidate, and you know them and believe in them, but the lesson holds. Dark ages recruiters would get their candidates interviews over the phone. Do you remember the scene from the film *The Wolf of Wall Street*, where DiCaprio is unemployed and sells penny stocks over the phone to 'schmucks', as they called them? Well, it's *nothing* like that because I told no lies, and you must tell no lies, but it's *everything* like that because it's all about phone influence. Today? We have become experts at sending emails with résumés attached. WTF?

Urgency

This makes me want to cry with nostalgia. Urgency! In the dark ages, if a great candidate came to see you, you *knew* that if they left your office, you had lost them. This happened literally straight away in some cases, because they would go across the road to a better recruiter than you, who would move fast and get the job done. However, even if they did not go to another recruiter, you had lost them for a day at least. Remember: no mobile phone, no email.

So, the dark ages recruiter was an urgency freak. If the person they just interviewed had the skills, and the client had the need, the two would be put together – fast! The candidate would be given a coffee and asked to wait. The recruiter then jumped on the phone to the client in a matter of seconds. The interview was set, there and then. The candidate was briefed, enthused and, if necessary, given the train fare to get there.

But wait! The candidate is not in her best interview clothes? No matter. I have seen with my own eyes a great dark ages recruiter take just such a candidate to the bathroom and swap her corporate clothes with the jeans of the candidate before sending her off to interview. She got the job, too. Today? Are we doing that? Or even thinking like that? Or are we stuck in the process with little regard for outcome?

Memory

One of the things I ask recruiters to this day is: *"Who are your three most placeable candidates with [...XYZ...] skills?"*

It is incredible how many automatically turn to their keyboard to work out that simple answer with the help of their database. The dark ages recruiter could quote you their best candidates in their sleep. They could tell you their skills and their qualifications and their availability. They could remember candidates they placed, and did not place, from ten years ago. There was no database other than the database of the brain.

Memory was a prized dark ages recruiter skill. Now? We can't even remember how to use our database search function in some cases, let alone recall our hot candidate profiles. Digital has made us lazy and hazy.

This 'memory' skill was hammered home to me not that long ago.

For about five years, I worked out of a great office in Pitt Street, Sydney, when I was running Aquent and Firebrand Talent Search (which I get to later in the book). At least twice a day, I would need a hit from Pronto, the coffee shop below our office, and that meant me nipping downstairs and putting in my order with the friendly crew. In 2012, I sold Firebrand and moved away from that end of town.

Five years passed since I'd been into Pronto. Then one week I was striding past, fancied a caffeine hit, and in I strolled, with no expectation of recognising anyone who worked there now.

How wrong I was.

"Hello Greg!" came the cheerful cry. There was David, the owner (I had forgotten his name, of course, but he was instantly recognisable).

"Flat white, no sugar, isn't it?"

I was gobsmacked! I had not been there for five years, and this place must serve a thousand people a day. And he remembered my name *and* my order?

We chatted. I had to ask for his name. He was unfazed.

It gets even better…

"How's your son's cricket going?" David asked. Had we even discussed that? All those years and coffees ago? *"Fast bowler, isn't he?"* Correct. *"Is he enjoying school?"* he continued with a smile, correctly naming the school my son attended.

We chatted some more, and I left with a handshake and a great coffee.

I walked out reflecting on David's talent. I remembered now that he had always greeted his customers by name. However, I was a five-year lapsed customer!

Great recruiters do what David does. They take enough interest to remember.

The ugly side of technology is that it has dumbed down recruitment. It has weakened the human skills that make great recruiters so special. So many recruiters today hide behind technology and avoid real interaction.

I am a firm believer that the more technology we see in the workplace, the more complex it gets, and the greater the need will be for human intervention.

David, I salute you. We must all take heed. There is nothing sweeter to the human ear than the sound of your own name.

CHAPTER 4

Learning to lead in London and Sydney

I HELD my own during my first year or so in the dog-eat-dog environment at Accountancy Personnel, but I wasn't a superstar. I never got near the top of the billing table, but (after my slightly shaky start) I did deliver good results and felt relatively secure. That was until a dry spell hit, and two quiet months had me on edge.

As mentioned, our office at Great Castle Street was tiny. There were no meeting rooms, so when the need for a serious discussion arose, privacy was a challenge. The Director's tactic was to walk around the block with whoever he wished to address. This particular morning, he entered our office and looked across at my manager. Don was summoned for a walk around the block, and the cold hard fact is he never came back. He was fired on the corner of Regent Street, outside the Wimpy Bar, and I never saw him again.

The Director came back in. *"Savage... walk with me."* I knew it was over. Don was gone, and Savage was going.

Instead, to my surprise, I was promoted. I was made manager outside Boots the Chemist on Great Portland Street, and returned to the office in my new role.

My salary was raised to the princely sum of £5,000 per year along with an individual commission of 5% of my perm placement fees above a standard requirement, as well as a team bonus of 5% of fees produced by my team members above a certain threshold, plus a managerial overrider of 2%.

The first lesson of management

The day I was made manager surprised yet pleased me, but I was also naive, with little experience. I assumed my fellow consultants would fall into line and follow my leadership. After all, we were mates. However, in actual fact, my mates were thinking, *"Wow, how cool, Greg is the manager and we can do whatever we like now."*

My first and biggest lesson of management was learned: you do not set out as a leader to be liked.

If you do, you will make compromises and inconsistencies that will undermine you and erode trust. Consultants don't need a friend in you. They need clarity, to respect you and be respected, to trust you and have ground rules and expectations made clear, and for you to remain consistent.

Good people will learn to work with you as a leader. Setting out to win loyalty via 'friendship' is a catastrophic error fraught with danger.

In London it was a tough lesson because the consultants, my mates, were shocked that I wanted things done well, and I was shocked that they did not respond as I thought they would. It was hard. You have to be brave. No one likes walking into a room then everyone goes silent. However, things slowly turned. Results improved. Trust grew. Lessons were learned on all sides.

I must have done OK as I still have a letter from the MD Dennis Waxman dated 22nd March 1984, which thanks me for my commitment and contribution since taking over as manager and announcing an increase in my base salary to £6,250.

As my third English winter approached at the end of 1984, however, my thoughts turned back to Australia. Accountancy Personnel had a sister business called Accountancy Placements in Australia, and I was offered a role as manager of the Sydney office, which I took sight unseen after a short meeting with Graham Whelan, the NSW Director, who was visiting the UK.

My farewell was in a West End pub. Consultants came from the various offices we had across London. As was customary at the time, a 'fatogram' was arranged (an obesely overweight lady) to humiliate me and entertain my colleagues as they watched me suffocate between her voluptuous breasts.

The interesting postscript to this is that five or so years later when I married my now wife, and relayed the story of that night to her, she claimed to have been there – at the farewell party, witness to the 'fatogrammery'! I knew she had worked for Accountancy Personnel in London, but laughed it off as I did not remember her from that time. Trust me, I should have. She is a stunner, way above my division. Years later I stumbled on some old pictures taken of that night and, sure enough, there she was in the photos – wine glass in hand, laughing at my embarrassment.

Stepping it up in Sydney

So, in 1985 I was back in Australia, this time in Sydney. I was in charge of a team of 20 consultants across permanent and temporary accounting, business support and banking. It was a big step up from the London role, which had been challenging enough.

I was also tasked with recruiting for chartered accountants, personally. The market was buoyant, and all of our advertising was done in the newspapers at the time, but imagine this… *The Sydney Morning Herald* divided job listings into two sections: 'men and boys' and 'women and girls'. Seriously. As I wrote this book, that fact was so weird I wondered if I had imagined it. So, I went to the *Herald* archives and, yes, that's how it was. Wow! How the world has changed.

I reported to Graham Whelan, whom I'd met in London and subsequently became the co-founder of Recruitment Solutions with me, and a lifelong friend.

I talk more about Graham later in this book. For now, let me say that Graham had a major influence on me and others in the office because of his humanity, his empathy, his leadership and his willingness to help. He is still the greatest recruiter I have ever met, with an incredible memory for people and their lives.

My job was huge, although I didn't fully realise it at the time: one-on-ones each week with 20 recruitment consultants, team meetings and a significant personal budget placing chartered accountants in 'big 6 firms' and smaller practices throughout Sydney. Soon we would open offices in Chatswood and South Sydney, expanding my responsibility.

It was a huge step up from my role in London, from the volume of people involved to the diversity of disciplines. London had taught me how to manage a group of five or six consultants in one room, but to lead four times that number – and with some in different locations – was quite another thing altogether.

I was billing, and billing well. Yet I also had to manage a large group. Without doubt, the billing manager is the toughest job in recruitment. It's an incredible challenge to make the transition from being a great consultant to managing other recruiters. As I talk more about in Chapter 11 (in Part II), this move can often be the undoing of some very good performers.

To manage a team while you continue to write significant fees yourself is extraordinarily tricky. Many people in this position gravitate back to fee-production – ignoring their management duties – at the cost of the team, while others see their time sucked up by people issues, and their fee-production plummets. Neither outcome is good.

The truth is that the great majority of people make that transition only by recognising that they must learn new skills (see the breakout box at the end of this chapter). Thankfully, I recognised this need and developed these skills, meeting my own fee targets while managing and building the success of my team.

Now I was getting into the 'meat' of my career, with six years of recruiting and managing under my belt. In 1986, at age 27, I was made an Associate Director at Accountancy Placements in Sydney, with a place on the board and a stellar career looming.

However, a year later I was unemployed with a giant mortgage. What happened?

The Savage Truth

Lessons learned from leading (and billing)

The key to being a great billing manager is to work out how you build a team that enhances your personal productivity (and billing potential), rather than hindering it. So, let's break it down.

Crunch the numbers

Before you start to add people who inevitably are going to take your time, analyse your current productivity:

- What fees do you generate?

- How much new business do you generate?

- On average, how many placements do you make per month?

This is crucial because you have to do some calculations. You need to estimate how having new people on the team will eat into your time and therefore reduce your personal revenue.

You then need to pin down what the new recruits must generate to compensate for your own drop in revenue.

And, of course, 'compensate' is not enough. The total fees generated by the new people must cover their direct expenses, cover incremental costs and exceed your own personal shortfall, or why are you hiring people at all?

The danger, of course, is profitless sales growth.

Determine your personal skills balance sheet

The second thing to consider when building a team while still billing fees is to work out a personal skills balance sheet.

What are you best at? You are the leader, but you are also part of the team. What are your strengths (assets); what are your weaknesses (liabilities)?

What do you like doing? What don't you like doing? Are you a great business developer – but bored with interviewing or

42

job filling? Or maybe you are a slick job-filler, but not a great rainmaker.

Here's the trick. Once you have an honest balance sheet and you decide to add staff, go for consultants who:

• complement your strengths

• shore up your weaknesses.

If this strategy is going to work, you need to be brutally honest with yourself.

Many managers hire people who are carbon copies of themselves. That could be fatal. If we have a team full of 'Gregs', for example, we will have a team that is very good at some things (and competing to do those things) and very weak at others. No one on the team can or will do the tasks we are not good at.

What you end up with is a lopsided skill-set. Many consulting teams I have seen have this handicap. It's a recipe for disaster.

Understand your management style

This applies to all managers and leaders. As you build a team that enhances your productivity – a team that you find easy to get the best out of, a team you have fun leading – you also must understand your own management style.

If you are directive in style, don't pretend you are not. Accept it and hire your consultants accordingly or, better still, adapt your approach to suit the modern mindset and ethos.

Building a team is like putting together a jigsaw puzzle. Make sure the pieces fit together properly and there's nothing missing.

If you hire people who are predisposed *not* to respond to your management style, you are pushing the proverbial uphill from day one. Hire people who will run with you – not pull against you.

Finally, in terms of building a team that enhances your productivity…

Stick to your hiring criteria

Don't compromise on the people you hire. Don't 'give it a go' if you have doubts. Don't get so busy that hiring your own people slips down the priority list.

Establish a set of criteria that you know works in your business and stick to it. Keep raising the bar, not lowering it. Shortage of quality is not a reason to lower standards. It's a reason to raise your hiring focus and up the intensity. I talk a great deal more about this is in Chapter 19 (Part II) 'Recruiting Recruiters'.

Be a manager, not a friend

Whether you are the boss when new team members arrive or you are promoted from the ranks, there is a golden rule which, if broken, will cause you much angst: Do not set out to 'ensure your people like you'.

Remember my mistake (my first lesson of management) when I was promoted in London? Many managers believe that if their team likes them and they are all 'mates', they will get greater co-operation and commitment from team members.

Unfortunately, human nature does not work this way. In fact, that strategy could not be more wrong. People work most effectively for a manager whom they respect and trust.

In the jungle of our industry, consultants want support, consistency and direction. They already have friends.

Your goal as a manager is to very quickly establish the ground rules of behaviour and expectations in the office. If your team grows to respect and trust you – you will succeed. If, at the end of the day, they like you too, that is a bonus – but it is not a goal in itself.

We are all human, after all, and we want to be liked. However, start out trying to achieve that and you will make half-hearted decisions, you will become inconsistent and end up a slave to your team.

Balance consulting and management

One of the fundamental requirements of a successful team leader who is also a consistent fee producer, is to get the balance between consulting and managing right.

This is not an easy thing to do. To achieve it, I believe you need to separate consulting time from management time.

Most managers come into work, sit down and 'work hard'. They have no structure and no plan and as a result they either gravitate completely into consulting – neglecting the coaching, managing and directing aspects of their role – or they spend all day with the consulting team, and of course their personal production falls.

The key to success as a billing manager is personal organisation. You have to be silky smooth in managing priorities and putting effort into where you get a swift return. You need to plan.

It is essential to set time aside in your diary for what you consider to be strictly management tasks. For example, set aside blocks of time to 'roam the office'. Actually, block out these times in your diary. Or, if it's a tiny team, kick back to talk. If it's a remote team, make time to call or Skype. This activity can be done in as little as a half an hour block; sit for a few minutes with each consultant, get a feel for what they are doing and provide input.

I am sure that all of us who are managers can think of times when we have hardly left our seat for days and haven't even been to the other side of the room for two or three days. This is a sign of poor time management.

Although it may seem to your consultants that you have very little to do if you spend time just wandering around the office, I believe it is an essential management tool. It is a way to keep yourself informed, to pick up problems before they get serious and it gives the added benefit of keeping your consultants on their toes.

The key is that you must discipline yourself to make time to do this.

Remember: your input, your energy, your knowledge can raise productivity across five or six people in just a few minutes. If you are stuck in a corner, face in a phone, placing engineers or accountants in jobs all day – you will not have this impact.

Be selective

One of the key skills great fee-earning managers have is the ability to cleverly select what consulting work they do.

They set themselves a target lower than the rest of the team to ensure that they can balance their managing with their consulting time. Leading from the front does not necessarily mean producing the most fees. To reach your own personal targets, you must be selective about the candidates you interview.

Don't make the mistake of picking up all the 'problem' or mediocre candidates to make your consultants' jobs easier. This will eat into your time in a dramatic way and will make achieving your own target far more difficult.

In fact, you should do quite the reverse. Work on a small group of quality candidates, probably no more than five to ten if you can. Make sure that these are serviced properly, and you will find two, three, four and five placements coming through a month in your name.

This will be achieved with the minimum of fuss and effort on your behalf and leave you enough time to manage.

It's also very important to keep control of your client time.

Do not cling to old clients in the belief that they will not work with anyone else. They will!

Slowly divest your clients to competent consultants who will do the work for you. You can still keep the relationship with clients going, but get your consultants to service the work.

Here's an important tip: get to know (personally) the top 20 clients in the office (other than your own). You must protect your assets. Should team members leave, it is important that you have established relationships with the key customers who give you the majority of your business.

Prioritise tasks

Highly effective billing managers do the right things at the right time.

Here is an example of a typical time trap:

"Tomorrow I must go through Jane's job orders in detail because I think she is losing track of them, and I also have five or six phone calls to make."

Typically, what happens is you arrive at work in the morning and start by making the five or six phone calls, which in turn lead to five or six other phone calls, and so on. Of course, the review of Jane's job orders doesn't happen at all. This is a classic case of poor prioritising.

Instead, you must put the five or six phone calls aside, because making sure that your consultant is handling her job competently is your highest priority. Once you have got that out of the way, you can go onto other things, comfortable in the knowledge that Jane is on the right track.

During your working day, constantly make yourself sit back from the situation and assess what is the most important thing for you, as a leader, to do at that time – and get on with that task.

Delegate

As a manager, you will have people coming up to you all day with questions, problems and enquiries.

When a consultant comes up to you with a question or a problem, what they are trying to do, in many cases, is leave you with that problem to sort out for them. But management, no matter the industry, is all about getting things done through other people.

For example, a consultant comes to you with a job board ad, or a client proposal they are having problems with. You look at the ad or proposal, and very quickly see in your own mind how you would write it. You've got two options.

The first is: *"OK, leave it with me and I will get back to you"* – in which case you actually rewrite the task for the consultant (who probably goes to lunch).

Do you see what has happened? You have taken the problem away from them and the consultant has delegated to you! These situations are massive time-eaters and will leave you working longer hours for less results.

The second, more preferable, option is to look through the ad or proposal and give the consultant some useful feedback. For example: *"It's a bit wordy, it rambles on a bit in this section and you haven't said very much about what you are looking for – go back and try again."*

Do you see the difference? The consultant has gained advice, has been guided by you, but the problem is still with them and your management time is 30 seconds rather than 30 minutes or more.

Understand this: because you can do something better than your consultants is not a good reason to do it for them.

Don't allow consultants to delegate to you. Rather, give them guidance, assistance and encouragement, but in most cases let them resolve their own problems. They will learn, you will have time to spend on other issues – and both of you will end up doing the tasks you should be doing and are getting paid for.

CHAPTER 5

Recruitment Solutions, recession and revival

SO, WHAT took me from career ascendency to unemployment? Well, Hays bought Accountancy Placements and that triggered a series of events that changed my career, and my life.

While there was absolutely no negativity about Hays per se (in fact, the people we met were very nice and positive about our future with the company), the status quo was changing. We were likely to be a very small part of a global business, and it all provoked serious thought about the future.

Ultimately, Accountancy Placements' three senior people (of whom I was the youngest and least experienced) – myself, John MacSmith and Graham Whelan – decided the time was right to strike out on our own. And so what became Recruitment Solutions was conceived under a Moreton Bay Fig tree in Sydney's Botanical Gardens.

Doing things our way

It was a momentous decision. As I mentioned in the previous chapter, I had only recently been elevated to the board, at age 27. My career was flying, and I was earning very well indeed.

I can only really speak for myself when I reflect on what our motivation was. I had a desire to be my own boss, to have more control of decision-making, to make a mark, achieve something memorable.

The three of us wanted to do things our own way and, perhaps naively, do it better than anyone else had done it before.

I am being perfectly candid when I say that making money was only a vague consideration at that point, and it really wasn't fully thought through. I certainly had no grand vision about 'becoming rich' from this venture. I borrowed $15,000 (AUD) for my equity in the business.

So, we handed in our notices. It was a difficult and emotional time. We were all immensely loyal to the Accountancy Placements that we knew, but we were doubtful about the new future being laid out before us.

Many discussions took place to entice us to stay. I was offered a salary four times that of my current package. I still have the handwritten 'new structure' in a bottom drawer. It contains a strong lesson about sticking to your dream. Being completely honest, I was definitely swept up by the massive financial inducement, and I strongly considered taking the offer and staying. *"Why not?"* I reasoned to myself. *"Four times the income, same job, bigger company…"*

Thankfully, the voice of true reason, in the form of my wife, spoke out. As I prevaricated and weakened, it was my wife who asked me what my original motivation had been when I'd decided to resign. I mentioned autonomy and decision-making and innovating our own way, and so she pointed out in no uncertain terms that those were unlikely to be available should I stay.

I may well have had a great career at Hays. It was one of those 'sliding doors' moments. However, I have certainly had a brilliant ride since I made that decision to strike out on my own, and so that little push by someone close was critical. The flash of clarity, the subtle prompt to be brave – even though she was nervous too, no doubt.

So, we held out (the others were offered more than I was!). We each sat out our three month non-compete period. Then in August 1987, when I was just 29, Recruitment Solutions began under its original brand name, Accountancy Careers. John was the financial guy, strategic and analytical. Graham was the people person – a brilliant recruiter and wonderful candidate-care guy, with an impeccable moral compass, an all-round brilliant example to others. And if I had anything to offer it was people management, coaching, building engagement and effort, and an innate understanding of what needed to be done to make a recruitment business profitable.

We were ambitious and we started big – ten people in two offices. We had big dreams and were not planning to muck around! We were taking on the world.

But the world (and the universe) does not always play nice. Almost immediately a horror story began to unfold.

Black Tuesday

Unlike most horror stories, this one is true in every single detail.

Eight weeks after we opened our doors, the world's stock markets went into free fall: on Black Monday, the 19th of October 1987. The Dow Jones on Wall Street dropped 23% in eight hours. In Australia – where it all came crashing down the next day, hence Black Tuesday – the All Ordinaries dropped an astonishing 46%, while the New Zealand Stock Exchange fell a cataclysmic 60%! That's right – over half the value of listed companies in Australia and New Zealand vanished in one day.

I was terrified. Mortgaged to the hilt, I had borrowed every single dollar to start the business. I had encouraged colleagues to leave great jobs, follow me and start Accountancy Careers. Yet now, I was sure, the economy would tank and our business would fail, ruining us all.

However, the business did not fail. Stock markets recovered. The real economy thrived. Our business boomed and by 1990, only three years later, the rebranded Recruitment Solutions had 75 staff, five offices and revenues of $13 million. (We'd rebranded to allow diversification beyond accounting recruitment as we grew.) It was all good. So where is the horror, you ask? As it turns out, it was still to come.

The 'recession we had to have'

By mid-1991, the Australian economy had fallen into deep recession. So too had New Zealand, of course. I won't quote you economic data. Let me tell you how it felt being a recruiter. In mid-1990, before the recession hit, our business was handling, on average, at any one time about 250 active perm job orders. I know this because each manager faxed me the job numbers every Monday morning.

By mid-1991, that number had dropped to 18 active jobs. Our revenues, which peaked at $13 million in 1990, fell to $9 million in 1991. However, even with those horrific numbers, Recruitment Solutions did far, far better than most. During 1991 and 1992, 60% of all recruitment companies in Australia and New Zealand went bust.

For us, it was still beyond tough. Our staff numbers dropped from 75 to about 30. We closed two of our five offices. Every person in the company had to take a 10% salary drop. Administration staff were eradicated, with consultants shouldering the load. None of our offices ended up with receptionists, and all consultants took turns on the front desk.

We stopped advertising totally because great candidates were queuing up in the foyer, without appointments, desperate to be seen. This is not an exaggeration.

Our Sydney temp desk, which had averaged 30 job orders a week, plumbed new depths. In one memorable week, we took one order. It came in at 4pm on a Friday, and it was for a one-day credit control clerk. Rented pot plants were wheeled out the door.

The breathtaking aspect of that time was the speed at which revenue dropped, the speed at which the market switched from job-rich to job-poor.

Recruitment Solutions would have been among the 60% that failed too, if it had not been for four key facts:

• We had a strong temporary business, which kept us afloat (more on this in the next chapter).

• We had no debt, so we were not crippled with repayments when revenue dropped.

- We had some great recruiters who saw the thing through – recruiters with character, recruiters who were not just boom-time show-offs, recruiters who could win business and foster relationships.

- We cut our expenses fast and very deep, early.

I remember a conversation I had with our finance guy, when I said we could *"sell our way out of this"*. He said, *"Fine – you do that, but we must get our cost base down."* And we did, from $450,000 a month to $225,000 a month – and still, in 1991, we only managed to break even.

What doesn't kill you makes you stronger

Oh, it was a full-on horror story, believe me. Yet it had a happy ending. When the market recovered, we found that many of our competitors had disappeared! I take no joy in the misfortunes of others, but the fact was the field was much clearer.

We found that our clients valued how we had persisted and felt bound to us as 'fellow survivors'. The consultants who survived had been burnished by the fire of true 'battle' and were tougher, more loyal and far more skilled. Some of those recruiters who worked through those tumultuous times work with me even today.

Subsequently, Recruitment Solutions boomed. In three years, our revenues were up to $18 million. By 1997, sales were over $35 million and the business was so profitable we could list it on the Australian Stock Exchange (ASX) the next year, at a value of over $60 million at its peak.

We learned some massive lessons during that horror story of a time. I don't want to scare anyone, and I have no special knowledge, but I feel another massive downturn is not too far away (at the time of writing). In fact, by the time you read this book, it may have happened.

I had a significant experience during the recession. I mentioned how revenues dropped and staff numbers halved. I operated out of an office at that time and, in the middle of the worst period, I closed and locked my office door and announced to the permanent recruiting team that I was coming to sit on the desk with them and recruit hands-on myself.

Many years later, after the market recovered, some of us 'old-timers' from the recession years were sitting around on a Friday night spinning yarns about the old days. Two consultants from that challenging era mentioned that the day I closed my office door was the day they decided to stay and see it out with Recruitment Solutions. They believed that if I was going to get in the trenches with them, shoulder to shoulder, that was a fight worth fighting.

I want to take credit for that brilliant leadership initiative, but the truth is I had nothing to do in my office. I was lonely, bored, feeling ineffective, scared of the business future, and so I decided to get back to recruiting, where at least I could look busy and maybe make a meaningful contribution.

Though certainly not something I was conscious of at the time, my decision to sit and work with my perm team was unwittingly pivotal. As I cover in much more detail in the second half of this book, leadership is action – and my action had a potent effect on morale and motivation at that tough time.

Lessons learned from managing in a downturn

The Recruitment Solutions experience, and subsequent downturn, have led me never to be seduced by the good times.

No matter how well things are going now, always ask: am I vulnerable?

Preparing for a downturn

I ask all my clients to consider the following question at board level. It always shocks them.

"What would happen if our permanent gross profit (GP or net fees) dropped by 50%, and temporary/contract GP by 25%? And the drop occurred in a month and GP did not recover for two years? Would we survive?"

I usually raise it when the going is good and profits are at record levels, because that is precisely the time we get complacent. We start to believe in a world of never-ending fat years. No thought is given to surviving the lean years.

The point of that question and the ensuing conversation is to test our fitness to adapt to a new world. Also, it ensures we are making decisions and building structures that allow for much lower revenue.

The following list runs through some possible scenarios your business might be facing, and in doing so provides a handy checklist for your business to prepare for a downturn. Recruitment history is littered with once highly profitable recruitment businesses that had feet of clay, which crumbled when the dark days descended.

So, consider these scenarios, and if they describe you or your business, consider making changes, now.

- You are a *permanent-only placement business*. It's tempting to head that way because perm in a buoyant market is highly profitable. (And at time of writing we have had ten years of growth, pretty much.) So, it feels good, and makes good money, and we love it, and things will never change, right? The only problem is it can drop 80% in a recessive environment. You have no ongoing annuity revenue stream, such as a substantial temporary or contractor business. That is a big problem. What is the ideal GP ratio? 65% to 70% temp or contract GP, with the remainder being perm.

- Your *niche specialisation is highly vulnerable* to economic downturn. You are recruiting in a 'bubble'. This is problematic because niche and being deep in a vertical can be good. It positions you as 'expert' and gives you access to networks of hard-to-find candidates. However, it can also be dangerous if you are too niche and that niche gets massively disrupted. Where do you go then? Evaluate and assess.

- Your *clients themselves are vulnerable*. In other words, you may be exposed to some types of banking clients or other

55

businesses that are at risk of being hit harder than others when the economy tightens. So, you may want to spread your risk more widely by diversifying your client base where possible.

- You have *no flagship clients* with whom revenues are entrenched and substantial and relationships are deep. All your client 'relationships' are superficial, 'retail' or piecemeal. Your company has 'shallow' consultant relationships, which are mostly transactional and not based on trust and credibility. When the flight to quality occurs, you will no longer have a seat at the table – unless you future-proof by changing your approach and developing deeper, two-way client relationships.

- You have too much *reliance on one/two clients* who, if they disappear, would leave you exposed entirely. This seems so obvious, but I have seen it happen countless times. Maybe 50% of your GP comes from one or two clients. The profit and loss (P&L) of the business looks great. However, in reality, it is being propped up by these one or two 'super-clients' who, while fabulous to have, often soak up all the resources and all the focus. The business is exposed as very weak once they 'go'.

  This can even happen in 'normal' economic times when a recruitment business becomes too dependent on one preferred supplier agreement (PSA) – in the UK known as preferred supplier list (PSL) – customer. Then, one day, that deal is lost. The smart thing to do is run a P&L on your business without the GP from those clients, right now. How does that look? Pretty ugly? In which case, grow out your 'non-elite client' portfolio. The diversity of revenue streams will save you.

- Your company has *high fixed costs* like real estate, job board advertising or other supplier contracts that you cannot reduce quickly as your revenues fall. I have seen this cripple businesses many times. It does not even take a recession to do it, merely an economic softening. I have said it before, and I will repeat it here. Fancy offices in recruitment are all about ego. The owner's ego. No one cares. Your clients rarely visit you, and frankly would be horrified to see their fees consumed by your marbled reception area. All you need are respectable offices that make your candidates feel confident and your staff comfortable. It's dead money otherwise and a noose around your neck in a revenue-drop scenario.

Be smart about the detail. Does your lease agreement allow sub-letting? (I have personally sublet office space on numerous occasions, halving rent as our business subsided.) Do we need *that* much space in the first place? (It's better to have five interview rooms full all the time, and one candidate being interviewed in the coffee shop downstairs, than ten interview rooms which languish empty most of the time.)

Is it better we pay slightly more per square metre for a four-year lease, which we can get out of, than do that super-deal on a ten-year lease that we rue all the way to the liquidator's office?

- Your company has too much *reliance on one or two recruiters.* You might be proud of your ten-person business that generates annual GP of $2.5 million. However, the reality is that you have two admin staff, and two of the recruiters bill $1.5 million between them. The market drops, one of the big billers leaves, and the tiny billers become almost zero billers. Turn out the light and shut the gate. Cherish and reward your big billers. However, do not live with serial mediocrity from the rest of your team, even if the profit line looks good. It's an illusion! Invest in upskilling your underperformers and diversifying your revenue stream across multiple consultants.

- Your *recruiters are lightweight.* This is harsh, but you have to be realistic in your assessment. Are they flat-track bullies? By this I mean recruiters who survive, even look good, when the orders are flowing and the times are merry. In truth, though, they have no depth of relationship. They are order-takers and résumé-flickers. They can't sell, network or open doors. You need to evaluate this now. If that revenue dropped as described, who would have to go? Who would you keep? Would anyone be able to survive the post-apocalyptic recruiting world?

- You have *lots of non-billing managers*. In other words, you have a fat layer around your belly, with these managers on high salaries, doing… what is it they are doing again? Review your staff mix and business needs along with the billings and costs, and ensure you only hire the people you need.

- You *don't read the signs*. History has taught us that speculation and bubbles are the prelude to collapse (recent examples being the dot.com crash and US housing crisis). I am not suggesting you can 'time the market' to perfection, or that you should be economic experts. However, be aware, sniff the air, be paranoid.

- You are *seduced by the good times*. You never talk about the possibility of a recession. You don't run scenarios like the GP questions and possible chain of events I described above. You have no downturn cash flow projections prepared. You don't consider your strategy. You sail on merrily, until you fall off the end of the earth.

- You get *seduced by revenue growth over profit*, and most importantly you forget the importance of cash. Remember this: revenue is vanity, profit is sanity, cash is reality. You allow your debtors days to blow out, when in fact you should be managing this like a rabid honey badger on crack. (I discuss these concepts in detail in Chapter 22.)

- You have *too much debt*. You borrow merrily because you have the profits and the cash to service the loans. You talk earnestly about a balance sheet that has good cash reserves as being 'lazy'. You even borrow money to pay dividends (God help us!). Smart borrowing to leverage opportunity and to gain profitable market share is clever. However, always run 'worst case scenarios' and leave room for survival on much lower revenues than forecast.

- You *act too slowly*. This is where you see revenue dropping. The signs are there. However, you convince yourself it's a 'blip'. You tighten the belt a little and let one person go. Two months later it's getting worse. You chip away at the expenses again but hold on to 'nice' people whom you know can't bill in a downturn.

  The next month it's even worse. You are haemorrhaging money. Yet still you believe things aren't as bad as all that, and you change the Friday beer from Asahi to VB as a nod to frugality. This is death by a thousand cuts. It destroys morale, and, in the end, you are chasing your tail, never getting costs down low enough. A quick, deep cut – a real restructure – while painful, will get you fighting fit again and, believe it or not, is better for morale. Not the day it happens, of course. However, once done and explained, you can move on leaner and better equipped to thrive in a world of less money.

Smart recruitment owners – actually, all smart business owners – always build a company that can reap significant profit in an upswing but can hunker down fast in a downturn and is highly resistant to revenue falls. Don't put it off – prepare now.

Managing in a downturn

Once the recession hits and the cruel reality bites, everything then hinges on effective leadership. Success in a slowdown – and in any aspect of business – is based on this.

Trust me on this. You have never had a true test of your leadership until you have managed through a recession. In my experience, there are three key areas you need to focus on to lead successfully in tough times.

Adopt laser-like focus

Desperation in bad times can lead to losing focus. I believe in specialisation, and that carving out a series of niches gives you power in the good times and is highly defensive in the bad.

My mantra in my businesses has always been: *"We are a mile deep and an inch wide."*

Winners in a downturn narrow their business portfolios. Do not try to become all things to all people. You must walk away from bad business. Allow losers to chase unprofitable sales in an attempt to hold market share. As a leader, you must encourage the business to focus on just a few critical priorities that you know will drive revenue.

There are many ways of driving revenue, but it may be as simple as the following (these are just examples, yours may well be different):

- We will grow temp sales in the clerical accounting sector.
- 70% of our time must be face-to-face or verbal customer contact.
- We will only work on qualified job orders.

Focus on the people

When the pressure is on, it's often true that recruiters become defensive and territorial. Your teams start seeing internal colleagues as threats. When that happens, they take their eye off the real targets – competitors and customers.

Leaders have to stop this self-destructive behaviour from catching on. As a first step, I recommend you spend as much time with your staff as you can, on the job. Run job meetings, take training sessions, go on client visits. Don't lock yourself in your office. Be more visible, not less visible.

However, you must do more than that. You need to actively encourage people to work together. That could include joint meetings of temp and perm teams to share ideas. It could mean encouraging people from different teams to go on joint visits. Alternatively, you could get a real 'gun' recruiter from one part of the business to share their success ideas with those from another part. These may be small steps, but they are important to keep people aligned with the common goal: winning business.

Ensure staff engagement – nothing is more important

It's crucial that during challenging times, you open up a dialogue about what is happening with people in your teams. Don't leave them in the dark. Lack of information promotes uncertainty and takes the focus off the job at hand. As you go about making change, you need to make sure that people understand the decisions you are making and the reasons for them.

So, at Recruitment Solutions and also at Aquent many years later, these were some of the actions I took that I like to think kept people engaged:

- Constant communications including mailing of results, successes and updates.

- In person or video 'fireside chats' where cutbacks were explained, results shared and updates given – this is a very powerful method.

- Coaching of change in tactics by recruiters and dedicated training sessions to deal with changed market conditions. Not more of the same old stuff, but bespoke tactics for what they were dealing with there and then.

- Repeats of the old stories of previous recessions and how for us, while painful, it would be a great thing in the long run.

- Candid talk about how the business was doing, keeping people informed.

- Telling staff the bad news (like people cutbacks or advertising freezes), including the why and the how.

- Celebrating the small victories publicly.

- Mixing it up – making it fun.

Keep these three areas – having a laser-like focus, focusing on your people and keeping them engaged – 'front and centre' as you lead through a downturn, to help your business survive and soar again when the economy recovers.

CHAPTER 6

Scaling for growth and listing on the ASX

WHEN WE started Recruitment Solutions in 1987 (at the time branded as Accountancy Careers), we began with seven permanent recruiters and just one temporary consultant.

This reflected the emphasis we put on the two potential revenue streams at that time. In fact, it fairly accurately represents how the industry and market viewed the two services; permanent recruitment was a 'serious business', while temp was somehow defined as clerical or office support, downmarket even, and so not to be taken so seriously.

One year later, in 1988, we hired an excellent temp manager, and the temporary business started to grow. Before too long, we realised the value of this stream of business – indeed, as I mentioned in the previous chapter, our strong temporary business helped us survive the early 1990s recession.

The birth of Temporary Solutions

We began to invest aggressively in the temporary side of the business. Writing this now, it seems logical, but back then our actions were a very different approach to the industry norm.

We took the offering to the nth degree; we set up the business name of Temporary Solutions to focus on the provision of temporary recruitment services. It even had its own logo and colours. It was for all intents and purposes a separate business.

All of the staff specialised in temporary recruitment and reported to the manager of the temp division. It even had a separate entrance to the permanent business at our office at 275 George Street, Sydney and in all the other offices around the country too.

For a period, I was appointed Director of Temporary Services while Graham ran the permanent business.

While a growing temporary business can be a drain on cash flow – because you have to pay your temps and contractors weekly, while your clients will pay monthly or take even longer – our permanent division was performing strongly and so provided the liquidity to grow our temporary business. And grow it we did!

Over the next few years, the strength of the temporary business meant we were able to expand into five offices in Sydney alone, as well as Melbourne, Brisbane Adelaide, Perth, and eventually Auckland.

Our core business was placing qualified accountants, and we also had a strong reputation for our work at assistant clerical level as well as with senior contractors.

The secret sauce

We marketed Temporary Solutions heavily, on railway posters, billboards and signage on taxis. However, our success was due to much more than just good marketing.

Our mark-up on the temporary hourly rate was significant: over 55% on average – something companies today would find hard to believe. We invested heavily on the candidate side. We held events for candidates, both social and professional. We produced newsletters, gave gifts and offered various ancillary free services, all to secure the best temporary talent available. Again, this approach was way before its time.

It seems like a trivial distinction now, but giving temp that focus and those resources was a ground-breaking initiative, I believe. It set up the business for significant profitability and growth. Even today, I speak to owners who say, "We take temp and contract seriously", but when you dig into it, all that is happening is that they allow their permanent recruiters to handle temp and contract as well. That never works in terms of building a strong temp and contract business. Never. The business will always retain a permanent GP bias.

We had a relentless and intense focus on skill development for our temp recruiters. Everyone likes to think they train their staff, but this was woven into our DNA. We had daily skills coaching and weekly formal training sessions – not just lectures, but role-plays and reliving real-life scenarios, with all recruiters participating.

We introduced video recordings of role-plays of client visits to develop recruiters' skills, and we practised impromptu public speaking to nurture confidence and articulation. This was done often to camera, so we could play back, review and coach. This might seem passé now, but trust me, 25 years ago it was ground-breaking. Remember, this was when video was very expensive, required heavy equipment, and years before I heard of any other recruitment agency making such an investment.

At Temporary Solutions we also assertively resisted the insidious trend to transform a temp/contract job-filling process into a de facto permanent recruitment process. This is not a good thing and minimises the role of the recruiter to consult, control and manage the process. So, a critical skill was filling a job over the phone. At Temporary Solutions we worshipped at the altar of the 'phone-fill'.

When a client hires a temp on the basis of the recruiter phone-sell, it proves that recruiter has credibility and trust.

We filled temp orders with no résumés and no interviews, where we could. We filled jobs quickly with excellent candidates, always looking to keep those in work who had worked for us before.

It's something I bemoan frequently now as I see temp/contract consultants default to a résumé/interview process without even attempting to assert their expertise and value. After all, who can describe the candidate's suitability better? The recruiter or a résumé?

'Recycling' our candidates was a commandment too. If a good temp of ours was finishing next week, we moved heaven and earth to make sure they were rolled into a new assignment, through us. This was for the obvious commercial reasons, but also because once working for another agent they could be lost to us altogether. We pushed hard the fact that the temp was 'our' employee, and gave benefits to the temporary workers to reinforce that, including training, entertainment and bonus pay for longevity.

We fought hard against margin degradation, moving our rates according to contractor supply and not allowing our margin to be squeezed. We turned bad business away without question. We worked on the critical skill of being able to handle and resist client requests for discounts, especially temp to perm fees which have cascaded into a farce in recent years (and which I explain in detail in Chapter 16).

We upsold higher-skilled, higher-margin temps when the assignment called for it, and we squeezed extra cents on each deal if it was warranted, knowing that a 50c extra margin per hour across 700 contractors was a lot of money by year end. (*"How much money?"* did I hear you ask? Well, if those 700 contractors averaged 35 hours a week, it's an extra $637,000 – a year, in gross profit, for no extra work. Thanks for asking.)

We never sent rate sheets to clients because we figured temp rates are determined by supply and demand so rate sheets were never up to date, as demand fluctuated weekly.

If the client wanted to give the temp a raise, or the client wanted to keep a temp who wanted a higher rate, we never absorbed this raise as a margin loss, instead we pushed up the rate to the client. We stood firm on fallacious arguments about us having 'made our money'. Our margins were sacred.

We built temp revenue to over $30 million at Temporary Solutions, and we did it with very few PSAs (or PSLs, as they are called in the UK). These so-called 'preferred' arrangements were often no more than a mechanism for clients to reduce fees, with no clear guarantees of extra volume for the recruiter. We saw through this ruse and only accepted 'special deals' when it was 'special' for both parties. I maintain the rage on that view to this day. We were not seduced by revenue. We wanted to make money through a combination of reasonable margins *and* volume – because lots of volume at an unprofitable margin just means lots of losses. Some people in our industry still don't get that.

Sure, we did some deals, but we walked away from bad business and so should you.

Our overall premise was to compete on value, not price, and we worked hard to prove that value through the only two things that clients really care about – quality temps, delivered fast.

We even had a sophisticated 'sleepers-catching' program – a system to check that our clients and candidates had not colluded behind our back to 'recommence' the assignment without our knowledge. That was very common then and is still happening now. The program did in fact extend to standing outside the building where we knew a lying temp and a dishonest client were working, ready to greet the startled and embarrassed temp on the doorstep of the company they were 'not working at', with a cheerful *"How is the new job going?"*

When we caught them out, we politely negotiated the proper fee and we sued recalcitrant clients with vigour, because we valued what we did. We went to court if required and I even spent money to gain less money on occasion, just to keep the bastards honest and send a message to our staff about how we value our service – and I feel good about it to this day.

We had a phobic hatred of ever losing a job order. Losing to another agency was the worst, but even on a cancelled order we took the blame. We had 'vacant job meetings' twice a day– at 8am and 12.15pm, every day. Reporting a lost job at those meeting was not your happiest moment. We detested losing a job and a thorough post mortem was carried out on every miss. There was no 'win some, lose some' vibe at Temporary Solutions. We sought to win every order we took.

We measured individual consultant 'fill rates'. We never allowed 'bad luck' to creep into the lexicon of lost jobs. We used every loss as a platform to assess what we could do better next time. We valued each job like the precious diamond it is, and spoke about *job-order perishability*' as the gospel it is. That being the fact that *every minute a temp job order is open, the more chance there is that you won't fill it*. Ponder on that truism, if you will.

We had regular, compulsory candidate calling nights in an era before mobile phones – where the whole team stayed back once per month to check in on candidates working elsewhere by calling them in the evening at home. Pizza all round was de rigueur, but the real hunt was for information. Where were they on assignment? Who were they working through? When were they finishing? What new or improved skills did they have? We loved to place a competitor agency's temp into one of our jobs.

Maintaining our focus

At Temporary Solutions we were all about focus. Accounting temps: that's who we wanted, that's who we hunted. A blog written by Ross Clennett, who worked at Temporary Solutions for ten years and rose to Associate Director status, tells the story:

> *Twenty-four years ago, I was in my fourth month of employment at Temporary Solutions in Sydney. I was an accounting temp consultant. Unemployment (7.9%) was continuing to rise, eventually peaking at 11.2% in November 1992. The market was tough. Jobs were hard to come by and good candidates were plentiful.*

> *One of the few things I had in my favour was that I had focus. My job was very clear; I was responsible for generating, and filling, temporary accounting jobs in the Sydney CBD and the light-industrial corridor to the airport, comprising Alexandria, Waterloo, Zetland, Mascot.*

> *My target market was predominantly medium-sized companies that had an accounting team of five to fifty people.*

> *With no open jobs to fill, my day was spent calling and visiting prospects (you could count my clients on the fingers of one hand).*

> *As an accounting temp consultant, I only had one person in each company I was interested in speaking to and meeting; the Financial Controller (or equivalent). The FC was the person who held the keys to any recruitment in his (rarely did I meet a woman FC in the early 1990s) department (no pesky internal recruiters in the 'olden days').*

I wasn't seeking to uncover perm jobs or office support temp jobs or any other type of job. My own future depended on me focusing solely on the hunt for temporary accounting jobs to fill.

This laser focus kept me my job.

My temp accounting desk colleagues and I were out there selling temp accounting services. Nothing else. That made us memorable when most of our competitors had consultants covering both temp and perm or covering a range of temp roles.

I took the job at Temporary Solutions because I was offered a job on the temporary accounting team, which I was assured was a big area of importance to the directors, compared to a vaguer job offer at Accountancy Placements (now Hays).

The three company directors, John MacSmith, Greg Savage and Graham Whelan, made a far-sighted decision to create a separate name for the temporary division of their company, Accountancy Careers Pty Ltd (later Recruitment Solutions Limited). In the late 1980s this was unheard of. All our competitors in the temporary accounting space operated under the same name for both perm and temp business.

How well did this focus work?

Well, here's the 1993–94 financial year result: three and a half years after I started a desk from scratch I achieved an annual temp gross profit of $670,000 against a target of $460,967.

It was my hard work. But it was also the machine that was Temporary Solutions and the focus we applied to our goals.

The force behind our success

We were also great target-setters at Temporary Solutions, both at an individual and team level, and we managed against those targets vigorously.

The targets were set using data and we backwards planned so every consultant knew the metrics they needed to hit to achieve the financial goals set (more on 'backwards planning' in

Chapter 21).This way we got buy-in to activity targets and financial goals. Success was vigorously celebrated while underperformance was coached and managed with a subtle mixture of empathy and consequences, which I have come to call 'managing with an iron fist in a velvet glove'.

The decision to focus on temps in this way was the force behind the Recruitment Solutions success. Finding data from those days is not easy (I wasn't planning on someday writing a book, back then!), but here are the numbers just for the Sydney City office at the end of the 1997 financial year, a year before we listed (remember we had at least seven other offices also driving temp placements).

Recruitment Solutions, Sydney, 1997 end of financial year

	AU$m
Total sales	19.90
Margin	5.10
Temp to perm	0.55
Total gross profit	5.65
Expenses	2.74
Total operating profit	2.94

The numbers are big, even by today's standards, but look at the ratios! Gross profit margin on temp sales of over 28% ($5.65 million against $19.90 million total sales). It's a gorgeous number, that... it makes me nostalgic, even now. With EBIT (earnings before interest and taxes: $2.94 million) as a percentage of sales of nearly 15%! And that's from a temp-only business, with no perms to inflate the numbers. That kind of profit margin is totally unheard of now and was then too.

My records show that temporary sales for Recruitment Solutions were $8 million in 1993 and reached $34 million in 1999. When we listed the business in July 1998, the temporary business was the platform for its valuation of $24 million. The prospectus for our listing shows that 85% of the company revenue came from

Temporary and Contract Services, a split at the gross profit line of approximately 70% temporary and 30% permanent.

Temporary Solutions: it's a permanent reminder of how a great contract business works.

Taking Recruitment Solutions to an IPO

As Recruitment Solutions grew, we began to attract the attention of potential buyers. Multinationals eager to enter the Australian market came courting, as did big local groups looking to amplify and grow. However, we were having fun, were highly profitable and we were still driven to achieve greater things.

We never took the prospect of exit seriously, until the institutional bankers began to take an interest. Listing meant a partial realisation of value for the founders, but at much higher multiples than a trade sale. It also assured us of capital to fund acquisitions and rapid growth. It was a very appealing prospect.

To my knowledge, only three recruitment companies had ever listed on the ASX at that time. Skilled Engineering, primarily labour hire, had done well, but Morgan & Banks was the standout. That business had thrived post-listing and provided shareholders with spectacular returns.

The advantages of being listed are huge: the profile, the publicity, the financial discipline, the credibility you earn with clients, the morale boost for your staff. Also, access to capital would give us the opportunity to make acquisitions.

Recruitment Solutions listed on the ASX in July 1998 with a highly successful initial public offering (IPO). The shares we sold into the float were valued at nine times multiple of EBIT, a number that would be unheard of in a trade sale, then or now. As the share price rose on the day we listed, shareholders saw the value of their shares move to 10 times EBIT and, in due course, our share price doubled as we hit all prospectus forecasts.

Listing brought with it some downsides. Although I did very little of it, the work leading up to listing was enormous and a major distraction. The due diligence, the compliance, communication to clients and staff, all required massive thought and executive time.

However, this didn't end with the initial listing. The big message that I would send to anyone considering an IPO as an exit strategy is to understand that listing your company on the stock exchange is not the end of the story. It's just the beginning. Shareholders invest with the expectation that you improve their share price and provide ongoing dividends through growth and profitability.

The scrutiny is relentless and the transparency is intimidating, to the point where one day I was accosted in the street by some punk questioning whether the salary I was being paid as COO of Recruitment Solutions was appropriate. He was half joking, but it's not what you want to deal with on your way to buying a sandwich for lunch.

In our case, only two of the founders ended up on the board (John MacSmith and myself), with the majority of board members being non-executive directors, not from recruitment, representing the shareholders. This is exactly as it should be, but it's a difficult transition from being a business owner with almost complete autonomy to having to justify every decision.

As well as listing being a very expensive process, it costs a lot to remain listed. The sword hanging over you concerning share price performance can lead to short-term decision-making, which I found challenging.

Quarterly and half-yearly analyst briefings, while challenging and interesting on the one hand, could also be irritating and time-consuming.

Post-listing, Recruitment Solutions grew strongly but, to be honest, did not reach its full potential because we were unable to make the acquisitions that would catapult the business to a new level and maintain the interest of the fund managers.

In the midst of these issues, it turned out that the board of Recruitment Solutions did not see me as the person to take the business where they thought it could go. My role was mooted to be downgraded.

That wasn't going to happen, so I resigned to great shock and hullabaloo.

I was high profile in the company and the industry at the time and, the day my impending departure was announced, the share price dropped more than 10%. No one likes instability in leadership of a small cap service company. It never recovered, and in fact that was the start of a steady decline over time from above $2 per share to under 20 cents.

It would be silly, egotistical and wrong to say the subsequent demise of Recruitment Solutions was because of my departure. It wasn't. The market softened and in my view poor decisions were subsequently made around senior management appointments, allowing the business to be bought by interests associated with John Plummer and Chandler Macleod a few years later, at a fraction of its listing value, and delisted in 2002.

Personally, my biggest mistake through that period was to leave a million shares in Recruitment Solutions after I left, naively thinking it was 'too big to fail'. That was a mistake I would never make again. The magic formula of the three managing founders had been broken, and the lesson that even substantial businesses can flounder when the key ingredients to success are ignored was there for all to see.

Yet, all that is a footnote. Recruitment Solutions was the love of my recruiting life. We achieved something special, we created financial stability for ourselves, real careers for hundreds of people and great gains for shareholders.

I believe we set the bar in many respects for recruitment businesses at the time, and we certainly hired, trained and developed a whole generation of recruiters who have gone on to great success in our industry.

I regret nothing – not even the way it ended. It opened up the door on a whole new recruiting world for me.

Lessons learned from building a great recruitment business

I am very proud of what was achieved at Recruitment Solutions. We started with nothing and took the company to an IPO, from ten people to almost 200, with up to ten offices at its peak. I was only one part of a cocktail that led to that success.

As I mentioned in Chapter 5, John, Graham and I, as the three owners, were fortunate in that our skill-sets and personalities complemented each other, for the most part. John focused on the financials, Graham was the people person and I covered team management and coaching.

Importantly, we also thought like a big business even when we were tiny. We innovated and we embraced marketing in recruitment well before it was really a 'thing'. We had salary surveys, client events, newsletters, incentives for temp hours worked, transport and radio advertising, mass mailings, candidate drinks nights, harbour cruises for our temps, newsletters and a box at the Sydney Football Stadium where we could take clients. None of this individually sounds innovative now, but this was 30 years ago, and we were doing them all at the same time!

Another example of our willingness to act bigger than we were was with hiring. Our fledging brand had no cachet in the early days, but we wanted to grow and hire recruiters. So, we got in a video production company, created a 'corporate video' and then ran adverts for recruiters in the UK and NZ, who wanted a new life and a fresh recruiting career in Australia. (That video still exists and gets dragged out by old Recruitment Solutions alumni keen for a laugh.)

An amusing aside was that the night before we made the video, my brother hit me in the eye with his racquet while playing squash. Nevertheless, production time was bought and paid for, so Kristen, my darling PA and friend (now so sadly lost to us, and forever missed), stepped in and applied something from her makeup kit which hid the worst of my black eye. The show must go on!

Anyway, I subsequently flew to London and NZ and interviewed recruiters, showed them our whiz-bang video (which in the 80s was quite groundbreaking) and hired four from the UK and at least three from NZ.

It's very hard analysing something of which you were an integral part, but Recruitment Solutions was no doubt not an 'easy' place to work. We managed via a heady mix of process and art. Expectations were high. Bullshit was not tolerated.

I was young and driven. I was very black and white. I was quick with the smart remark, not a bully, but lacking in empathy at times. I was brash, confident, relentless in the expectations of myself and the team. I think I could be too demanding at times. I like to think I have mellowed considerably.

Having said that, we built a great business where the right people thrived, and many of them now own great businesses themselves. Many work with me today in my affiliated businesses.

Yet I was definitely a hard nut, a stickler for doing what we agreed to do. You followed through on your commitments. Accountability was a religion – consequences a given. Meetings started on time. Everyone has an 'I was late for a meeting with Greg' story.

Simon Gressier, with whom I subsequently founded people2people in 2004 (which I cover in Chapter 9) and who is still a close friend, has a story from 25 years ago. I don't remember it. I am not particularly proud of it – but I bet it's true.

Simon explains:

> *"Let me set the scene…*
>
> *I am only a few weeks into my new career as a recruitment consultant, at Recruitment Solutions. Things seem to be going*

well. My colleagues are supportive, and the work is interesting. One of my senior managers and a director of the business, let's call him Greg, has booked me in for a 2pm meeting.

At 1.55pm I receive a call from an old boss, who has called to see how the new role is going. At about 2.05pm I feel an uneasy sensation that is hard to define. I look up and note that Greg is standing at his doorway looking with serious intent in my direction. I wrap up my conversation and promptly apologise to Greg, but compound my mistake by asking if there is anything, in particular, he wants to talk about (as in what should I bring).

'Simon, we are going to talk about whether you have a f#@%ing job or not!!'

The lesson was real.

No matter how particular you are about being on time, your reputation for timeliness, or anything else for that matter, is only as good as your last effort.

Nearly 25 years later, and still working with Greg, would indicate that his bark was worse than his bite, thankfully."

That's a bit embarrassing. I sound like a real jerk. I was sometimes. Though guess what? At Recruitment Solutions, you never spent 20 minutes waiting for people to arrive for meetings. You never had one-on-ones start late. Things got done. In retrospect, I think being a bit of a jerk and running a great business is better than being a nice guy all the time.

Still, I cringe a little when I read stuff like that.

CHAPTER 7

Going global with Aquent

I RESIGNED from Recruitment Solutions and took 18 months away from work, enjoying my time out from the recruitment industry. I was at home for the birth of my third child, had four months in Italy and France, travelled down the Amazon with a mate, spent a month at the Rugby World Cup in the UK (Australia won, thanks for asking) as well as enjoying a wide range of other adventures.

I was on Balmoral Beach in Sydney with my children when my phone rang. I found myself speaking with a recruiter. Was I interested in a CEO role? I wasn't really, life was chilled, but of course I asked who it was with.

She told me it was Aquent and in a classic case of Savage arrogance and ignorance, I replied that as I'd never heard of them before, it couldn't possibly be of interest to me. She persisted. She told me Aquent were different. Slowly I got reeled in. Soon I was meeting their Asia Pacific (APAC) leader, and subsequently had a lengthy telephone interview with John Chuang, the CEO and founder in Boston.

Aquent was different. It still is.

It was started in Boston 35 years ago by a trio of quirky undergrads who taught themselves desktop publishing and then hired themselves out as creative talent. Over time, they saw a gap in the market for designers using the Mac and the group transitioned into staffing. MacTemps was born and grew rapidly across the US.

In fact, within five years, MacTemps became the 12th fastest growing private company in America (ranked in *Inc. Magazine's* 'America's Fastest Growing Private Companies').

Innovation was in their DNA. In 1992, they became the first US national staffing firm to provide comprehensive medical and retirement benefits to temporary employees – a big deal in that country.

With 18 offices in the US by the early 90s, they expanded to the UK first, then France and Australia. MacTemps became Aquent in 1999. By 2001, when they approached me, Aquent had several offices in Europe and seven very small offices in the APAC region. The company was still deeply embedded in the creative space; particularly graphic designers and web designers.

I was to be the APAC CEO based in Sydney and I started in the role in April 2001. The title of the job was big, and so was the geographical footprint, with offices in Sydney, Melbourne, Brisbane, Auckland, Singapore, Osaka and Tokyo. In fact, that was part of the initial allure of the job – I had never worked across a global region, and this was an exciting opportunity to learn.

However, the business was actually quite small; each office typically had about five people, and the revenues when I joined were only around $5 million. My brief was to steady the ship and then ensure incremental growth. I had no idea of the exhilarating ride that was to come.

The Aquent difference

Aquent was different from my previous experience, in many ways.

First, they never refer to 'candidates'. They talk about 'Talent'. They consider 'Talent' to be the primary customer and that they act as the agent for 'Talent' in the marketplace. Indeed, their recruiters are called 'Agents'. This in itself was a significant shift from 99% of recruitment organisations who treat candidates like cattle and consider the client to be king.

Aquent also offers a unique 110% money-back guarantee – the premise being that *"if the person doesn't work out, we just give you your money back and 10% extra for your trouble."* This was introduced for all clients in 1994, and as far as I am aware is unmatched in the industry even today.

I vividly remember my first trip to the Boston head office, only a week or so after I started with the company. It's a long trip, 24 hours in total, but the next morning I was up bright and early, dressed for business in a dark suit, crisp white shirt and tie – my usual business attire during my entire recruiting life.

I entered the Aquent Boston offices in Boylston Street, only to find 50 people all dressed in jeans and t-shirts. However, I soon learned it wasn't just the superficial things, like dress code, that were different, or even just the way they framed candidates and recruiters.

The business was led by John Chuang, a man whom I would describe as highly intelligent, hugely innovative, somewhat eccentric and definitely unpredictable. I learned a great deal from his style, despite the fact that it is almost the polar opposite of my own.

He asked brilliant questions and, if you were going to make a statement, you had to be prepared to defend it with data. If you had an idea, he would quickly let you run with it if he liked it, and decisions were often made on the spot. And I mean big decisions, like opening an office or changing strategy.

His mind was always running way ahead of everyone else's. He had high expectations of people and, I think, a very short attention span when it came to the day-to-day aspects of the staffing industry.

One of John's greatest assets and something I learned a lot from was his willingness to invest. Of course, he always had one eye on the profit like any business leader, but I never felt that was his primary objective. He valued innovation, disruption, improvement and challenging the status quo. In an industry dominated by people stuck in their paradigms, I often felt his paradigm was that there was no paradigm. That was challenging and invigorating at the same time.

It was good for me to see someone so open to innovate and take a risk and ask 'why' so often.

The Aquent Boot Camp is a good example. This is a one-week intensive training course for all new hires – new 'Agents' – in the business, covering many of the skills required. Many recruitment companies would do something similar. However, Aquent flew all recruits, no matter where they were hired, to Boot Camp in Boston. They were flown from all over America, all over the world. There are plenty of Australian, UK, European and Asian recruiters working in the market now who were flown to Boston for a week of Aquent Boot Camp, as total rookies.

Although I was far from a rookie, I did have some initial teething problems. When I started, I had a one-week handover with my predecessor who was returning to the US, and we used it to do a tour of the offices including Singapore and Japan.

I was not well received initially. Not personally, because everyone was lovely, but with scepticism about my 'fit' for the company. I was a career 'recruiting guy', who wore a suit some days. I was not a 'creative'. Many Aquenters were trained designers and creatives who had morphed into recruitment. To me, they loved design more than recruitment, which was very suspect. To them, I was a commercial recruiting hard-case, who could not be fully trusted to appreciate what 'creative' staffing was about. We were both a little bit right, and a lot wrong.

One particularly arrogant pillock, sent out from Dallas to train Australian staff, freely told all and sundry in Australia, including my local manager, that I didn't 'understand the business', that I was wrong for the role, was a bad hire and would fail very shortly. I sent him back to the US on the next plane and called John Chuang to request he stop sending arseholes to my region. (I was not happy, and I have to say John handled that call pretty well, and the guy ended up being fired a few months later.)

While mutual respect and trust grew the longer I worked for Aquent, some misunderstandings continued – although the consequences were not as severe. Along with the Aquent Boot Camp, there was the famous BTS – which stood for 'Back To School'. It was a two- or three-day training, socialising and strategising extravaganza usually held in Boston, although I do recall going to one in Las Vegas... and I think I am one of the few who were there those three days who can remember much! (We should be grateful for that, perhaps.)

BTS included training, speeches, ideas sharing, case studies, updates on the market and the company and, of course, plenty of frivolity and carousing. One quirky time we had a seafood dinner, including Maine lobster, served in the function room of the Boston Aquarium, which seemed somewhat macabre at the time, but still, a great time was had by all.

As my credibility grew within the business, I featured as the keynote speaker at several BTSs – I think people liked the relaxed Australian delivery, and the hard-core recruiting experience I had to share. They also noted the Australian vernacular. I admit, I did throw everyone into a frenzy once when I was talking about negotiating fees and suggested that if we *"lower our pants or lift our skirts"* by dropping margins, we deserved what we got. I realised then how conservative, on the surface, the American business culture is.

That comment wouldn't raise an eyebrow in Australia. However, in the US, it raised concern about whether I needed to meet with HR for serious counselling. I laughed it off, reminding them I was never likely to change, that I was on a plane home the next day and everyone needed to chill. Which they did, but it served as a clear reminder of the cultural differences that prevail.

I learned that lesson again when I was attending one of my bi-annual board meetings with John Chuang and the very senior management team in Boston. Our results in the APAC region had been very good, and John remarked, *"Well done Greg, great results."* (That's high praise from him, I assure you!)

I replied in a traditional Australian way, dripping with irony, when I said, *"Thanks John, I did it all myself, with no help from anyone."* Of course, what that means in Australia is the absolute opposite of the actual words. What I intended to convey was that I was not the reason for our success: it was, of course, the work of everyone else, which was obvious, as we had over 100 staff!

Suddenly, I found myself staring at four blank faces, all shocked that someone could be so arrogant as to suggest that the corporate results across ten offices were all due to his own brilliance. I stammered and stuttered, trying to explain myself, but I learned at that moment that Australians and Americans have a different appreciation of irony.

Nevertheless, overall, it all worked out OK. As I said, the guy who was sure I didn't understand the business ended up being fired. Conversely, I was at Aquent for ten years, was made International CEO in charge of all Europe, Asia and ANZ, and was subsequently offered the role of Group Global CEO in Boston, which I declined because it's cold there and they don't play rugby. So one-nil to me, I guess.

Hire and promote on potential

Over time, I worked out who were the 'guns' in my region and began to build a good rapport with them. My observation was that we were niche in creative staffing, both web and print. This was 2001, and the proliferation of internet jobs was beginning. All the Aquent offices were small, and most of the consultants were from the creative industry.

It wasn't a very sales-oriented culture, although service levels were high and consultants had a deep understanding of their markets and the skills required by candidates. There were other problems: we lacked scale, we lacked critical mass and in some cases we weren't making any money at all. We also had a dearth of quality leadership across the business.

A particular case in point was Melbourne. At that office, we had four staff including a non-billing manager and one consultant who was generating 62% of the GP. Unsurprisingly, we were losing over $100,000 a year.

I had few options, and I decided to roll the dice with a person who appeared to have great potential, but on paper had zero qualifications to take on the role of manager and build the Melbourne business. Michelle Tickle had joined the Sydney office in an admin role, and she had recently been moved into the position of an Agent in Sydney and showed great potential. I saw something in her; she had courage, she had sales ability and she had coachability.

I distinctly remember inviting her for a coffee near Town Hall in Sydney and saying to her, *"Michelle, I need you to go to Melbourne."* She smiled and replied, *"Sure thing, Greg, for a few days?"* I replied, *"No Michelle, for the rest of your life."*

Well, as it's turned out so far, that request and prediction are accurate. She still lives in Melbourne 17 years later.

Within a few months, she was down there as the new manager. From the figures, it's pretty clear to see what the impact of the right kind of leadership can do. Three years later, the Melbourne office was six people strong with Michelle, the manager, billing 22% of the GP. That high performing consultant who was billing 62% of the GP before was now billing 31% of total GP, but her 31% represented a personal increase of nearly $200,000 per year. We had several other consultants all billing consistently and the office had moved into a profit of $440,000 in that third year.

However, the story gets better. Five years later, the Melbourne office had 20 staff, including 16 billers, and the operating profit was $1.2 million. Michelle was still billing $250,000 a year herself, but now had an emerging second tier of management in her team leaders. We had moved into a market-dominant position in Melbourne and were growing steadily and cranking out excellent profits.

At about the same time, and perhaps through a little overconfidence and hubris, I convinced the Boston board to buy out one of our primary competitors in Melbourne. I think we managed to negotiate an appropriate price and an appropriate earn-out, but frankly, it wasn't the best decision I have ever made. It wasn't a cultural fit, people left, and while the business was undoubtedly bigger afterwards, I don't think we got the big leap forward that we were after.

However, Michelle managed this entire thing, and it's a wonderful lesson for me and all of us – in several areas.

First of all, you need to hire people for a role on their potential, not only on their experience and skills. I was lucky enough to recognise something in Michelle, and she actually exceeded all my expectations and possibly her own too, through applying her determination and talent.

The second thing is that a billing manager who can pay their way through their billings, and is also able to coach and develop others, is critical to running a successful recruitment business.

And the final lesson? Be careful about acquisitions – they involve a lot more than making sure the price is right, a lesson I was slow to learn.

Hire people better than you are

I also went about making some key strategic hires, who contributed to our rapid growth. These were some of the most impactful I have made in my life.

Simon Lusty in Auckland is a standout. Qualified as a chef and then as a recruiter with the Lampen Group and Hudson, Simon had the energy and the passion I was looking for, and I hired him as soon as I could. He repaid that faith by turning the Auckland business around from a loss-making business to one that made close to $1 million just a few years later.

In due course, as I was building a very significant Sydney business, I offered Simon the opportunity to come to Australia and manage that business, which he did highly successfully, eventually becoming the Australian director responsible for all five offices.

Simon continued to be a key person throughout the ten years I was at Aquent. An interesting footnote is that in 2019 Simon is still with Aquent and now based in the US running a big part of their operations. Personally I believe his stellar journey is nowhere near complete.

We also had to get better at marketing the Aquent business and so, with limited resources, I looked around for someone to be my right-hand person. Carolyn Hyams was a graphic designer, but a graphic designer with a lot more to offer. I hired her as the marketing coordinator, and eventually she elevated herself to the position of marketing director of the entire Aquent business outside of North America.

Carolyn is an excellent example of somebody who had the passion and drive required to excel. I also admired her courage. Encouraged to think big, she did. If she didn't know, she would find out. I am immensely proud of the initiative Aquent (and later Firebrand) showed in a fresh approach to recruitment marketing.

I genuinely believe we led the industry as marketing moved online, and Carolyn was front and centre in that.

Another strategic hire was Jenny Gottlieb, who had worked for me before at Recruitment Solutions, when I hired her as an ex-teacher fresh off the plane from Johannesburg sometime in the early 90s. When she became available, I snapped her up for Aquent, to work initially on our big outsourcing project Sensis with Jolene Andrews, also an outstanding person to have on your team.

Jenny was a known quantity to me but, of course, as with most people she had far more potential and she subsequently emerged from a recruitment role to that of being Aquent's HR director.

These three hires had an important impact on Aquent's success – and all three went on to be founding members of Firebrand Talent Search (which I talk more about in the next chapter).

I cover this in many parts of this book: the real role of a leader is to hire people around you who are actually better than you at delivering the jobs you've hired them to do. In all these cases, these people not only achieved what I asked them to do, but surpassed my expectations and ended up being far better at their roles than I ever could have been.

All of them became leaders, which at the end of the day is the role of any good leader – not only to create more followers, but in fact to promote and develop more leaders.

Rolling the dice on diversification

The APAC business was now beginning to grow for Aquent. New managers were in place in many cases, and a different style of recruiter was joining. So, I turned my mind to a longer-term strategy. Aquent had always focused on creative staffing only and, to be perfectly honest, almost their entire business was focused on temporary and contract. That was their ethos, that was what they were good at, and that was what led to enormous growth across America particularly.

However, it began to occur to me that there were tremendous diversification and cross-selling opportunities that we were missing. We had good relationships in the advertising and creative industries, but we were also placing creative people in-house in large corporations – some of Australia's and the region's top 500 companies.

Yet, all we were doing was placing web and print candidates on a temp basis, with the occasional temp to perm. So, I sat down with Carolyn and some of the other senior people and we started to develop a plan.

The first thing was that our flexible staffing solutions around temp contract and temp to perm, or 'talent bridge' as we called it, were going to stay fundamental to our business. We love temp, I love temp and you should love temp. We wanted to dominate that area, and we wanted the majority of our gross profit to come from it. However, why not place permanent roles, on a contingent basis (where a fee is only payable on successful placement) or even retained (where an upfront and sometimes staged fee structure is agreed)? We had the candidates, we had the clients – we just needed a structure and perhaps some specialised recruiters.

I also saw an opportunity at executive search level, and we discussed project and outsourcing solutions as well.

Then we looked at disciplines. We were doing creative staffing pretty well, and if the roles weren't in advertising/design, often they sat within the marketing department of large corporates. But what about marketing roles, from trainee to director, in corporate organisations?

We also looked at advertising and media, account managers and account directors, and the general managers of advertising agencies. We were already working with ad agencies, but we were very, very niche. As we were working with ad agencies, why not the sister businesses: PR, communications and media, both in-house and agency?

At Recruitment Solutions, we had built a substantial business support and admin recruitment business off the back of our accounting staffing heritage. Yet, here we were at Aquent with hundreds of clients, placing creatives but not stepping across and placing the admin and communications support people around those roles.

The plan was hatched: we wanted to diversify across advertising, marketing, media and PR. We wanted to do contract and temp, but also permanent, executive search, as well as payroll transfer, outsourcing and project solutions. This was the plan that I was to fly to Boston with and present to the board.

I will never forget flying to Boston to sit opposite John Chuang and the board. I'm quite sure none of them would remember that meeting now; it was 15 years ago and one of many such meetings.

However, I went in with what was quite a controversial pitch. I was suggesting that Aquent change its strategy outside North America. I was asking that they give me permission, and resources, to hire dozens of new people in new roles and disciplines, focus on permanent as well as temporary, and pick up the outsourcing model that they were already doing well with in the US.

I went in with a PowerPoint presentation. I have the slides in front of me now. I spoke for 30 minutes. There were no questions; there was no interaction at all. The board all listened intently. There was no feedback.

So I finished by saying: *"What Aquent will become is the largest provider of marketing communications and advertising staff across the Asia Pacific region, both in-house and agency. We will dominate temp, contract and perm and will provide a range of other outsourced staffing solutions."*

The first person to speak was Chris Moody, who was the CIO and subsequently the COO. He said just one sentence: *"Greg, what are you thinking?"*

My heart sank. Had I blown it? For a few seconds, I thought he was serious. He was joking. There were smiles all round. The mood lifted.

This was something that had crossed their minds before, but no one had put it into one lucid format. By the end of the meeting, it was agreed. I had the brief to go out and diversify, hire and grow the business. That was a typical John Chuang reaction. If he liked the idea and trusted the person, he gave you lots of room to move.

And boy, did I move! I dug through my old records when writing this book, and I found the following revenue figures, which show the growth of the APAC business over six years.

Aquent Asia Pacific

Year	Revenue (US$m)	Gross profit (US$m)	Operating profit (US$m)
2003	18	7	0.5
2004	29	11	2.1
2005	39	16	2.2
2006	43	19	2.3
2007	51	23	4.7
2008	53	24	2.7

The APAC results from this period make interesting reading. We saw healthy revenue and gross profit growth as we added staff and opened new offices. Profit grew vigorously too, initially, from break-even to over US$4.7 million, but the 'drop through' was slow as the cost of growth weighed us down.

By 2007, we had taken a US$5 million business (in 2001) to US$50 million in revenue, and US$4.7 million in operating profit, a very healthy 9.4% EBIT margin. So, the numbers show that after the Aquent board in Boston accepted my growth and diversification pitch, we moved ahead with purpose.

Lessons learned from Aquent

Job boards don't find people jobs – people find people jobs

I loved the innovation at Aquent. Sacred cows were slaughtered all the time.

For example, we recognised that a big negative for candidates was going to company job sites, scrolling through jobs, applying blindly and never being able to connect with a human.

We also found that the job board mentality from candidates was to 'have a go at anything vaguely appropriate'. It was only a click, after all. So, we were flooded with inappropriate résumés, we could not cope and didn't respond fast enough, and so the vicious cycle of discontent continues.

We totally changed the job board paradigm. We made the recruiter accessible to the candidate and accountable for each application. Indeed, the candidate had the recruiter's name, email and phone number as well as all their work social sites. Plus, the candidate had to search by skills and discipline to find the right recruiter. We found we got fewer applications. However, they were better quality.

This interview from the Aquent blog sums up what we were gunning for:

"With the main aim being connectivity and visibility, candidates will now be directed to search for an agent (Consultant) who specialises in their area of interest first. Based on each agent's profile – via a personal URL – applicants will have the ability to connect with the consultant directly either by phone, email or social network, or apply to any of the specialised jobs that the consultant lists on their profile.

'Candidates are tired of applying to jobs via info@cyberspace.com, where their application disappears into the ether, and they never hear back', explains International CEO, Greg Savage. 'They don't know who to contact, how to contact, or where to contact the person responsible. They don't even know if the job is still open or even whether it even existed in the first place. And worst of all, they don't know who the person is who is handling their personal data.'

Aquent is taking the concept of connectivity and visibility to a whole new level, embracing the social media model as an intrinsic way of doing business.

'Lack of personal interaction is doing our industry no favours and now is the time to do something different,' continues Savage. 'Instead of searching for jobs on our website, candidates will first search for an agent who specialises in their area of expertise within

either marketing or design and who can demonstrate the right sector knowledge.'

On the agent's profile, visitors will see their face, all their contact details, including any social networks they belong to, find out what they are passionate about, read their testimonials and be able to apply for jobs via this person's profile.

'We've turned the tables in the way the recruitment industry is moving. With more and more recruiters going out of their way to be un-contactable and hiding behind job reference numbers and e-mail addresses, we have created a totally transparent way for talent and clients to connect with our people. Besides, job boards don't find people jobs. People find people jobs,' Savage concludes."

It's ironic that this issue in our industry is as bad now, or worse, than it ever was.

Linking recruiter pay to customer satisfaction

I loved that at Aquent there was no fear of trying new ideas. Things not working was not a 'disaster'.

So perhaps it was not surprising that we tackled the 'candidate experience'. I was passionate about it then, as I am now.

However, the way we pay people in our industry and the way clients pay us (contingent fees) leads to overworked recruiters unable to service candidates as they should, or in some cases merely not caring about those who 'don't make the cut'.

So, in conjunction with exclusive assignments (see the next chapter), I rolled the dice and started to link consultant salaries to customer satisfaction (not only billings),

My reasoning was sound. Read the websites of any ten random recruitment companies from any country. You will almost certainly find glowing and poetic prose about 'customer service', and the 'customer comes first' and 'exceptional standards of service delivery' and many other cliché-ridden phrases.

These claims were not written without sincerity. The companies professing to provide flawless service intended that to be the case, I am sure. The desire to be excellent is, in most cases, genuine.

It is the delivery on the service promise that is the problem. All companies, in all industries, find it challenging to deliver top service across a broad customer base consistently. Indeed, it takes an exceptional business to do that.

However, recruitment is in a class of its own when it comes to over-promising and under-delivering.

Recruitment and staffing are a special case because we ask our recruiters to deliver on the customer experience, but then we reward them largely for the dollars they individually generate, regardless of how many candidates and clients they burn along the way. So, there is a mismatch of the message and motivation.

At Aquent, we wanted to demonstrate the best customer service and loyalty in the staffing industry worldwide. However, that lofty goal can't be measured by self-acclamation. It has to be empirical and unbiased. So, we engaged a specialist customer-satisfaction survey firm – focusing on the staffing and professional service arena – to survey our customer base, in every one of our 70 offices, every six months (using the Net Promoter Score, or NPS, system).

We got an overall customer satisfaction score for each business unit, and we could track regular improvement and change. That was super cool! However, we went one step further. All Aquent agents (consultants) in the international business under my management now had a big chunk of their compensation linked to improvements in these customer service scores.

So, our vision was to compensate people with a fair base salary, and exceptional results would attract meaningful bonuses, as is true of most of our industry. Now our recruiters would also earn a 25% 'kicker' on top of their bonus, if their NPS customer score met the set benchmark of improvement and excellence.

We learned that there were many points of potential failure in candidate (and client) experience, but these are three of the biggest:

- *The period between the initial interview with us and the first temp assignment (or perm role referral).* This is critical. The candidate (the talent) has taken time to come and see us. We have spent an hour together. A relationship is established. Communications expectations are set. This is when the recruiter must deliver. The candidate is vulnerable and keen to hear the next steps. The recruiter needs to actively engage with the talent, whether there is an assignment on offer or not. Keep them informed. Advise on the market. Advise on progress with their job search.

- *The post-first-interview stage after a permanent role interview.* This is a burning moment of truth. The candidate has seen the client. They are 'dying' to know more. Many recruiters leave them hanging. This is especially true if the recruiter learns that the client does not favour a particular candidate. That is the time to communicate with the talent and manage their expectations.

- *On a long-term temp assignment.* It is an irony, but a long-term temp will make more money for the recruiter than the biggest of perm fees. However, often the temp is never contacted by the agency who placed them. It's a significant criticism of the staffing industry. Moreover, it's dumb business. That contractor is generating income for you every day. Nurture them. Keep in touch. Show appreciation. They can be your most prominent advocate or your most vocal critic… to your client.

So, in our view 'customer experience' was a key differentiator for recruiters going forward. It still is.

At Aquent, we did not want to be duped by our own PR. We measured what the customers thought. We copped what they told us on the chin. And we worked out ways to fix the problems.

Then we rewarded our staff when the customers were happy.

CHAPTER 8

Rapid growth, catastrophic fall

AFTER THE Aquent board in Boston green-lighted my pitch for growth and diversification, I hired an executive search professional and set up Aquent Executive Search. I started to open offices across the APAC region. We hired aggressively. We scouted acquisitions.

It worked. Initial success was fast and robust (as the figures I outlined in the previous chapter show). Subsequently, the board decided that they liked what I was doing and extended my role beyond APAC to take responsibility for Europe as well, where we had six or seven offices.

Going global

Now I was International CEO for Aquent. At its peak we had 30 offices in 17 countries. I visited every single one of them, and most of them multiple times. It was a massive job, covering at least half the world geographically. The travel is hard to describe now, especially when you add in Boston where I needed to be at least twice a year as well.

The business covered a huge diversity of cultures, business ethos and market conditions, and the legislation matrices were almost impossible to fathom. *(Can we fire someone in this country? We have to pay how much social security loading?! France, I am looking at you.)*

We operated in at least ten different languages. Think about the challenges we faced – with the applicant tracking software (ATS), the website, the marketing campaigns… even in-company communications.

It was suggested I move to somewhere 'more central to my region'. London, Paris, even Singapore were mooted. We discussed it at length at home and decided it wasn't right for the kids. I slightly regret that missed opportunity now, but regardless, my expanded role meant a great deal of travel. I soon became quite chummy with Qantas Lounge staff around the world; we were on a first name basis, and still are in some cases. It's bizarre, really.

It was frenetic, but the results were there as you can see from the numbers in the following table. Revenue and profit grew exponentially. We were on a golden run. I took over as CEO of the combined APAC and Europe business in 2005, and that year we hit revenues of US$64 million. These climbed to US$107 million in 2007, a good effort by most measures, especially when profits followed – from US$3 million to US$9 million three years later.

Aquent International* Europe and Asia Pacific

Year	Revenue (US$m)	Gross profit (US$m)	Operating profit (US$m)
2005	64	25	3
2006	76	32	4
2007	107	47	9

However, as I am fond of lecturing to people now, we should never be taken in by our own PR. Pride comes before a fall, as the cliché warns us. Success breeds overconfidence.

I don't believe I was ever complacent, but I certainly know I began to think we could do little wrong – that everything would 'work'. Naively, even though I really knew better, I began to give

---

* My sincere thanks to Larry Bartlett, CFO of Aquent during my tenure, and still there today, who provided the audited numbers for all the Aquent tables. So we know they are right!

all the credit for our success to ourselves, and none to the buoyant market and the healthy hiring conditions.

That was to prove telling when the market turned – and wow, did it turn! (More on that soon.) However, while it lasted, growth was exhilarating.

We grew into prominent Asian markets first. In Hong Kong, I hired Duncan Cunningham, a staffing professional who built the business from the ground up. From a greenfield start-up, Hong Kong was making US$250,000 a few years later. Duncan subsequently went on to open offices for us in Beijing and Shanghai.

It was a tremendous tragedy when Duncan passed away a few years ago at a young age. I think about him often – a gentle, humorous and loyal man.

Our expansion in Australia was aggressive and rapid. We hired in large numbers in Sydney, Melbourne and Brisbane, and we made small acquisitions in Adelaide and Perth to become a national business. The diversification strategy in Australia took off. We got traction in marketing recruitment in corporates. PR and communications were strong sectors for us, and we acquired a small business support agency with a strong leader; she built up an excellent business which we later re-branded Eloquent Staffing.

(Years later, under the Firebrand regime, which I talk about later in this chapter, we decided Eloquent was not part of our strategy, so I sold it to people2people, of all companies. I talk about my involvement in people2people in more detail in the next chapter, so let me just say for now this was a bizarre little manoeuvre, where I was both a buyer and seller on the same transaction. That needed a lot of transparency and visibility for all parties. It was a success though. There are staff at people2people still now who came across in that transaction, and it was at least eight years ago.)

Back to Aquent: we opened in Malaysia and did well there for many years. At that time, it was an underserviced market in our sector, and we took full advantage.

Malaysia was a case in point when it came to business ethos differences. We hired a manager and were setting up the office. At the time, Malaysia needed all staffing companies to have a staffing agency licence. This was a so-called formality, but it took weeks to come through, then months. In frustration, I called the manager. *"Where the **** is this licence?"* I gently enquired. *"Greg, authorise me to spend $10,000 today on 'charity', and we will have it by tomorrow,"* she sadly replied.

This was her way of explaining that an 'inducement' to the official would do it. It was tempting, but it was a crossroads. One justification was to view this as 'business as usual in a foreign country' – you know, 'when in Rome…'. However, I felt that once you offer a bribe, you are on a slippery slope. Where does it stop?

I decided it would stop before it started. I instructed her to hassle the official until we got it. *"Go and sit in his office all day,"* was my closing advice. We got it weeks later – no bribe. It cost us quite a bit in money terms because of delays. However, I sleep well.

Many mistakes along the way…

Even in the golden times, we did make some mistakes. We opened an office in Taiwan which frankly wasn't very successful, and we set up in Korea, despite a mistake by me.

The plan to open the office in Seoul may not have been an error in itself, but our entry was flawed because of the leadership I appointed. It's not possible to outline details here, but the business was left vulnerable until I appointed Kay Lee, a decent and hardworking man who stabilised the business and settled the staff and the client relationships.

Ultimately, the office was closed in cutbacks caused by the global financial crisis (GFC) – which was nothing to do with Kay's management – but not before Kay and his team engineered the biggest fee generated by Aquent International in my ten years there. I think it's still the biggest single placement fee by any company I have ever managed or worked at.

The client was Innocean, the in-house agency of the Hyundai Group. Aquent Seoul was asked to recruit an executive creative director. The ideal candidate was sourced via search methodology and approached, but declined the opportunity to consider a move.

It sounds incredible, but Aquent negotiated with Innocean to make an offer to the candidate based solely on his résumé, and also to agree to an 'open salary package'. In other words, *"Whatever it takes, we want him!"*

The candidate was understandably impressed with this approach, agreed to meet the CEO, and a deal was struck.

The fee of KRW $100 million (approximately US$100,000) was celebrated as an Aquent record, and I doubt it has been beaten since. So there were some wins there.

I looked at acquisitions in South Africa which didn't come through, but did make a small acquisition in India, so we had a presence in Mumbai for five years which frankly was another of my poor decisions, as the leadership was not right, nor was our local strategy.

Singapore grew to over 20 staff and was highly profitable. We tried to build contract and temp in Singapore, and even sent one of our best Sydney recruiters to drive it, but either we got it wrong or the market just wasn't there, and it never really took off the way it had in Australia, New Zealand, the UK, Japan and elsewhere.

In Europe we had a significant London business of over 40 people, one in Manchester and then also in Paris, Amsterdam, Munich and the Czech Republic. We subsequently opened in Poland and Spain as well.

Frankly, when I look back, some of those smaller businesses were not well enough planned. We didn't hire the right people or apply the right resources to make them sustainable. London, however, is a massive market, and we eventually made three acquisitions there, taking the business to more than 70 people.

...And a big success

Apart from Australia and London, the 'jewel' in the Aquent International 'crown' was probably Japan. In Japan, we grew the temp and contract business at excellent margins under the leadership of Yoshiko Fujii, who was not my hire; she was the incumbent when I joined.

Yoshiko revelled in the growth push; in Tokyo to 40 staff, and Osaka to 15. We opened offices in Fukuoka, Sapporo and Nagoya. Japan was one of the most sustainable of the businesses in my region because most of our gross profit was from high-margin, long-term contract placements. We added buckets of permanent revenue too, but the bedrock was always sound, as it is to this day.

Unlike most non-Japanese recruitment companies, which are mainly staffed by ex-pats, Aquent's Japan branch was a very 'Japanese business' with 90% of our staff being locals, many of whom could not speak English. I spent a lot of time in Japan and loved learning the business culture, although it is true that the more time you spend in Japan, the more you realise how little you understand Japan.

Yoshiko Fujii was one of the most determined, hardest working individuals I have ever met. She was a strong, independent woman, but she also did take advice, and this combination was good for us as we grew from about ten people when I joined the company to well over 80.

She probably won't like me saying it, but she was a workaholic, dedicated to the Aquent cause and regularly staying in the office till midnight and beyond. I counselled her on this for years, not only for her own sake but for that of the staff, who tended to want to leave only after the boss had. That was problematic and, although she tried to adjust her work patterns, she was one of the most dedicated people I have ever encountered.

The contrast in business culture across countries was brought home to me so many times when I was at Aquent. Like my 'Australian irony' that went down like a lead balloon in Boston at the board meeting (see the previous chapter), so too did I see many other differences in the way people thought and behaved in these different environments.

For instance, take Sydney and Tokyo…

I was asked by one of our Sydney recruiters to join her on a client visit to a high-profile Australian advertising agency group. I jumped at the chance because I love speaking with clients. We were booked to meet two very senior people, both at executive creative director level.

We arrived on time and waited in the trendy, borderline pretentiously creative reception.

And we waited.

And waited.

At ten past the meeting hour we asked the receptionist for an update. She looked a little confused. She made a call. She clearly got a disconcerting answer, and then disappeared out of sight.

We continued to wait.

Eventually, she came back, and it was clear she had bad news.

The creative duo had been *"called into a meeting"*. She paused, and then added (in what I could see was a moment of embarrassed inspiration) *"by the CEO."*

We explained that we had an appointment, confirmed the day before. She offered to call the HR manager, and she did, but that person was unavailable. I could see she was the innocent party here, and very uncomfortable, so I asked if we could have a two-minute chat with one of the executive creative directors, to set up another time. However, she got even more flustered, and we left on the basis that they would call to reset the meeting.

Neither of them did. Ever.

They never contacted us again. Not to apologise for wasting our time, not to reset the meeting – a meeting they had both firmly agreed to at the outset, verbally and via a follow-up email.

Then, three weeks later, I spent five days in Tokyo. On that trip, I met with seven clients, all at CEO, marketing director or VP HR level. Most of the clients were Japanese, but two of the people we visited were Westerners who had been living in Japan for some time. I was struck by the demeanour of these clients when dealing with us, their supplier, and the contrast between this and what I had recently experienced in Australia.

On each occasion, we were expected and were greeted as honoured guests. The receptionist buzzed, and within a few moments a PA or assistant greeted us and showed us to a meeting room. We were rarely left in the reception area for more than a few minutes.

Refreshments were always offered: water, tea and many times small cakes and biscuits as well.

On not a single occasion did the person we were there to meet keep us waiting. CEO or not, the meeting started on time.

The shortest meeting we had lasted an hour. The length of a meeting does not dictate its quality, of course, but it does mean that your presence there is taken seriously, and that time has been allocated.

To cap it off, I was struck by one final act of good old-fashioned manners.

After every meeting, the senior person saw us not only to the door, not only to the reception but actually walked us to the lift and waited till it arrived. They then shook hands, thanked us for our time and pressed the ground floor button for us, and waited there until the door closed.

Compare this to those super-cool executive creative directors in Sydney who stood us up without a second thought, or even the courtesy of coming to reception to tell us why.

Being 'the client' does not make you special. Being special is what makes you special.

This lesson from Japan reinforced what I like to think I already knew. Whether in a position of 'power' or not, being rude is being rude. Thus, being a jerk is just, well… being a jerk.

Below, Yoshiko Fujii remembers a visit we did together in Japan. (English is not her first language, obviously, and I have not tried to polish her note.)

A business development campaign happened every quarter involving all offices in Japan. One day, Greg was there coincidentally during his business trip from Sydney, so he joined in!

Many managers talk and talk, but never actually do the work. On that very day, Greg demonstrated he could still do calls, and got an appointment with CEO of Grey Worldwide, one of the biggest advertising agencies in Japan, and I accompanied him to the meeting.

The Grey CEO kept on talking how bad the situation was in the market at that time. His Japan subsidiary was not doing well. The tone was totally negative. I felt it hopeless and no alternative but to politely leave.

Then suddenly, Greg spoke, "By the way, are you hiring?" Of course not! I thought to myself. But next moment, the CEO replied "Yes, we are."

In Japan, there is a term 'read the air'. We are expected to respect the mood and follow accordingly. However, Greg did not read the air at all. Actually ignored it. Or maybe he read it better than I did!

I am quite confident that the good manager must be the best player, when you lead the team. People can be brave and challenge the difficult task, when they know there is a reliable boss to learn from somewhere around you.

Thank you, Greg, my dearest leader in that era :)

So it seems at least on that occasion I was following my oft-given advice, *"Ask for the business."*

Hey recruiter, can you put the fee up, please?

Let me share another story from our success in Japan. Permanent recruitment fees in Japan often shock outsiders: 30% is standard, 35% common. However, Japan gave me my most incredible ever client fee story in recruitment. Not about haggling the fee down. No, it was the reverse!

Also, it is proof that when it comes to price, market forces will prevail.

On one memorable and much-celebrated occasion (in 2010) our client in Tokyo, a gaming software business, offered us a 60% fee (on a US$60,000 job!) and our Tokyo team promptly filled the order, securing a fee in the vicinity of $40,000.

This was fascinating to me. I have never really seen a situation where the client is driving fees upwards. We would *never* suggest a 60% fee.

Yet this client's rationale was: *"Top talent is hard to find. We want the best. We are competing with other employers. We want the recruiter to be motivated to find us the best."*

And it worked. The candidate we placed into this role had scarce user interface skills, and our team found him, a Japanese speaker, in Melbourne!

Once again, the real value of our business was laid bare – finding talent that others cannot. We took that seriously at Aquent, as I have my entire recruiting life.

Client commitment – an Aquent gamble that worked

I talk more about the importance of gaining client commitment and exclusivity in Chapter 15, but let me be clear here. We need to get paid more often for the work we do. We need to have more belief in our value.

With this very much in mind, in January 2010, as International CEO of Aquent, I launched a new strategy for engaging with clients on permanent hiring assignments, only accepting assignments in design, digital and marketing on a retained or exclusive basis.

When this was announced to the broader recruiting community, the move provoked considerable industry debate. A few months later (18 March 2010) industry news service Shortlist.net.au reported on our progress as follows.

Aquent taking fewer jobs under exclusivity program but fill rates up

Aquent is turning away up to five permanent job orders a week as a result of its new push to take only exclusive work, but fill rates have more than doubled, says CEO Greg Savage.

Savage told *Shortlist* in Aquent's Australian business, where it had taken "a very hard line" on only accepting permanent recruitment work if it was on an exclusive basis for an agreed period, the three-month-old strategy had so far had a positive response from 60% of clients.

"We're turning away between three and five job orders a week right now, and that's frustrating because we think we could fill them, but we want to build on the momentum we're getting."

Although Aquent was doing about 40% fewer permanent assignments in Australia, he added, its fill rate for these jobs had gone from around 30% up to between 60% and 70%.

Savage said all of the permanent recruitment staff still had enough work to keep them busy and reach their targets, but also had the capacity to increase their workload.

"There are plenty who can handle more work, but they're not idle because they're doing a much more thorough job on the work that they are doing now.

"A consultant may have been handling 16 jobs, and they're now handling seven, so it allows them to give more attention to both the client and candidates."

Truthfully, it was not as brave as it sounds because 70% of our gross profit in Australia came from contract and temporary placements, so we had our 'factory' churning the revenue for us. I doubt I would have done this if we were a permanent-only business.

It's also important to note that in the October of that year, a few senior Aquent executives and I were involved in a management buyout of ten Aquent offices, and we created Firebrand Talent Search, so I never got to see what would happen if the 'exclusive only' strategy had been maintained long term. I strongly suspect we would have stuck with it, with universal benefits!

Indeed, years later, the message still resonates.

Elizabeth Kingston, Executive Director of Kingston Human Capital in Brisbane, sent me the following note in 2017. Its relevance to this topic is evident and compelling.

Hi Greg

Before we close out the year, I needed to email you and thank you.

Eons ago you posted about contingent work.

Since that post, I've re-engineered our offering.

We're only taking exclusive or retained work on our perm desks... (with a few exceptions that I need to tighten up).

You know what?

- *Our permanent desks are more profitable*
- *Our conversion rates are so much better*
- *My consultants are less stressed because they are spending time on the roles that truly deserve their attention*
- *Our clients are thrilled with the service*
- *Our costs per project are down*
- *And there is a tangible increase in the level of self-respect my consultants have.*

So, thanks for the light bulb moment.

Thanks for being the catalyst to one of the best decisions we've taken this year.

Elizabeth Kingston

Then... we hit the wall!

In September 2008, Lehman Brothers collapsed. Global financial markets reacted and to us it felt as though hiring across the world just basically stopped.

In one year. our revenues dropped $50 million. Of course, we had no hope of cutting our expenses to keep pace, so we went from massive profit to significant losses. Declining revenues exposed weaknesses I had previously glossed over. Some of these I've already mentioned, such as the quality of some of the management, but other weaknesses included the shallowness of some of our client relationships, the skill levels of many agents and the reliance on perm in many markets.

After the 2008 Lehman Brothers collapse, its inevitable impact on the staffing industry worldwide can be seen in the full numbers for Aquent International from 2005 to 2009. I've mentioned the massive growth to 2007; the following figures also show the drop in profits and then revenue to 2009.

Aquent International Europe and Asia Pacific

Year	Revenue (US$m)	Gross profit (US$m)	Operating profit (US$m)
2005	64	25	3
2006	76	32	4
2007	107	46	9
2008	114	50	5
2009	64	22	(-7)

Figures given to me by Simon Lusty concerning the Australian business of Aquent at the time show the knock-on effect in Australia. In October 2008, Aquent Australia had its best profit month ever. However, let's just examine the permanent placement revenue. (The business was mainly temp and contract.) Permanent gross profit in Australia for October was $585,000, about the monthly average of the year to date. After Lehman Brothers, permanent hiring ground to an abrupt halt. Clients were making optimistic noises about hiring again in January, but the fact was that permanent gross profit in November, normally one of our strongest months, dropped to $184,000! And December was worse, at $112,000.

Simon tells me that in November 2008 when the perm fees dropped like a lead balloon, I said to him, *"Don't worry mate, it will all recover by February, and then it will be biz as normal."*

Well, in January things got worse, and our perm business showed no growth at all till 2010 and didn't really get back to anywhere like 'normal' till 2013. Great forecast, Greg!

As already mentioned, it wasn't only Australia though, and Europe was particularly hard hit. It was at this time that I re-learned the hard lessons that I'd learned at Recruitment Solutions all those years before in the early 1990s (which I discussed in Chapter 5).

It wasn't just Aquent, of course. We probably did better than most! There was global carnage in the staffing industry.

Good times don't last forever. Sustainable businesses have components that protect them in an economic downturn, and we realised that many of our offices simply did not have these things.

All the offices with a majority of revenue from permanent placements came under immediate pressure. Offices where consultants had shallow client relationships or no ability to sell and had been merely transacting at a superficial level, saw revenue drop. The quality of some of our management was exposed as individuals without the necessary drive, sales focus and staff motivation skills, retreated behind their desks and buried their heads in their computers.

Hard decisions had to be made. As our revenues across the world dropped dramatically, it quickly became clear we had to take drastic action. This included shutting some of the small, underperforming offices, reducing staff numbers, cutting advertising, and a wide range of the usual cost-cutting processes.

Jenny Gottlieb, still at Aquent now, who worked with me on redundancies and closures at that time, told me recently that after a dismal week of distressing conversations, she was sitting shell-shocked at her desk, when I approached her with the comforting words, "There is no crying in recruitment".

What a guy. Even so, she still loves me apparently.

Our profit-making machine stumbled. It was a chastening period for me as I'd experienced eight or nine years of continued success at the helm of Aquent outside the US, hard on the success of the Recruitment Solutions listing. There is no doubt that I had begun to believe my own PR and started to feel that everything I would touch, staffing-wise, would turn to gold.

That proved to be an illusion as I found myself on the back foot grappling with falling revenues, distressed staff and no real light at the end of the tunnel – that is, until a bright idea came my way.

Firebrand Talent Search

We had been battling the severe economic conditions of the financial crisis for over a year. The international business, while still overall in sound health, was full of weak points and needed a rethink. It was at this time that an idea was put to me by Mike Smith from the Aquent board. It was big, but it was simple.

The senior management of Aquent International would engineer a management buyout of ten of the Aquent offices across Europe and APAC. I would be the major shareholder, and several key managers would take a significant stake too. Aquent would remain a minority shareholder and provide some back-office support as the new company, soon to be named Firebrand Talent Search, rode the 'imminent recovery' and built a significant business for sale at some point in the future.

I could see the logic: the business that had been so strong was now at a low point; I had a good track record of growing businesses significantly, so why couldn't I do it again with this excellent team?

Aquent had excellent infrastructure and back office to support us. They would stick to their temp and contract business globally, which had always been their heritage, while we would grow Firebrand Talent Search in the UK, France, Hong Kong, Singapore, Malaysia, Australia, New Zealand and Japan.

The idea was fraught with risks, and it was also opportunistic. In truth, we were trying to 'time the market', which any share trader or property investor will know is a dangerous thing to do. We had seen our permanent revenues drop by over 60%; we had also seen those same offices be highly profitable. Surely we could build them back and ride the wave of the economic upturn?

The communication of this idea to the staff was a delicate and challenging thing. I flew to every office and explained what was going to happen. In some cases, half the team would be staying with Aquent, while the other half would be part of Firebrand. That required honesty and transparency but also something of a sales pitch to both parties.

We assembled a team of managers in Sydney, and we met at my home around my dining table. We got in a brand expert and created the brand. We decided on an ATS (database) system. In this way, on 11th October 2010 Firebrand Talent Search was born.

After that began the toughest two years of my recruiting life. We were selling a whole new brand, both externally and to our staff. We no longer had a big brother in Aquent underwriting our every move, although they were tremendously supportive overall.

The truth is that the idea did not fully work. Yes, we built a successful business. Yes, many of the offices were highly profitable. However, the reality is that Firebrand Talent Search only had its peak at about 80 staff, and we had ten offices, so in many cases we had fewer than six or seven staff in an office. Thus, rather than being a company of 80 to 100 people, we were a conglomeration of affiliated small businesses, all very far apart! And all of which had the problems that small companies face – such as lack of critical mass. So, if you were sitting in Hong Kong with five people and two people resigned, you were suddenly facing an almost deserted business.

The permanent market did not come back as quickly as we had hoped. In retrospect, the smarter thing to do would have been to just take the four or five biggest countries and put all of our resources into building those businesses, rather than spreading all of our management and our money and our time across ten small offices in eight countries and speaking three different languages.

I loved the Firebrand experiment and appreciated Aquent's support for doing it. I am deeply grateful for the unstinting loyalty of the management and the consultants who made that business the quality operation it was.

However, in the end, the road to making it profitable and valuable was far too long. So, we sold the majority of the businesses at the end of 2012 and Firebrand now exists as an Aquent brand in Australia alone.

More lessons learned from Aquent

Golden times at the Golden Club

Owners of recruitment businesses often ask me about incentives other than commission for their consultants. Dinners, trips, awards… do they help?

Mostly I don't think they work, but the Golden Club, a brainchild of the management team of Aquent in Sydney, and designed for the business under my management, might be the exception. As we grew and started making significant profits, we wanted to drive top performers to peak achievement. We also wanted to become an employer of choice. Aquent is a truly international company, so we wanted people to mingle and collaborate. Golden Club members from across Aquent APAC and Europe met once a year at an exotic location to share learning and socialise, and enjoyed other ongoing benefits.

Golden Club was for peak billers, yes. You had to achieve a certain dollar value fee production in the year to be 'in'. However, it also required behavioural standards – it was for collaborators, sharers and those who supported the 'Aquent way'.

This was real. One of the more difficult conversations I had was eight or nine months into the year with a high performing Sydney agent (consultant) who was on track to hit the Golden Club entry level as far as billed fees were concerned. I told her she wasn't going to be accepted, regardless of the number. I explained why. Her attitude, behaviour and treatment of others was a problem. You can't be in Golden unless you are 'golden'.

She was understandably disappointed. Many managers would not have had that conversation for fear of losing a big biller. To be honest, I was a bit nervous. However, fees do not beat ethos in my book, and it had to be addressed. To her credit, she changed, improved and joined Golden Club the next year.

Golden Club was really 'something else'. Locations were memorable: Shanghai, Siem Reap and Bangkok, for starters. There were between 15 and 30 Golden 'Clubbers' there, from all over our part of the Aquent world. We invited a few of our colleagues from the US, and the learning, the bonding and the fun was on for three or four days.

Being in the Golden Club was special. It went beyond the trip away. There was ongoing advanced training, Golden Clubbers were asked for input on strategy and were given other perks.

The reward for high performers was significant, and the benefits for the company in terms of motivation and engagement were genuine.

CHAPTER 9

people2people

IN THE midst of all the growth I was experiencing at Aquent, another avenue opened up that I couldn't help exploring. It proved to be one of my most successful recruiting ventures of all, and I can take little real credit for it – although, of course, I often do!

Conceived over a Sunday Shiraz

One day in late 2004, when I was still CEO of Aquent APAC, I was enjoying a BBQ at home with old work colleagues from my Recruitment Solutions days, Manda Milling and Simon Gressier. Hired as rookies, these two were now ten-year recruiting veterans. They had seen Recruitment Solutions in its heyday, including the IPO, then subsequently taken over by Chandler Macleod and absorbed into a much bigger organisation with a different ethos.

The history behind the actual 'birth' of people2people has several versions. However, at the exact moment of its conception, there were only three people present, and I was one of them. So I am confident in my version.

Simon and Manda (who had met at Recruitment Solutions and were now married – my pleasure, guys, no need to thank me) were not happy about the decline of Recruitment Solutions. After about the fifth glass of Shiraz, and many hours of hearing how *"It wasn't like the old days of Recruitment Solutions anymore, but we treat it like our own company,"* I suggested that they start their own business.

This comment resulted in much hilarity, but after a little debate it was decided it wasn't such a silly idea. Indeed, Simon and Manda had discussed the idea before with another Recruitment Solutions stalwart, Mark Smith, but they had never actually acted on it.

So, I believe I made two contributions to the founding of people2people.

First, I contributed enough money to make sure they had the resources to get it going (and to take 40% of the equity) but, far more importantly, I think I gave the three founders the belief that they *could* do it, that they *should* do it, and that they *would* succeed if they did it.

The three of them had worked with me for a combined 30 years, and no doubt took some comfort from my confidence in them. They had toyed with the idea before, but now they had the catalyst to take the leap.

My motivation? The same as always: fun and money. I loved the idea of Recruitment Solutions alumni 'having a go'. These people were friends as well as ex-colleagues, so playing a part in their future success was very appealing.

Moreover, it was a chance to help a business succeed without having to run that business – leveraging my experience to some degree, I guess. I believed they would succeed, and vaguely I hoped for a steady stream of dividends 'at some time'. I most certainly did not envisage the scale of the success that was to follow.

After months of planning, people2people was born and commenced trading on 1 February 2005.

Mark Smith, Simon Gressier and Manda Milling, plus two more Recruitment Solutions alumni – Kirsten Garrett, and the much loved and now so sadly late Maria Mexis – began operations, perched around some second-hand desks, behind the Italian National Tourist Board, upstairs in Market Street in Sydney.

I was a shareholder, director and avuncular advisor – but my most significant contribution on day one was to turn up with a crate of beer and a bottle of champagne on a stinking hot Sydney afternoon, and distract everyone by pouring drinks and telling stories about start-ups past.

It was a long time ago, but I do remember one of the other critical roles I played was to encourage the company to place a significant emphasis on growing the temporary business.

Mark Smith had started as a temporary consultant, and then went on to hire others. This focus on annuity revenue was to hold us in excellent stead in 2008/9 when the GFC crippled recruitment companies around the world, and was particularly vicious on those companies that had a majority of income from permanent placements. We didn't. So people2people made money through 2009, 2010 and 2011, going on to grow exponentially.

Mark Smith takes up the story:

Greg's value as a true advisor came into real focus in the aftermath of the Lehman Brothers collapse in October 2008, a time of considerable uncertainty.

Our business was growing fast, but was still small and vulnerable. None of us had been in the recruitment industry during a downturn. We were frightened that we could lose everything we had worked hard for.

Greg had steered a course during the recession of 1991, and this experience proved invaluable to us. We felt more secure in the decisions that we made during that time.

I remember vividly sitting in a small Sydney wine bar near Town Hall in December 2008 with Greg, Manda and Simon discussing our course of action for the GFC. Greg led us to decisions that I believe set us up to take full advantage of the GFC. With his advice, people2people prepared to gain market share in the upswing after the GFC, which we did.

Exceptional growth

The people2people story is extraordinary.

The company has grown to be one of Australia's pre-eminent large generalist recruiters, independent and Australian owned, with revenues of $100 million per year. This is an extraordinary feat when you consider that 80% of recruitment companies in Australia can't grow beyond ten people, let alone to a multi-office, multi-faceted, multi-million-dollar profit, privately held business like this one.

The annual revenues produced by people2people over 14 years tell the story. As you read them, consider that this business started with $300,000 funding and five people on day one.

people2people Annual Revenue 2005–2019 (AU$m)

2005	2006	2007	2008	2009
1	3	5	8	6
2010	2011	2012	2013	2014
12	17	17	23	30
2015	2016	2017	2018	2019
39	66	103	118	96

In its first ten months of operations, the company generated just under $1 million in revenue, climbing rapidly to $8 million only three years later. The Lehman Brothers collapse, and the subsequent global downturn, hurt revenues in 2009, but afterwards there was a strong bounce back and then relentless growth, highlighted by some massive jumps in 2016 and 2017, as some very large contractor and outsourcing contracts were won.

2019 has dipped, but this is actually a good thing. people2people did not renew a massive low-margin payrolling deal with Optus (which I had been badgering them to do for years), and that decision wiped $32 million off the top line, but the rest of the business grew as usual.

The 'loss' of the Optus deal, by the way, increased profitability and relieved massive pressure on cash flow. It also released consultants to work on better quality business. (See Chapter 22 for more on high-volume, low-margin deals, and why it's good to avoid them.)

Mark recalls:

Following the GFC, people2people was profitable and cashed up. I was ready to take risks and grow rapidly. Having Greg on the board, as an advisor but also as an investor, meant risks I would have otherwise taken were always undertaken in conjunction with the board. Manda Milling and I were always pretty gung-ho, but we were always counterbalanced by Simon (who was nearly always more conservative).

Greg brought an investor's point of view. I, as Managing Director, might neglect the return on investment for the shareholders but Greg would always say, "We don't make vanity investments" and ask why we would put at risk cash that could otherwise be returned to investors. The result was that we were unlikely to overpay for acquisitions and sought only to grow in markets that provided a strategic advantage.

Growing our own

For many years, people2people found it challenging to attract recruiters from other agencies. We didn't have a strong brand or a compellingly different story, and the market was hot, so good recruiters were spoilt for choice.

This turned out, though, to be a blessing in disguise as it pushed us to hire graduates and junior people who were not from the industry.

Here's Mark Smith again:

people2people developed a 'para consultant graduate scheme' which took green and untested graduates on a journey to a 360-recruitment consultant. The results of this scheme surpassed anything any of us ever envisaged.

Recruiting graduates means taking greater risk, so at p2p we took some time to consider the behaviours of the successful recruiters we knew, both inside p2p and in the market, and developed a testing regime.

However, we used the psych test as part of the process and not as a determinant to hire the graduate.

We also used an aptitude test to benchmark the graduate against their peers. This is to establish innate intelligence of the graduate, and experience has proven that anyone without sufficient 'smarts', won't be a successful recruiter.

We often start the graduate as the 'people manager', physically based at the reception. It grounds them well in customer service and the office process. The respect given to the front desk by experienced consultants is enhanced by the fact that they have worked in this role.

Phase two is to move into a 'para consultant' role, ideally supporting one consultant or a small team, exposing the newbie to taking the brief, sourcing, controlling the process and negotiating the placement. The training is one on one and directive. We support this with an external 'rookie' program and online tools.

The amount of time that someone stays in the para consultant role is dependent on their performance but is around six to twelve months.

At people2people, this program has been running since 2006. The return on what is clearly a considerable investment of training time and resources has been beyond any of our initial expectations.

As the company has grown, it hasn't all been roses. At least 50% of graduate hires have not 'worked out'. On the other hand, hiring people with a degree and a couple of years of experience, sometimes less, has resulted in some exceptional success stories. Elizabeth Punshon has been with the company for more than ten years and is now a shareholder and director in Melbourne. Christina Sclavos currently manages the 35-person Sydney business. Catherine Kennedy is a director and shareholder, and manages the entire New South Wales business.

These are just some of the people who were hired without any industry experience and have gone on to forge exceptional careers with people2people – making an enormous contribution to this business. Many others are making a considerable contribution and on a stellar journey.

Melbourne: I love it when a plan comes together

The establishment of the people2people Melbourne office (in 2015) is one of my favourite recruitment stories because it began as one of those rare situations where quite a convoluted plan comes together, and everyone ends up happy.

It started when a broker suggested that people2people consider acquiring a very small recruitment business called Devlin Alliance. We assessed the opportunity and met with the owner, Erin Devlin, whom I already knew. Although we liked her a lot, we had so much else on that the board decided to pass up on the acquisition.

I agreed with that decision, but the opportunity we had missed started to bug me. Mostly, I liked Erin and believed she had tremendous energy and potential. So I hatched a cunning plan.

Even though I was a director and shareholder of people2people, I suggested to Erin and the board of people2people that we should create a new entity that would be people2people Victoria. I would put a third of the funding into that entity and Erin Devlin would roll her company into it, for which she would get a third of the equity. Mark and the other shareholders of people2people would put in the remainder of the investment.

The secret formula was this: Erin would bring her network of contacts, her energy and her determination as well as her recruitment skill. people2people would bring its brand, its technology, its marketing, training and the expertise of its executives in other states, as well as the opportunity to cross-sell to clients across the country. In addition, I would act as a mentor and manager to Erin, to help her grow a business beyond a size that she had experienced before.

The deal was simple and was struck on the back of an envelope. After between three and five years, I would sell my shares back at an agreed multiple to people2people and they would take ownership of the business, with Erin having a one-third share of the company, which would have by that time grown exponentially.

So, guess what? It worked!

Three years later the business had 20 staff, sales of $10 million and an appropriate EBIT return on that number. I, along with the other shareholders, sold my shares to people2people, and Erin continues to lead the business with Mark as her CEO. Thus, people2people acquired a healthy, vibrant and very profitable Melbourne branch.

Erin Devlin, director of people2people Victoria and founder of the branch, shares her views:

The growth of people2people Recruitment Victoria has been incredibly successful, rewarding and fulfilling. From my perspective, the ingredients to this success have included the marriage of two businesses with aligned values, and three business leaders with highly complementary strengths and experience.

Bringing together people2people, a forward-thinking, financially successful and well-known recruitment agency, and Devlin Alliance, a small, but locally established recruitment agency, gave the business a starting client base, local reputation, and momentum. This was underpinned by the seamless and complementary interaction of the three business leaders that brought the business's successes to life.

In addition to my contribution, Mark Smith provided unique people2people knowledge, innovation, business acumen and an optimistic outlook, while Greg Savage brought the proven success of experience, executive mentoring and coaching to the table. With Greg guiding on critical decisions and supporting with leadership coaching and development weekly, we were able to execute the board's plans to great success, achieving sales, gross profit and net profit growth above 70% year on year.

The experience has been exceptionally professionally and personally rewarding, has created jobs for an outstanding group of Melbourne consultants, and has set people2people Victoria on a path for long-term success.

Crazily, they decided to keep me on the board even though I'm no longer a shareholder, so I am still involved to this day. Moreover, I love it. I'm immensely proud of the achievements of people2people Victoria even though my contribution was tiny.

Erin herself evolved from an excellent recruiter to an outstanding leader, something that is not necessarily a natural course of events.

people2people came to the party in providing tremendous support and, as a result, a business now worth many millions of dollars was created. As I write this, the staff is at 25 in Melbourne, and the business continues to thrive.

As someone else once said, *"it's a beautiful thing when a plan comes together"*.

The phenomenon continues

As this book goes to publication, I remain an advisor to all the people2people Australian companies (there are four: NSW, Victoria, West Australia and Queensland and South Australia is on the way) and a shareholder in the Western Australian entity where we are embarking on a Melbourne 2.0 strategy with a young up-and-coming recruiter/manager, Kim Padmore.

It's been 14 years since people2people started and it's tough for me to honestly assess what contribution I have made. In many ways it has been minimal; I'm hardly ever there and I've never done a day's real work in the business.

On the other hand, I do think it's true that I ensured mistakes I had made in other businesses were not made at people2people and I helped to craft a strategy, especially around marketing and expansion, which has worked. I've also been involved in numerous acquisition discussions and the inevitable discussions around people that a business of this size will have to undertake.

Perhaps it's best I leave it to Mark Smith, who is now the MD and majority shareholder of people2people – having bought the shares of Manda Milling, Simon Gressier and myself some years ago – to explain why he has kept me hanging around all this time:

As a business owner or manager, you need to understand the limits of your knowledge and acknowledge just how inexperienced you really are.

In the early days of people2people, I found real value in having a distinction between everyday operational management and a board of directors. This meant that the daily decisions had to be in line with the strategic objectives set down by the board. As Greg was not in the 'everyday', the board meetings were a mechanism to rate our performance, demonstrate our success or to articulate our failures. I learned that I would have to explain my decisions. Having Greg on the people2people board provided discipline to our decision-making.

To this day, Greg adds considerable value to people2people, via his ability to ask the right questions. He has an uncanny ability to ask the one question I don't want him to in the board meetings. Greg always seems able to perceive what our underlying issues are. He is not side-tracked by rhetoric. Having Greg in the room asking prudent questions meant that we couldn't avoid these issues that I was prepared to 'paper over'.

Another advantage of having Greg available during this time was to listen to, learn from and participate in conversations that were not part of my lexicon before – particularly around acquisitions. I started to determine how recruitment firms were valued, and how deals were negotiated.

In any relationship, it's not all smooth going. There are conflicts and issues, and you should be aware that a non-executive director will challenge and question. This is not always easy, but if there is mutual respect, the process gives any decision you make a certain rigour.

Even today, people2people is a phenomenon.

As a founder, investor and initially a major shareholder, I obviously had confidence in its potential. However, it has exceeded all my wildest expectations. The growth story you have read here hasn't stopped, and now the company is among a very small group of large Australian owned recruitment companies.

For perspective, consider that in the whole of the biggest staffing market in the world, the USA, out of 19,408 staffing firms, almost 85% have less than $5 million in annual revenue. According to *Breaking Through*, by Mike Cleland and Barry Asin (Charted Path, 2018), only 140 companies in that giant market have managed to exceed $100 million in annual revenues. The number in Australia would be a tiny fraction of that. Yet, people2people has broken that barrier and has done so while remaining totally independent and highly profitable.

It is a success story I can take very little credit for. I feel immense pride nonetheless.

Lessons learned from people2people

If you are good enough…

people2people has always been a business that champions diversity. Women, in particular, have thrived in an environment without glass ceilings.

The company currently has eight branches or 'Business Units'. Women run seven of these.

At director level it's a similar story. The board of the NSW business, for example (a $60 million p.a. turnover), has two men and four women. All the women are shareholders as well as directors, and all have 'risen from the ranks' through effort, results and subsequent recognition.

Our director and shareholder in Perth is a woman and is 28 years old. She thinks she is young, and people judge her for that. We think she is good and judge her on her potential, skills, results and attitude.

It's not unique, but it is an integral part of the company success story – respect for all who contribute, recognition of results and no artificial hurdles.

We are who we are

people2people may have started as a mini version of Recruitment Solutions, which is not that surprising given it was founded by four people who had spent a combined 40 years plus there – and our first two paid employees were ex Recruitment Solutions. However, people2people quickly developed its own culture and company ethos.

Small things seemed to make a big difference. The concept of a Strategy Day every year, where everyone in the company was flown to one location, successes were communicated and input to initiatives were sought and acted on, really did work.

Frankly, my initial view was that these trips were a junket and a waste of money, but as with many similar ideas over the years, I found out I was wrong. They do mean a great deal to the staff, who feel valued and heard, and excellent ideas are always uncovered and implemented.

Something small happened at the tenth anniversary of people2people in 2015, which for me indicated that the company is a little different to most. It was a huge celebration; black tie, best location, great food and wine. The company had survived ten years and was thriving. Staff partners were invited, I acted as MC that night, and it was a pleasure to take on the task.

I was surprised and delighted to see among the guests many people2people alumni; consultants and managers who had worked with the company previously then had moved on to other roles, even other recruitment companies and, indeed, in-house roles.

Yet, here at the tenth anniversary, the business was acknowledging their contribution by literally 'inviting them to the party'.

Any recruiter reading this will know there are not many companies that would have had this attitude.

Loving the Longevity Lunch

Another people2people tradition is the Longevity Lunch. This is simple, but it's one of my favourites.

If you've been with the company for five years, then you get to come to the Longevity Lunch. The lunch celebrates the fact that these people have had a long career with the business, but it also has a beautiful and ironic double meaning because these lunches can sometimes go on for 12 hours, given a chance.

I very rarely miss these lunches, as it's a wonderful occasion to sit with people whom you have known for a long time who have made an enormous contribution to an excellent business and are friends as well as colleagues. The last lunch I went to had 30 people there, an indication of how much longevity there actually is at people2people.

It's just lunch. Everyone who attends can afford their own lunch, but it's a tremendous atmosphere, and it's always coupled with marking achievements, milestones and a few bloopers around the table which makes it something entirely different.

That most recent lunch (at the time of writing) was held in The Rocks in Sydney, starting at midday. Lunchers came from around the country and also from New Zealand. A few hours later the party moved further down the road. In the end I vaguely recall heading home, catching a cab from a somewhat dubious pub in Oxford Street at around 10pm, and getting loudly booed from the entire gang of Longevity Lunchers for being the first to leave! It's that kind of lunch. It's that kind of company.

CHAPTER 10

Taking recruitment on the road

MY PRIMARY activity these days is acting as an advisor to recruitment companies. It's a little ironic, then, that I'm probably better known as a public speaker on the topic of recruitment matters.

I never set out with that goal in mind.

A gift of the gab

We can trace the early foundations of my speaking success right back to the 1990s. I was running Recruitment Solutions and at the same time trying to contribute to the greater industry by supporting the RCSA (Recruitment, Consulting and Staffing Association of Australia & NZ).

I served for several years on the RCSA Membership and Ethics committees, and then found myself on the State Council of NSW. Eventually, I became Vice President of the Association, nationally.

It was both a privilege and an honour, but it also thrust me onto the broader public stage to share my knowledge and experiences with others in the industry. It turned out I had a reasonable 'gift of the gab'. I was more than willing to share what I had learned, and it seems I was able to do it with clarity and the odd splash of humour.

Slowly I started to be asked to speak at more and more RCSA and other recruiting events and conferences. I won't lie – I enjoyed the spotlight. I thrived on having a platform for my views. I was pleased to be able to contribute to the industry. However, it was all 'extra-curricular' – for fun, pro-bono, part of being a member of the recruiting community.

Nevertheless, I quickly translated this new-found speaking prowess into my commercial activities. At Recruitment Solutions we developed a very sophisticated events program which culminated in the annual launch of our well-known salary survey – which at its peak involved a keynote address in eight or nine locations to over 1,000 clients and prospective clients. I was always the keynote speaker and that, combined with the hard copy survey itself, was our most powerful marketing tool, which drove many client meetings, job orders and a considerable amount of revenue as a result.

Later, at Aquent and Firebrand this continued, and I spoke at dozens of industry events, client events and a broad range of recruiting events as well.

My reputation had grown as a good public speaker. I got lots of requests, but at that point they were still mostly limited to Australia and New Zealand.

Social media and going global

In 2010, I began to grow my digital footprint as social media emerged as a force, and that's when things took off.

We had just started Firebrand, an international company in eight countries (as I talked about in Chapter 8). It was a start-up with no funds for marketing, so we planned to use the nascent social media platforms – believe it or not, a radical idea at the time. So, I started blogging and using Twitter, published content and engaged on LinkedIn, which back then was not very common at all, especially for a CEO.

In 2013, when I struck out on my own as a consultant to the recruitment industry, I started to pay more attention to my brand and quickly realised that my audience was recruiters and recruitment company owners.

Through a content marketing program – which was my blog 'The Savage Truth', a consistent profile on Twitter, regular posts on LinkedIn, as well as an active Facebook page, and more recently

Instagram – my audience started to grow. It has become an extraordinary marketing tool.

My speaking events through the RCSA in Australia routinely draw up to 2,000 people across seven or eight events. The last event drew 500 paying attendees in Sydney alone. We have subsequently taken them to New Zealand, South Africa, Ireland and Asia.

Through the REC (Recruitment & Employment Confederation) I have delivered four or five speaking tours across the UK, which sold out.

A few years ago, my brother Chris Savage joined me on some masterclasses where he added his marketing and business development expertise to the mix. It turns out that the audiences loved 'double the Savage', and Chris proved exceedingly popular, so we have taken multiple events all around Australia and New Zealand, as well South Africa and the UK several times. It's true that his involvement added new spice, not only to the material but also to my enthusiasm. Chris halved my workload on stage, but also we developed a 'bantering brothers' routine, which frankly is a reflection of our normal interaction. We must have done it too well on occasion because sometimes concerned attendees would come up to me after the event and entreat me to be kinder to him! The fun irony of all this is that I got to see more of him on these projects than I did in the normal course of our busy lives. That was a welcome bonus, even though publicly I moaned about him dragging me down and me having to carry him even after 50 years.

The fact that I am a very popular and successful speaker still bemuses me a little because there are plenty of people who have my knowledge of recruitment, and there are also many who are willing to share this knowledge. The extra bit of feedback I get from time to time is that often I share real and relevant financial (and other) data about offices, consultants, leaders and companies. This is not common in an industry paranoid about the 'competition'. Perhaps naively, I always believed the competitive edge was in the 'doing' not so much the talking, and I do feel that if the industry rises we all rise with it.

In any event, I believe the combination of a willingness to share the real truth, to deliver it with clarity and credibility based on track record, and the extraordinary power of a social footprint which has built a global community, is the reason for my success.

I have spoken at events all over the world now, and yet still find to my shock that people are prepared to pay to come and listen. It's a daunting responsibility, especially at that moment when they call your name and you stand in front of the crowd with four long hours in front of you!

Of course, speaking brings with it its own rewards. The opportunity to mix with and learn from a wide variety of others across the globe has been priceless.

Any thorough examination of my speaking schedule would see a close correlation with international rugby, cricket and football fixtures, particularly in the UK, NZ and South Africa. Totally by good fortune, my talks always seem to be in the same week as key fixtures.

My profile as a public speaker has also led to a wide range of in-house presentations. This is most definitely not my 'main game', and I do routinely turn down offers to deliver 'training' (because I have had 40 years of that!).

However, sometimes the opportunity to deliver something in a cool location, with an exciting company and on a topic that I'm genuinely passionate about, comes about. So, I've done in-house presentations in the UK, Ireland, South Africa, New Zealand, all over Australia, in Japan, Singapore and Hong Kong. Some have been at smaller companies, but many are giants of our industry such as Robert Walters, Randstad, Morgan McKinley and Gattaca. They are great people, doing great things – so I am in there, sharing my stuff and learning new things myself. It's great fun!

I do love speaking to recruiters. It's a heady mix of my love for the industry, the fact that I'm a little bit of a show-off, and also that I have plenty of opinions to share.

Moreover, I would add with complete sincerity, I honestly do love seeing information shared for the greater good. My biggest ever buzz is someone coming up to me in the street, at an event or via email and telling me that something I said in a talk made a difference to them. It really is the most gratifying experience.

Vanessa Raath, a South African recruiter whom I would now call a friend, remembers some of my talks there:

Greg has visited South Africa three times. I made sure that I took my whole team with me to hear him speak.

I was blown away by how 'straight-talking and no-nonsense' Greg was. He really called a spade a bloody shovel! His advice was great, and he took the time to encourage South African recruiters to get a firmer grasp of their recruitment processes.

Albeit by default, becoming a public speaker taught me a great deal about communications, but also exceptional lessons around brand, credibility and thought leadership and how these concepts are authentic and can be converted into business and personal relationships, as well as commercial success.

Is great recruiting universal?

As I touched on above, my in-house gigs have taken me to a wide range of cool and unusual places, such as…

… an Indigenous art gallery in Alice Springs in the Australian outback, a converted Victorian post office in Singapore, Cockatoo Island in the middle of Sydney Harbour, a floating event centre on Auckland Harbour, the flashy Westin Hotel in Tokyo, a converted barn in Birmingham, a function room above a massage parlour in Wan Chai in Hong Kong, upstairs at the Hard Rock Cafe Glasgow, the top floor of a skyscraper above the Bund in Shanghai, a Guinness pub in Dublin, the Sydney Cricket Ground (the events room, not on the centre wicket, sadly), the Melbourne Cricket Ground (same deal), the casino in Hobart, a theatre in Johannesburg, above the Nelson Mandela Robben Island Ferry Terminal in Cape Town, under the grandstand at the Moses Mabhida Stadium in Durban, Sea World on the Gold Coast in Queensland, a hotel (name forgotten) on the strip in Las Vegas, the Taj Mahal Hotel in Mumbai (subsequently the site of the appalling terrorist attack), a brewery in London, upstairs in the events rooms at Harrods in Knightsbridge, a 200-year-old hotel in Prague, a café just off the

Champs-Élysées, a converted castle in Bratislava, the RSL in Dubbo in NSW, a gentleman's club in Berkeley Square in London (no, not *that* sort of gentleman's club!) and hundreds more in Bali, Fiji, China, Malaysia, the US and Europe.

People often ask me: *"Is recruitment different in all these places? Are your messages and your experience valid when you go to another country?"*

To answer that, I draw on not only my speaking experience around the world, but my recruitment company management history. My recruitment career has allowed me the tremendous privilege of running and owning recruitment businesses all over the world. Literally. At one stage it was 30 offices in 17 countries (while I was at Aquent, from 2001 to 2010).

I made some almighty cockups while doing that, but I also learned at least one golden rule: great recruiting is great recruiting. Anywhere!

The core tactics and competencies that make for a great recruiter are the same everywhere.

If I had a dollar for every time I have been told, *"Oh, but that won't work here, Greg!"* or *"Things are different here"*... You don't even have to cross borders to hear it. Try going to Brisbane with an idea born 'down south'. Or tell someone in Manchester, *"This is how the London office does things."* Tell a Capetonian that *"the dudes in Jo'Burg do things this way."* Everyone believes that where they are is 'different' – usually harder, somehow more complex... in a word, special.

At a certain level, of course, they are right. A client visit in Japan follows a different path in terms of manners and protocol to the free-flowing style of Australia, for example. Yes, every country has its traditions, etiquette, habits and nuances, for sure.

However, the core aspect of recruiting? The ability to sell? The crucial need to focus on activity? The importance of prioritising, qualifying and talent picking? The need to know and deliver on critical metrics? Deep understanding of your clients? The need for continuous learning? The ability to manage stress? The ability to plan? A candidate care ethos? Winning exclusivity? The resilience required to survive?

These elements are universal.

One special mention

It's been a privilege to attend and speak at recruiting events all over the world, and every one of them has been a fun learning experience. However, sometimes, you do see something different.

A few years ago, I was the keynote speaker at the excellent Evolve Summit in Brno, Czech Republic. This was a first for me, speaking to 250 Central and Eastern European recruiters, so I was pleased to be involved (and I have been back since – the beer is so good and the people so friendly).

Every conference has its nuances, but most follow a fairly predictable pattern. This conference had all the usual buzz, social and learning-wise, but a few things happened that were unusual, to say the least.

The conference venue *served alcohol to attendees*. That is not a surprise, you say, we always have a drink after our conferences, right? Yes, except here the bar was open all day, was *in* the conference room, and many attendees had their first tipple at morning tea and continued all day!

Two babies attended the event, in both cases cared for by their recruiter mothers. I have never seen that before. They were gorgeous and well behaved, by the way (the mothers too), and I for one thought that was a practical and excellent solution.

One recruiter *brought her dog*, in a handbag. It kept on eyeing me while I was speaking. I've never spoken to a dog audience before, either.

Within 20 minutes of the last speaker wrapping up, the stage had been re-set, and *a full-on rock band* was blasting out tunes, with two raunchy female lead singers pumping out what I was told were classic Czech rock standards. The party only sped up from there.

The organisers had prepared for my arrival with large printed signs, which read "I Love Greg Savage", which were enthusiastically waved by attendees throughout the day. This does not happen to me very often (i.e. never!). I sent a picture of this to my wife. Her response is not printable here.

My speech was in English. Most of the other addresses were in Czech. Every attendee had a headset, and *instant, simultaneous translations* of every speaker was available. English to Czech. Czech to English. I could listen to the entire day.

Halfway through my second presentation, at about 2.30pm, the considerate organising team *brought me a cold beer* which I proceeded to consume while presenting my ideas on candidate acquisition. I have no complaints about that, by the way – it's just never happened before.

Beer and recruitment? A perfect match!

Lessons learnt from public speaking

As my reputation and experience as a public speaker grew, more and more people would remark on how easy it was for me, and how I must no longer be nervous.

Neither statement could be less accurate. It's not easy. I prepare meticulously, and each audience, each event, brings fresh challenges – and a fresh bout of nerves and self-doubt.

It is true, after all these years, that once I have prepared, I am confident I can deliver a good presentation. However, what about the content? Will it be relevant? Will the audience be interested? Mostly, these people have paid to hear me speak. You can't wing that.

So, even though advice on public speaking is commonplace, I thought I would share what I have learned about presenting powerfully. I am not only talking about formal speeches. Most of us have many platforms where getting a message across is important, whether it be a staff meeting, a client presentation, a farewell speech or something else again.

Here are a few things I learned, which I practise to this day.

Prepare every word. I prepare every word of a major presentation, typing out the whole thing. On the day itself, I may well then ad-lib big chunks. I go where my mind takes me, and to the audience, it may look as though a 60-minute presentation was done without a single note. However, I have the security of knowing I can refer back to the full transcript. It is my 'safety device', and it's a critical psychological and practical aid.

Plan your key points. Your presentation needs structure. Work out what it is you really want to get across to your audience. It may only be two or three key points. Make those clear and communicate them hard and often.

Tell stories. People love true stories, anecdotes that support your key points. Make sure they are true, relevant and sometimes amusing. I include them all the time and, years after the presentation, people remember the story.

Don't tell pre-planned jokes. Unless you are Jerry Seinfeld, don't do it. It's a rare skill to tell a joke well, and almost always they fall flat and are not entirely appropriate anyway. Humour is good, but it is best off the cuff and always self-deprecating.

Rehearse like crazy. I admit it. I rehearse my speeches, aloud and many times. I time them, so I know I won't be rushing to meet the allotted time allowed for the presentation. In earlier days, my long-suffering wife would be asked to hear every speech before D-Day. Her feedback was noted and changes made. I practise the punchlines of pithy stories and I make sure the words flow. Maybe these days I don't put as much into rehearsing as I did before, as I have 30 years' experience of public speaking now – but I still rehearse every speech at least once… all the way through.

Start strongly. Write your opening lines carefully and rewrite them until you like them a lot. Make sure you start strongly. It grabs people's attention. It also gives you the confidence to know you have captured the audience early.

Even prepare for the 'small' talks. Giving a farewell speech? Announcing a new policy? Explaining the monthly team results? Prepare as if it's a major speech. Work out your key points and prepare a strong opening. List whom to thank or congratulate. All these small occasions build your brand and your leadership credentials, and allow you to influence morale and opinion.

Use PowerPoint sparingly. I use PowerPoint, but mostly as a teaser. Words are few and just give a taste of what I am going to elaborate on. If I use a graph or chart, it's very sparse and only shows a trend or direction that I will explain orally. Make sure 90% of the audience time remains focused on you, 10% on the screen.

Warm up. Sportspeople warm up. Singers warm up. Musicians do too. Seriously, before every speech, I 'warm up'. I find a quiet place (hotel room or at home before I leave, or often just before the audience files in), and practise tongue twisters. Say these fast and repeatedly: *"Red lorry, yellow lorry, green lorry."* Then try: *"She sells sea shells on the seashore."* Finish with: *"Peter Piper picked a peck of pickled peppers."* Say them over and over, until you can get them word perfect at speed. Guess what? When you hit the podium, there is no stumbling over words, and your brain and tongue are in synch!

End strongly. Sum up your main points and end with a phrase or thought that people take away with them. It takes planning, but it's important to leave them with a key message.

Prepare the logistics. I take a copy of my speech in my briefcase and another in my suitcase if it's an interstate trip. I have the PowerPoint on my laptop and on a memory stick. I bring both to the venue. If my laptop does not work for some reason (it has happened) I can use my memory stick on someone else's. I make sure I know the location of the presentation and I plan the trip there, so I know I will be on time. The last thing you want is to be flustered because you lost your notes, your PowerPoint is on the fritz or you arrive ten minutes late.

They say public speaking is the number two fear human beings have, after death! It does not have to be the case.

A little hard preparation before your speech will save tons of perspiration during it.

PART II
The Savage Truth on your career and business

For the past six years, I have been an advisor.
Right now I am on the board of 14 recruitment and HR tech companies, and I consult to many more. It's a privilege to share the growth journey with these businesses and, while I like to think my experience helps them, it's true that I am still learning every day from smart people doing exciting things.

Even so, I feel I have some insights – and hard truths – to share, regardless of whether you're just starting out on your recruitment career or are the leader in your own business.

The chapters in this part take you through all aspects of recruitment, from just starting out, building your personal brand and negotiating fees, to being a leader that others will follow, and steering your business towards becoming a market leader, and preparing for exit by creating sustainable value.

Hopefully, I can help you avoid some of the mistakes I made – and, equally, help you enjoy some similar successes.

CHAPTER 11

Managing your recruitment career

RECRUITMENT IS a real career, and for the right person it is gratifying and fulfilling.

However, I have a bitter pill for you to swallow – but trust me, it's true. Nobody anywhere (apart maybe from your Mum) cares about your career. Not really.

If you work for a great company, they will create an environment in which you can thrive. Opportunities will arise, and the company may even actively facilitate those opportunities. However, success in your recruitment career will *never* be just a matter of qualifications or skills. It will *always* be a matter of motivation. You have to get off your butt and take charge of your future. You don't outsource your career.

What happens to you at work is 90% because of what *you do* at work – or what *you do not do.*

Don't leave your career in the hands of someone else. Find a company that supports you, definitely – but you have to drive your career.

Often I hear candidates say they want to leave a job because their current employer is not *"looking after my career"*. However, just having qualifications is not enough anymore. Gone are the days where getting the 'right' degree would set up your career. A degree only gets you the chance to get on the field, not win the game.

So, as clichéd or obvious as it sounds, the starting point is to **find what you like doing**. A career without passion and enthusiasm will have no meaning, no joy and little hope of long-term success.

Indeed, does your career goal keep you awake at night? If not, maybe you need to start worrying. You have perhaps 30 (or more) years left in which to work and, trust me on this, no one else is having sleepless nights about what happens to your recruitment career. It's up to you.

So, with that in mind, this chapter provides some tips on managing your own recruitment career, starting with your first job and moving through to becoming a manager of other recruiters (or perhaps not). Many of the principles and tips provided here, of course, can be applied to other industries.

Starting your first job as a recruiter

Here is my best road-map for somebody starting in agency recruitment for the first time. Follow these guidelines and you give yourself every chance of getting through the first six months, which frankly, at least 50% of new recruiters don't manage.

Here's what to stay focused on:

- *Do the small things well.* For example, turn up to work on time. (Believe it or not, I see brand-new hires strolling in late all the time.) Wear the appropriate clothes for the environment you are joining. Take short lunch breaks. Get to meetings on time.

- *Be a willing learner.* 'Coachability' is a crucial recruiter requirement. Poor listeners, know-it-alls, and those who can't focus on learning different ways in their new environment are likely to fail.

- *Keep your head down.* I don't mean be a shrinking violet. However, don't be too cocky too early. Resist the temptation on day three to tell a hilarious story about how drunk you all got in Bali. Listen far more than you talk. Of course, engage and be responsive – but know your place until you know your place.

- *Don't join a tribe.* Every office has them: alliances, cliques and factions. It's tempting to 'join' one, as when you are new, you feel alone. However, don't. Treat everyone with respect and be open to help and guidance from everywhere.

- *Be brave.* Make that cold-call when it's time to do so. Interview that candidate for the first time. Negotiate a fee if you have to. I have noticed that new recruiters show their 'courage colours' early. A good employer will not throw you in the deep end too soon, but they will be delighted to see your willingness to tackle the task head-on.

- *Treat candidates like gold.* Actually, no, treat them like *human beings with feelings.* Develop your own 'candidate response charter' which includes empathy, respect and consistency.

- *Build your digital online brand from day one.* Learn about LinkedIn as a branding platform, get on Twitter if that's where your target community hangs out, blog and build an online community of fans (see Chapter 14 for more on this).

- *Compete with yourself.* Don't get caught up in office ego fights. Your biggest competition is not your 'competitor', your clients, technology, the recruiter sitting next to you, or anyone/anything else. Your competition is you. You have to *be better than you were yesterday.* Make that your daily goal.

- *Never stop learning.* You are never 'done' as a recruiter. Read articles and blogs. Learn from more experienced folks. Ask questions. Attend seminars. Add new skills, always.

- *Look for mentors.* Your company will have some great operators, hopefully. Some will be more helpful than others, but all will enjoy an ego stroke when you ask, *"Can I learn from you, please?"*

- *Ask.* Listen, learn, and try new things. However, don't suffer in silence. If you don't understand, ask. Be polite; make sure the person you are asking is not in the middle of a critical call. Then ask your question. The answer will be in the room.

- *Take notes.* For example, when in training, when being coached, when your mentor gives a tip. Write it down. Review it later. Then implement it!

- *Get on the phone.* No matter what others do in the office, this should be your mantra. Think about the outcome you want. Is it better achieved via an email or on the phone? Usually, it's the latter. Pick. It. Up.

- *Don't take it personally.* People are going to let you down. Things will go wrong. Clients and candidates will be rude and ungrateful. Learn to deal with it.

- *Don't get pissed at your first work function* – or your second, or your third. In fact, never get drunk at a work function. I have never seen anyone enhance their career, reputation or credibility by drinking too much at a work event. And I have been to infinitely more of those than you have.

- *Develop an ethos of networking from day one.* When your first candidate interview goes well, ask the candidate who else they know may be looking to move. Always be ferreting out new contacts and expanding your network of contacts.

I've saved perhaps my biggest tip till last. From the beginning, follow this golden secret that even experienced recruiters don't know, and I'm telling you for the price of this book!

The success formula is lots of *activity* of a high *quality* – *with the right people.* You have to do enough of the right activities, consistently, to succeed as a recruiter. However, the quality of those activities is critical too. Then, once you have mastered volume and quality, you have to make sure that your target market, with whom you do those activities, is the right market. I expand on this secret to recruiting success in Chapter 21.

Becoming 'senior'

So, you continue to learn as a recruiter. You are on the 'edge' (flip two sections forward for how I define this) and you start to rise to the top of the leader board. Where is your career going now? Surely you have 'earned' the next step?

I've had countless conversations with experienced recruiters who feel they have been unfairly passed over for promotion or a cool opportunity. I've been told, *"It's not fair. I am a senior person in this company."*

So often, it's time for a reality check. You see, you have to behave according to the job you want, long before you are ready for that job. If you want to be senior, you have to act senior. Indeed, your happiness at work is not only up to your current employer, or any employer – it's mostly your responsibility.

We like to perceive ourselves, and be perceived, as 'senior'. However, being 'senior' has little to do with how long you have been with the company. Being 'senior' is not a title or a rank or a category. It is a state of mind and level of maturity. It is a pattern of behaviours that ultimately will be the foundation for achieving career and financial progress in a business.

Here are some meaningful action steps, behaviour changes and attitudes you can adopt to get yourself ready for your next career step:

- *Build your brand.* However, on this occasion, I do not mean a digital brand. I mean what people say about you when you are not in the room. Are you 'Greg the Grumpy'? 'Sally the Selfish'? Or does your name elicit more positive vibes? 'Colin the Collaborator'? Think about it. What's your 'brand' in these terms? Because this will weigh heavily on decisions to award you the best projects and set you up for promotion opportunities as they occur… or not.

- *Understand what you are known for.* What's your 'superpower'? Are you the woman they always want on a big client pitch because you always nail it? Are you the guy who steps in to help when a counter-offer looms? Be known for something – preferably several things, and share them.

- *Cleanse your online brand.* This is not a joke. People miss out on jobs because of an unsavoury comment on their Facebook page. I have made decisions based on that. Even a 'joke' out of context can look awful for you. So too with online 'fights'. You usually look bad. Be careful what you post and remember that it never goes away, and can hurt you well into the future.

- *Smash your paradigms.* Recruitment can often breed selfish behaviour. The way we reward people can actually foster that too. However, if you want to evolve into seniority, even leadership, you need to cut back on the 'what's in it for me' focus and think more about 'what's in it for them'. This is not easy.

- *Step forward.* Look for the projects that count. Volunteer to be on the working group or the newbie training or organising the event. Don't think about the short-term rewards. Give before you take.

- *Chase the learning.* Be a sponge. It won't always come to you. Identify your skills and knowledge gaps and make it your job to fill them.

- *Be great at 'new'.* Don't be the dinosaur. *"It was always better in the old days." "We have always done it this way."* Always be asking, *"Why do we do it like this?" "Is there a better way?"* Embrace change.

Moving into management... or not

It's one of the biggest mistakes I have made, and many others are making it right now. What is it? Promoting your top recruiter into a manager role.

The thing is, great recruiters often make dud managers. Of course, a great recruiter *can* become a great manager – but it's not a given. It's actually unlikely, for one straightforward, but compelling, reason: they are totally different jobs, which require a very different set of skills, competencies and mindset.

The best billers are often 'lone wolves'. They thrive on the hunt and the 'kill'. They revel in the spotlight. They are inherently 'self-ish' (not always in a bad way) and they get their jollies from instant gratification, 'deals done', being top of the leader board and the fat bonus for personal results. The motivation of a top biller is always personal success.

On the other hand, great managers of recruiters get their kicks *through the success of others*. I am not saying managers are pure altruists who exist for the benefit of others. They will have their own interests at heart, but they see the route to fulfilment through growing the skills and success of people around them. They enjoy the coaching, nurturing, developing and motivating that this requires. The very best leaders rejoice in the success of others.

A big biller and a great recruitment leader are different species, originating from different DNA. These differences may not be obvious early in a recruiter's career, but they do emerge, and managers should foster and encourage them.

It is true that to manage recruiters, you need to know the job and have a track record of credibility in order to lead them. However, it's not necessary to have been a world-beater. Like me, for example. I was a good recruiter, sure. Better than most, I guess. Yet I was no superstar. For all my (many) faults as a manager, though, I was better at helping others thrive than I was at doing it myself. I enjoyed it more too.

However, often I see the top biller lobby for the manager job, be given it, and all hell breaks loose. It can be a double disaster. The promoted big biller hates the new role, and sees their personal billings drop as they spend time with team members. The team resents the poor leadership, performance falls and people leave. I have even seen entire teams disintegrate in these circumstances.

So, this means you must think hard about what 'floats your boat'. Management may seem cool, with a better title and bigger salary, but the reality is that it's hard, requires skills you probably do not have, and often there is more money in being the highest biller anyway! Work out what you love, and chase that, not a title.

Hopefully, your senior management has managed the aspirations of the consulting team from the early days. If not, truly think about what role will best serve you and what 'career' really means for you as a recruiter. Managing may not be it. If you're a big biller, don't be tempted by promises of management roles if you suspect you can't perform them. Careers can be had without hierarchical promotion, so if you're an ambitious recruiter with little interest in leadership, talk to management about a different career path.

If, however, you can see your strengths are in helping other recruiters thrive, by all means go for management.

Great recruiters live on the 'edge'

Regardless of whether or not you move into management, today's recruiter is never *'done'*. You are never *'trained'*, *'expert'*, or *'finished with learning'*. It's a process of constant renewal, upskilling and starting again. That is the ongoing challenge for all of us.

I like the concept of *'living on the edge'* because it suggests being alert, being dexterous, being nimble. I encourage you to adopt as your mantra, from today, that you will live on the *'edge'*.

The word *edge* means 'sharp', and that is what modern recruiters must be if they are to be future-fit.

Again, this also applies to anyone who wants to stay relevant in the modern workforce – which makes it hard for many of us who are very set in our ways. That needs to change.

You need to be a recruiter who:

- *embodies the 'cutting edge'* – is in touch with new tools, always learning and sharpening your ability, all the time.

- understands that to succeed you *need an edge on competitors, but also on clients and new technologies.* You have to know more than your clients about talent acquisition – and more than your competitors, more than the next generation of recruiters breathing down your neck.

- *knows 5% more than anyone else* in the room about your specialty – talent acquisition.

- *moves first* – does not follow behind, is an experimenter, tries things, self-disrupts. Indeed, a great recruiter stays paranoid, always on the lookout for some new threat, never entirely comfortable.

- *sharpens skills*, is always improving – never staying satisfied with what you 'know'.

Past success as a recruiter is no longer a reliable indicator of future success. You cannot rely on your track record.

Complacency is your enemy. Inertia will kill you. Be edgy.

Do not mess with your reputation

Throughout your career, your reputation is the only thing you will take with you when you leave a role. Every contact with candidates, clients and colleagues is a moment of truth.

Ask yourself after every interaction: *"Did what I just did, or said, enhance or damage my reputation?"*

Remember, it's not only the candidates you help – it's those you *don't* help. That goes for clients too, and colleagues, and suppliers.

Treat people with respect, do what you say you're going to do, never screw anyone over, and in the long run your reputation will get you there. Your reputation is your elixir of eternal recruitment career life. Protect it and burnish it, through your actions.

My biggest recruiting blunder

Throughout this book I outline many cataclysmic errors I've made in my career as a recruiter, but here's my biggest blunder (in my opinion). In terms of impact on my subsequent behaviour, it was even more significant than sending a candidate résumé to her own employer (which I owned up to in Chapter 3). The incident I'm about to describe has held me in good stead throughout my personal and professional life.

Many years ago, when we were about three years into building Recruitment Solutions and while I was a director and owner, I was also recruiting. My colleague Graham Whelan was handling an assignment for a major corporation, and the candidate was down to the last interview.

Graham was going away on a long weekend and so he asked me to take the feedback from the client and, if necessary, make the offer to the candidate – who was, by the way, chomping at the bit for the role.

Of course, if the candidate missed out, my job was to convey the bad news.

Sure enough, the company came back, but with negative news. I buckled and lost the courage to relay the news, lying to the candidate that he was still in the running, preferring it be Graham to break the news.

Not only was I weak, but I was stupid. You see, I'd also run another advert for the same role that weekend and, of course, the candidate saw it and needless to say worked everything out.

Later he told Graham, *"Greg Savage is not a man you can trust."* That still burns me today, but I vowed then never to have that said about me ever again.

That incident has guided my actions in business and my inter-actions with people over the years. Trust me. I've done some challenging things: fired people, not promoted people, upset people when offices closed. Deals have fallen through, and I've disappointed people and failed at many things, but I've never duped anyone, never cheated, and so I've never had to hide behind the proverbial pillar in the street when someone was coming the other way.

I chose to be transparent in my dealings because I wanted to sleep soundly at night, but this turned out to be my biggest asset.

In business deals and difficult situations or matters of trust, having a reputation for being a straight shooter will open many doors. Referrals have come, staff have come, recommendations have come and many opportunities have emerged. Many situations have been diffused because of my reputation for straight dealing.

The important message here is: don't mess with your reputation. By that, I mean your personal reputation, not your online reputation – what people say about you when you are not in the room.

What I've learned in this era of fake news and spin is that people value authenticity and loyalty. Every interaction builds or harms your reputation. Don't mess with it, it's the only thing you truly own.

Don't let the bastards drag you down!

As the recruiting world (and many other white-collar industries) is challenged by automation, AI and machine learning, as well as evolving models like recruitment process outsourcing, vendor management software and managed service providers, it's even more critical that we don't get sucked into competing on the basis of who can commoditise what we do the best. Don't play the low-margin, transactional game.

While your competitors may claim, *"We are bigger, have cooler technology, and do it faster and cheaper"* and technology-driven platforms push to cut out recruiters altogether, your premise for doing business should be: *"I can solve your problem because I under-stand your need, I know where the talent is hidden and I can bring them to the hiring table."*

As I talked about in Chapter 2, when I was at John P. Young, the 'profession' of recruitment was virtually unknown. I usually had to explain what I did to anyone who asked. However, in London a few years later, as the industry evolved, I became exposed to the criticism that all of us in recruitment have inevitably had to face. We are, so we're told, 'lazy, sleazy, pushy and incompetent' – and those are just the *nicer* things said.

It's worse now than ever before. Everyone has a 'terrible recruiter' story. LinkedIn is littered with horror stories and gratuitous recruiter insults. Every day brings more abuse and, increasingly, gleeful predictions of the demise of the agency recruiter.

The problem is, many recruiters find it hard to combat such negativity about the industry and, worse still, some have started to believe it! Moreover, if a recruiter has shaky self-belief, the end is inevitably nigh.

Well, stop – we've had enough!

There is an army of recruiters across the world who will *always* put the person before the dollar, and have had a positive effect on thousands of lives. I know dozens of such recruiters myself. Let's talk about *these* recruiters for a change. Let's make sure we don't tar every recruiter with the broad brush of disdain that often paints our industry.

While we are at it, let's shine a light on some of the reasons recruiters deserve respect instead of derision.

For a start, it's a tough job! It's one of the toughest around. It's brutally competitive and hugely stressful. It comes with long hours. Salaries are usually low, with upswing pegged to great results, and very often recruiters work long and hard for a tiny return.

It's scary too. Cold-calling is not fun. Also, as much as clients complain about unreliable recruiters, try working the other side of the fence… dealing with clients who tell you it's urgent, make you jump through hoops, then don't return your calls. Clients who invite you for a meeting, and don't have the manners to show up! Where job requirements change in mid-search or are cancelled when weeks of work have been done. Clients who lie about their commitment to the brief. Candidates who play one job off against another and leverage job offers for salary increases. Candidates who beg for a chance, and then don't turn up for the hard-won interview, leaving the recruiter to cop the flak, for 'flakiness'.

If every client or candidate who heaps abuse on recruiters for 'wasting my time' did an honest balance sheet of who wasted whose time the most, I know where the deficit would be.

However, let's bring it back to what's most important of all: recruiters do good. We find people work, and that's a good thing. It's something to be proud of. It makes an impact.

We change people's lives. We solve companies' staffing issues. We help people achieve their career ambitions.

How about a little nod of appreciation from clients who may make a living selling cigarettes or alcohol or junk bonds or dubious insurance or life-saving medicine at obscene profits, or who defend criminals?

How is it that these people call *our* profession 'bottom-feeders'? Pot... Kettle... Black?

I am not saying that what they do is 'bad' (even though it often bloody well is!) but that what we do is honourable, it's positive and there is no collateral damage in our work.

We create jobs. The frequent criticism of our industry having 'no barriers to entry' has an upside. Our sector breeds entrepreneurs who dare to start their own businesses and go on to hire people.

As I talked about in Chapter 5, I remember doing that myself, at 29 years old (and several times since), and having endless sleepless nights, paying myself a pittance, while employing people to get the business going. I have no complaints. I reaped the rewards. Yet I took the risk, as do thousands of other recruiters, many of whom are women by the way, who leave the restraints and discrimination of bigger corporates to create their own businesses and secure their futures.

That is something to be proud of, surely.

If you think this is spin, then reflect on the fact that globally, in 2017, agencies placed 53 million individuals in jobs. That was done through a network of 165,000 agencies employing 2.7 million staff (as CIETT reported).

Also, how about the service we provide candidates? Our industry gets hammered for poor 'candidate care', and in fairness, it's often deserved.

However, let's have a reality check. Recruiters invest millions of hours advising, counselling and supporting candidates on their job search. Some of that is material assistance, like résumé preparation, salary information or interview training, but often it's a morale boost or good career advice, or just providing a sane sounding-board.

We act as an advocate for the candidate who does not shine through the résumé but can in the interview. We make that happen – and candidates don't even get charged!

So, to all my fellow and future recruiters, I encourage you to stand proud!

Maintaining perspective – on yourself

This tip is important no matter what stage you are at in your recruitment career. It took me 30 years to learn this, but I believe it will save you a world of pain (so hopefully you can pick it up a bit more quickly than I did).

When things are going well, when the results are good, when it seems you can do no wrong, be sure you don't get taken in by your own bullshit. We are seldom as good as we think we are.

Be careful, too, not to surround yourself with yes-men, sycophants and brown-nosing acolytes, who feed you what you want to hear and seduce you into complacency and arrogance. For it's just at that time that the biggest fall is imminent. Self-satisfaction is what stifles growth, innovation, risk and hunger.

Equally, when everything goes wrong, every decision seems to backfire and your dreams are crumbling, do not believe you have no talent just because at that moment others around you are not able to recognise it. Before you write yourself off as a failure, as wrong, as mediocre, as 'not up to it', check you have not surrounded yourself with deadbeats, dingbats, dropkicks and doomsayers, who bring you down and stunt your dreams.

That's it. Maintain perspective – on yourself.

The very best recruiter I have ever known

Graham Whelan is the best recruiter I've ever met.

No matter that he has been placing people in finance jobs since 1978. There is no worn-out apathy or cynicism with this man. His love of the chase, his desire to make the match, and his interest in the welfare of his clients and candidates has not waned over four decades.

I worked with Graham for more than 15 years, including 12 as partners in building Recruitment Solutions, which (as I talk about in Chapters 5 and 6) went from a start-up to an IPO on the Australian Stock Exchange.

To me, Graham epitomises what a great recruiter should be. I am in awe of his longevity in this most demanding of businesses, but also his passion and commitment to service.

So, what is it that makes Graham special? Most importantly, it is the way he works with his clients and his candidates. He has all the technical recruiting skills, of course. However, he has more too. Let me count the ways:

1. **He cares.** About his clients, of course, but also about every candidate he deals with. Sure, he is looking to make the placement, and the fee, but Graham has never lost sight of the human element of our business. He treats every person he deals with, with kindness and attention to detail.

2. **He has incredible energy.** I don't want to break any privacy laws, but the man is on the far (far) side of 60, and he still works with the pace of the Energizer bunny. Graham is a shorter man than me, but when we went on client visits together I had almost to run to keep up with him. He strides around the office, he often stands when speaking on the phone during important conversations, he moves quickly from one call, one meeting, to the next. He is a little whirlwind of action,

149

and he inspires action around him. Typically, he works from 8am to 6pm, starting with a booming *"Bore da"* (Welsh for *"Good morning"*) across the office as he strides in. Lunch is a sandwich at the desk, and every other minute is spent engaging in conversations with clients, candidates and colleagues.

3. **He is honest.** Of course, he has impeccable business integrity, but he is honest at a deeper level. He tells clients when he can't help; he tells candidates their exact status. If the news is bad, he still gives it, directly, but with compassion.

4. **He does what he says he is going to do.** This alone separates Graham from the vast majority of recruiters. If he says he will call you back, he does. If he tells you that he will keep you in mind for a specific kind of role, he will, and you can expect a call, maybe four months later.

5. **He listens.** Again, so many recruiters can learn from this. Graham asks lots of questions, he digs, he listens, and he is purposely 'slow to understand'. He does not make assumptions. As a result, he inevitably develops a better search brief with the client than anyone else. He always gets to the core reason a candidate is looking to move jobs, which every good recruiter knows is often not the reason they initially give.

6. **He has a memory like an elephant.** If he interviewed you as an accounts clerk 20 years ago, Graham would remember not only you, but also your company and probably your salary and the person you reported to. There is a good chance he will remember your family too. I'm serious. Sit in a restaurant with Graham and he will be nodding to, and shaking hands with, every second person. This is not only because of his longevity as a recruiter in the same city, but also because he remembers everybody; and as he's never burned anyone in business, he has no enemies.

7. **He is the embodiment of PMA (positive mental attitude).** Graham believes and behaves as though good things will happen. Then he works hard to make sure they do. I believe so much in this trait. To Graham, his candidates *will* get the job, and, as a result, they usually do.

8. **He makes you feel special.** And he does this without even knowing or trying. He is interested – in you. You are his focus when you are talking to him. He remembers your wife's name, your kids' names. He asks how they are. You can tell he is actually interested. He sends handwritten thank you notes and he calls on your birthday. He cries when a friend is having a bad time or is seriously ill. What a great man.

Graham is the best hard-core recruiter I have ever worked with or against, and he has made an immeasurable contribution to countless lives, and to our industry as a whole.

So, to my old mate 'Wheels'… I salute you!

CHAPTER 12

How recruiters destroy their own careers

YOU MAY be a big biller. You may have been with the same company a few years. However, a few (unfortunately common) traits can ruin your career and negatively impact your life. They can destroy your job satisfaction and have led an army of recruiters to burn out and fade into the sunset. So, they are what this chapter is all about – avoid them at all costs.

Wasted emotion

Don't get me wrong. Being emotional about placing people in jobs is normal. In fact, it's essential. I love the passion of a recruiter on a mission to fill a role or place a candidate. I am cool about screams of joy or moans of despair. I love a placement dance!

That is healthy emotion. It's wasted emotion you have to curb and eliminate.

The days of moping because a placement fell through. The bitterness and angst over a temp who bombed out. The tears and recriminations over some meaningless in-office spat. The self-pity and 'woe is me' because a candidate got a counter-offer. The slumped shoulders and defeatist language that follows a bad month or quarter.

All that is 'wasted' emotion. It's dragging you down. It's wearing out your battery. It's eating away at your self-esteem. Also, it's dragging those around you down too.

You have chosen a tough career. In this job, people *will* let you down. People *will* lie to you. People *will* back out of commitments. People *will* be rude and ungrateful. 'Certainties' *will* crumble. There – now you know.

I don't expect you to be a recruiting robot. Have a quick cry. Kick the desk. Have a few beers. Then leave it there. Move on. Don't waste your emotion on stuff that's dead and gone. Save the emotion for the next placement dance.

Allowing stress to get to you

So, wasted emotion is not on. However, recruitment is stressful – and that is dangerous. Seriously. It can lead to medical issues, and maybe harm your relationships and overall quality of life.

I have seen recruiters reduced to highly destructive and anti-social behaviour as a result of the stress they feel, as they fight to achieve targets, deal with significant disappointments and cope with rude clients and ungrateful candidates. Behaviour like drinking too much, drug abuse, directing their anger at colleagues, wild mood swings, dishonest dealings, depression, rapid weight gain or loss. All of this is unfortunate, and all harmful.

The reality is that we need to learn to cope, to have some releases that ease the pressure and redress the balance.

Here are a few things I recommend, when it comes to battling the stress tsunami:

- *Have a good cry.* Yes, I am serious. Or, once the phone is put down, let off some steam. As long as it's not directed at a colleague. As long as it's quick. As long as you bounce back fast, it's OK! In fact, given our job, it would be weird *not* to melt down occasionally. It's OK. Let it go. You will feel better afterwards. But then… move on!

- *Get perspective.* Breathe. Again, I am serious. Push back from your desk. Suck in the big ones. Deliberately and consciously

153

shift your thinking. Dump the negatives. Say *"It will go well"*, not *"It's all going down the gurgler."* I believe in PMA. I also believe that we *can* control how we react to situations. Jump off the stress treadmill. Take a chill pill. Recalibrate your attitude. Whatever crappy thing just happened, it's not that serious.

- *Recognise the warning signs.* If stress is building, sometimes discretion is the greater part of valour. Take evasive action. Avoid that irritating client call. Stop making sales calls for an hour when you are getting nowhere with rude clients and call ten of your best talent instead. They will be pleased to hear from you, and that will cheer you up right there. Leave the office early. You can make it up tomorrow. Call someone else who will cheer you up.

- *Set an achievable goal.* Choose a goal you can hit, and which will make you feel good. This is key. A massive ocean of work is piling up all around you. You can see no way you can get it done. The 'to do' list is getting ever longer. So here is the trick. Cross out everything on the 'to do' list except the top three big, hairy important things that *must* get done. Forget the rest. You were not going to get to them anyway. Get the big three to five things done. Then go home – successful.

- *Sweat a little.* Exercise reduces stress exponentially. When I had my most stressful role, CEO of a global recruiter (with Aquent and then Firebrand), I had a month's worth of gym sessions in my diary ahead of time – three or four a week – and I didn't change them for anybody (unless my wife told me to, obviously). For you, it might be different, but if you feel the stress building, don't hit the grog or buy that burger to give you the comfort you crave. Run, gym, bike or even just take a fast walk. For me, it's a lifesaver. Someone even told me that if they needed to have an awkward meeting with me, they always tried to arrange it after my gym session because, inevitably, I was 'much calmer' then.

Being a recruiter means stress. It never entirely goes away, no matter how good you are. You have to manage it.

Looking for a quick fix

Too many up-and-coming recruiters are looking for the quick fix. So, I am frequently asked, *"What are the one or two things I can do to become a top biller?"*

The answer is often not what they want to hear: I tell them a great recruiter is like an iceberg.

I ask them, *"Have you ever seen an iceberg?"* Most of it is hidden. The part under the water, the unseen part, supports and holds up the part you can see – in fact, 90% of an iceberg is underwater.

When you see a highly successful recruiter who seems to sail through life and for whom everything seems to fall into place, don't believe that for one second. It took work and sacrifice to get there.

You see the success, money, status. However, really what you need to look at to understand that recruiter is the *journey*. The 90%: the rejection, the long hours, the fear, the hard work, the courage, the sacrifices, the focus on activity, the stress, the discipline, the huge learning curve, the many failures and disappointments…

Don't focus on the part of the iceberg that's visible. What you see there is the end game, the result. Focus on the part you don't see unless you look beneath the surface. Then replicate that behaviour, activity and effort.

Work on the bit of your career 'iceberg' that is underwater. That is where success is born.

Disastrous work behaviours that hold you back

Even if you do learn the craft of recruitment and produce outstanding results, your career can still flounder. Your manager wants results, but they also want collaboration and support. All managers want that, not just those in recruitment.

Be honest now. Do you recognise yourself at all here?

- You contradict or argue with your manager in front of the team. Or, at best, you show your disdain for their ideas and initiatives with negative body language, smirks, and audible sighs.

- You are negative about new ideas, cynical about change, and undermine initiatives.

- You come late to meetings, and often arrive late to work too.

- You inflate your potential billings, and always fall short on what you promise to deliver.

- If there is a dress code, you flaunt it, or push it to the limit, putting your manager in the awful position of having to counsel you on how you dress.

- You repeat the same recruiting mistakes time and again, and appear to be immune to coaching and mentoring.

- You don't comply with even the most basic admin requirements, and seldom complete the required data updates on your customer relationship management (CRM) or ATS system.

- In meetings, or any discussion about the business, *all* your ideas involve the company spending more money. None of them are about how you can work smarter or differently. You sulk when your ideas don't fly.

- You fan the flames of gossip and discontent, instead of dousing them where you can.

- You muck around on your phone during meetings when your manager is trying to convey a message or enthuse the team.

- You take the credit for new clients and deals done, even when you had little real involvement.

- You don't prepare for your weekly meetings with your manager, and you put almost nothing into your performance review preparation. Yet, you complain bitterly that your *"career is going nowhere"*.

- You are cynical and uninterested in training. You often find a reason not to attend sessions which management runs. If you do attend, you dominate the session with 'war stories' about the way you do things.

- When you do well, you are smug and insufferably arrogant, prancing around like a prima ballerina on smack. Yet, when your numbers are shocking, you blame the market, or the database, or the admin staff, or something else… just never yourself.

- You squabble with your colleagues over the tiniest of incidents, hold grudges for a long time and spend a good chunk of your time 'in a huff'.

- Two or three disappointments in a week will throw you into a downward dive of despair, wasted emotion, and 'woe is me'. You mope around the office, looking for sympathy and reassurance, dragging down the team with you.

- You complain bitterly that *"No one ever gives me any leads"* and demand access to everyone else's clients, but guard your own clients with the intensity of a rabid honey badger, hissing at anyone who even hints at an approach with a vicious, *"That's my client!"*

- You take so much for granted – training, bonuses, marketing expenditure, benefits, company-paid team beers. Pretty much everything, really.

- You never, ever, ever say thank you.

I am sure you don't want to admit to being guilty of all these. To be fair, it's a pretty long list. However, be honest. Can you see yourself in any of these behaviours? Resist the temptation to justify your behaviours because the fact is, it's this that's holding you back.

I know. I have been in a thousand meetings where the decision not to promote you was based around these transgressions.

Not thinking like an immigrant

I am an immigrant myself, arriving in Australia two weeks before my 21st birthday. I am the son of an immigrant too (I recounted the story of Major Ron Savage in Chapter 1).

When you are an immigrant, an outsider, you think and behave differently. It's a bit like the first week at a new school. Everyone else is chilled, knows the ropes, is very familiar with things and one another, complacent even. You, on the other hand, are alert, watchful, looking to learn, needing to be brave.

Recruiters need to think like immigrants, for these reasons:

- *Immigrants are massive optimists.* By definition – they have moved somewhere new because they perceive a better life. They want to be here. They need to succeed. It gives them an edge.

- *Immigrants are brave.* They need to be. Every step, every corner rounded, is a new experience. They need to experiment, to ask a lot, to be prepared to fail a few times, to bounce back. They act as if they have no safety net because, typically, they don't.

- *Immigrants learn new skills.* They have to. It may be the language, or driving on the right side of the road, the cuisine, local traditions, sports, and so on.

- *Immigrants are opportunists.* They typically don't have a lot, so they are alert to a 'chance'. They don't have the luxury of waiting for something to 'turn up'. They seek it out. Immigrants do not have the sense of entitlement that locals might.

- *Immigrants embrace new ideas.* They still hold on to what is dear to them from the past, but they absorb the new. They search for new ways. Their paradigms are not set in concrete. They don't limit themselves, because they don't assume limits on what is achievable.

- *Immigrants are humble.* They will do any job that sets them on their way. (Me? I was cleaning toilets at a caravan park in Coolangatta, barman at the Arkaba hotel in Adelaide, storeman/packer at R.M. Williams.) They know that they don't know what they don't know. They don't limit what they are prepared to do for success.

• *Immigrants work harder to get ahead.* They have to. They are 'on their own', with no 'old boys' network. It's make or break. Persistence is in their DNA.

All these immigrant traits are also those of the successful modern recruiter. In a sense, *all* recruiters are immigrants because we have just arrived in this 'new world of recruitment', where everything is changing. We need to embrace this world, using the skills we learned in the 'old country' if they still apply, but wide open to change, hard work and fresh thinking.

Twenty years ago, a client said to me, *"Greg, I only hire people who have at least one grandparent who cannot speak English."* A baffling remark at first, and certainly politically incorrect and probably illegal too. However, what he was alluding to is that he liked to hire sons and daughters of immigrants because he valued the way they thought and the values they brought. This is hardly scientific or unbiased recruitment methodology, but I admit I have never forgotten that comment, and I dare say it has influenced my hiring decisions since.

Do not work for a company that discriminates based on what language family members speak, obviously, but try to think like an immigrant and work with others who do too.

Want to really succeed as a recruiter? Create 'Recruiter Equity'

Why do some recruiters forge long and successful careers while others struggle and fade away, or experience 'burnout'?

All the training and experience you have had as a recruiter is a total waste of time unless the skills and techniques you learn are built on a platform of self-belief.

In business, as in life, you get treated the way you allow yourself to be treated. We all know people who are always 'the victim'. Bad things are 'always happening to them'. If something can go wrong with a client or candidate, it does. It's all so unfair! However, as already covered in this chapter, the reality is, it's their behaviour and attitude that's the problem. They waste emotion, becoming failure magnets.

You see, the foundation to being a great recruiter is self-belief. You are the expert. Your client may be an executive director of a listed company or the CEO of a multinational conglomerate, but who knows more about the permanent recruiting market? You or her?

Who interviews hundreds of candidates each year? Who negotiates salaries every day? Who knows what motivates staff in today's marketplace? Who knows contractor rates and what they look for in a 'cool gig'? Who knows permanent market-rate salaries, or how to handle a counter-offer situation?

You do!

You are the expert. Believe in that and behave so. If you do, your client will believe you too.

Of course, if you behave like a processor of résumés or a clerical resourcer, then that is what you become.

You have the power to set the tone of the relationship with your client. Too many of us are forever apologising for our industry and trying to justify our role. We must be proud of what we do and fiercely protective of our value. Any other way means you lose respect – and therefore control.

Your relationship with your client is one of equality. It is not a 'master/servant' dynamic. Through your credibility, your communication skills and your self-belief, you impose on your client a process that you know will benefit them.

Treat all contact with clients respectfully but always on an equal professional basis. If you are subservient, apologetic or lacking in confidence, the client will take control and you will be lost.

To be a winner in the recruitment business, you must have the attitude of a winner. You need the skills, of course, but only through the right approach can you grow what I call your 'Recruiter Equity'.

Recruiter Equity is the trust, the buy-in and the belief that your clients have in your ability and judgement. It is built from the combination of your experience and your knowledge, but it's also the personal confidence you show in delivering that expertise. It gives you the power to advise clients, and truly impact the outcomes of your interaction with them.

While equity in the traditional sense means ownership or a share of ownership, Recruiter Equity is the joint ownership of the problem and the solution.

Recruiter Equity is the fundamental difference between winners and losers in this business. Do clients trust your judgement? Do they interview every candidate you refer? Do they build questions into their recruitment process based on your advice? Do they adjust their hiring process and refine their offer letters, and add extra benefits, because you counsel them that this is the way to attract better talent?

No? Then your Recruiter Equity is low, maybe non-existent. It takes hard work to build. It takes determination, study and practice. Think about the best recruiters you know. The relationships they have with clients amount to shared equity. Sharing the problem. Sharing the solution. Sharing the rewards.

If you want to build Recruiter Equity, your service needs to be consultative rather than transactional, and your survival depends on your ability to offer something your clients currently lack.

Hiring managers need your wisdom. It's just that in so many cases, we have not yet learned how to sell that fact to them.

This is how great recruiters succeed in our business: through Recruiter Equity.

CHAPTER 13

Recruitment is marketing

AGENCY RECRUITERS and recruitment business owners who want to thrive need to understand and act on a new reality. Clients are not going to pay your business to screen candidates that they can get from job boards, LinkedIn or other traditional sources.

Any recruitment business model that relies on candidates making proactive applications for jobs is destined to fail. If the only candidates you have are those who come to you when *they* are ready, you will only have candidates that other people have too.

Your job is to unearth unique candidates. That means candidates not available to your clients, and candidates who have not yet started their job search, through a competitor or by themselves.

You and your team have to build long-term relationships with candidates who have not yet started to apply for jobs. Candidate relationship is now a long game, which takes patience, communication and relationship building.

It's a seduction – a romance.

'Creating' candidates

Think about the 'job applicant', a person who makes the conscious decision to look for a job change, and then executes a strategy to achieve that. Examine the psychology, and the process they go through.

When an applicant responds to you from a job board, there is every chance that person is already registered with other agencies, responding to client adverts directly and engaging with employers on social media. This means that you are not likely to place them.

In an increasingly tight candidate market, a good talent that you have exclusively is a virtually certain placement.

Let's consider the candidate 'placeability' life cycle, while conscious of the bigger question: at what point do you need to engage with a candidate to increase your chances of placing them?

75% of candidates on LinkedIn are 'not looking', but at the same time they are 'open to an approach from a recruiter'. What tactics do you have to engage with those people? Remember, they are not coming to you, not responding to you as a potential candidate – but they are placeable.

Recruitment is not a résumé race anymore. It's a talent acquisition business. The juiciest candidates are those who have made the decision to move but have not acted yet. The skilled recruiter will have developed systems to engage with those candidates, and know they are at that pre-job-search stage.

It's no longer your job to screen applicants. It's your job to create candidates!

We have to rethink the very way we view our job function. We have to reinvent how we define a 'candidate'. We have to adjust our skills and tactics accordingly.

We also have to change the candidate view of us as 'body-shops'. We must engage via technology, through social media and CRM, and in real life. Give the best candidates a reason to view us as their agent.

Recruitment as marketing

We must accept, indeed embrace, the fact that recruitment is merging with marketing.

When I say that most recruiter databases are candidate graveyards, my words need to be taken seriously. So many recruitment companies are spending money on job boards to recruit candidates they *already have* on their database – that's a massive own-goal.

It seems incredible to me that my local bottle shop is better at automated database marketing than most recruitment companies. They keep in touch with me, send me specials on my favourite tipple, send me updates. Yet, most recruiters have zero interaction with candidates, except those currently being 'managed'. True candidate care always involves the human element, but branding, marketing and engagement can and should be automated.

We have so much to learn from skilled consumer marketers. We need to use consumer marketing techniques to amplify our brand with a wide pool of both candidates and prospective clients.

Sure, you have your active candidates 'in the pipe', so to speak, those who are out on interview for you. However, you also have your 'reservoir in reserve', candidates with whom you and your team are building relationships, and funnelling into your pipe for the future.

That relationship building means marketing. That means your business targeting appropriate – and engaging – content at candidates, so they are interested in what you have to say. We have to identify them, connect with them, engage with them and then 'seduce' them.

The fact is that candidates have started behaving like consumers. Thus we now need to use consumer marketing tactics to win them over.

Consider your recruitment agency clients. Do you find them harder to reach these days? How many voicemail messages are you leaving for them? Clients say that they can't differentiate between recruiters. We know people are generally less trusting of being 'sold to' and more influenced by brand, reputation, reviews and referrals.

Clients want to deal with 'experts' – and how will they know we are experts unless we are positioned that way through branding, marketing and, most crucially, content?

We have always said recruitment is all about sales. Sales will continue to be important, but maybe for now, recruitment is all about marketing. Are you and your business ready for that?

Brand starts with reputation

Recruiters are now in marketing, whether we like it or not. More specifically, we are in the business of brand-building.

Building a personal and business brand starts in real life and is amplified by digital (see the next chapter for how to build an online brand), not the other way around, in my opinion. Moreover, your personal and business brand is really your 'reputation'. This applies no matter the industry. I spoke about reputation at length in Chapter 11.

You are not in 'recruitment' at all; you are in 'rejection'

What stronger driver of your reputation, and therefore your brand, can there be than the way you and your team deal with candidates? There is no larger or more influential set of stakeholders, surely?

Yet, from a broader perspective, which industry disappoints a higher percentage of customers than ours? We think of ourselves as 'recruiters', but what is the ratio of candidates we actually *do* recruit into roles, compared to the number we screen, interview, or even submit?

Our industry is obsessed with the number of placements we make *(I have run recruitment businesses all my life, I am one of the most guilty)*. We need to apply equal attention to the number of people we *do not* place, and more crucially to the treatment they get during that process. Certainly, from a reputation and branding perspective, it's key.

What is your business's 'rejection' process? Also, what documented automation process do you and your team have to ensure no-one falls through the cracks?

The successful candidate gets showered with love and attention, including flowers and a bottle of wine sometimes – and gets a new job.

What about the also-ran shortlisted candidates?

What about those who did not make the shortlist but still believe they might? (That's because you kept them warm – 'on the bench', so to speak – in case your real shortlist fell through, right?)

What about those you dismissed at first résumé read, but who are home waiting for your call, because you never got around to communicating that to them? (That's a terrible job, explaining to a keen candidate why they are not going forward, right?)

Even if you ignore the basic manners and human kindness aspects of this situation, the commercial reality of pissing off a high percentage of customers is a disaster.

Remember, even no news *is* news to a candidate who is waiting…

Your business needs great recruiters, yes. However, you also need empathetic, consistent and morale-building 'rejecters'.

The big 'secret' of candidate care is this (and I am paraphrasing Maya Angelou here): job or not, candidates *will remember how you made them feel*, long after they remember what you gave them or even said to them.

It's critical to understand and believe that candidate care is a recruiter responsibility, not a corporate responsibility. Recruiters don't need a candidate care department. They need a candidate care ethos.

A seven-point candidate care plan

Your business doesn't have to do that much to be very different from most recruiters. You can build a brand through professionalism and consistency by sticking to some straightforward rules. In fact, the following seven simple mantras, executed consistently over time, will make you a very unusual recruiter indeed – in a good way.

1. *Respond.* The biggest criticism of our industry is that we don't respond to résumés, to tweets, to applications on our website, to phone calls. Your first goal is to get back to everyone – fast.

2. *Don't keep them waiting.* Whether that be in reception, for news, for your call – you know what I mean.

3. *Manage expectations.* We are often poor at managing expectations. Don't say, *"When I get a cool job in for you, I will give you a call."* The candidate hears, *"I will give you a call."* Thus you have set the scene for disappointment. Tell the candidate you will call if you have a great job, but given the current market that's unlikely – and that they should call you once a week for an update if that's what they want.

4. *Return phone calls.* I know you don't. You know you don't... not always.

5. *Tell them the bad news.* Don't be a coward. Don't be selfish. A candidate wants to know they have been unsuccessful if that is the case. Don't leave them hanging, and not just after an interview. Also, after you have told the candidate you will be representing them to your client.

6. *Shut up and listen a little.* Yes, be slow to understand what the candidate wants and thinks. You already know what you want and think.

7. *Give a little.* That means thanks, advice, encouragement, respect.

It seems simple. In reality, though, that manifesto will be very hard to maintain. However, it will give your team and business a real edge.

CHAPTER 14

Building a personal online brand

THE MODERN recruiter knows that 'brand' is vital.

Moreover, the smart modern recruiter knows how to amplify that brand via 'personal digital marketing'. It's not cliché, it's not marketing babble, it's not the blathering of some pony-tailed, ear-ringed digital acolyte. It's a deal-breaker for recruiting success – and, indeed, for success in any industry in which personal brand and reputation is vital.

Personal digital marketing will become the recruiter's biggest asset. This claim is based on the social branding experience of an old-school, hard-case recruiter (me!). An old-school recruiter who was also voted the most influential Australian business person on Twitter and one of only 342 people out of LinkedIn's six million members nominated as a LinkedIn 'Top Voice' in 2018, for online influence. So you can be old-school and stay updated, it seems.

The real secret to building a personal online brand

So, how do you do it? Start by taking a professional, long-term approach to creating your personal brand, and use the following pointers to help you get it right online.

Get serious

If you have decided you will use Twitter, LinkedIn or Instagram for business, behave that way from the start. Create a professional looking profile, with a good picture of your face and a full biography that has the right keywords (to help with your site's visibility in Google searches). We don't care if you love cats, support Arsenal or have a cute baby. This is not Facebook. We want to know what we can learn from you, and what we can teach you. Include a URL link to your company website, your LinkedIn profile or your blog.

Find your voice

Post in your own style, using your own language, but frame it for a business environment. So, if you would not say *"Our Prime Minister is a tosser"* or *"I hate my job"* in a client meeting, then you do not say it on Twitter or LinkedIn. Being casual, conversational and even comical is OK. However, it's not OK to be racist, sexist, gratuitously crude or confrontational. It's not smart to be overtly political or strident about your particular cause or beliefs either, because you will alienate more people than you will win over. Be authentic, yet stay professional.

It's a two-way street

Having an opinion is good. People want to be informed and challenged. That is the way to provoke engagement. However, be a 'listener' too. Be prepared to be persuaded. Thank and acknowledge. Share the excellent content put out by others. However, do not self-endorse. Shine the light on others, not yourself.

Take a long-term view

You don't get fit, and stay fit, with one week's gym work. It's the same with building a digital brand. It takes persistence and patience. It takes time for people to become aware of your content, start to follow you, share your content and in that way build up the interest and awareness.

Be consistent

You must publish content every day: LinkedIn status updates, tweets, blogs. Twitter and LinkedIn are 'streams', not inboxes. People are not there all the time. They won't see everything you post. You have to be visible. Remember, though, that thought leaders choose quality over quantity (see the next tip but one).

Post for your audience, not for you

Do you love rugby? Great, so do I. However, if you post all day about rugby, you will lose your target following, most of whom could not give a continental about the game played in heaven. I need to emphasise this. You are tweeting to entertain, inform, help and share – for the community you want to engage with. It's for *them* you post, not for you.

Quality content is the key

Content is an opportunity to differentiate. You are different from the vast mass of recruiters whom clients perceive as bland and beige. You are interesting, with a point of view, a thought leader even! To show that, most of your content must be unique to you.

You must build an audience

You must have targeted followers. There are ways to do that. Remember that no matter how great your content, how witty your updates, they are all wasted unless you have followers and connections. Posting to a handful of followers is like putting on a musical in an empty theatre. It might be great, but who knows?

So how do you build your following? There are three ways:

1. Post good stuff consistently

2. Share and engage with influential people in your sector

3. The most crucial of all – follow people you want to follow you back, and connect with the key people in your audience.

Be generous

Yes, this is a key to social media that so few seem to understand. Think *"What can I give?"* – not always *"What can I get?"* Share ideas and insights. Give away research and tips and tactics. Answer questions. Introduce people to each other. Open doors. Be kind.

Be authentic

Be real. I don't mean blunt or rude. However, be yourself. Be 'you'. People can tell if you're not being authentic and will switch off.

Engagement

Some people use social media to 'broadcast' only, just pumping out links and content. Others spend all their time 'engaging', using Twitter almost like a chat room. Well, I believe in 'brengagement'. Broadcast a lot of great stuff and engage with people who like your stuff. That's the secret! 'Brengagement'. You need to interact.

Resist the temptation to fight

This is easier said than done because the social digi-sphere is packed with idiots, cowards and bullies who like to provoke or who are just plain ignorant (as in life generally, really). My approach, for the most part, is to try to answer with a reasoned reply. If the next response is obnoxious I usually block the person. Life is far too short to spend your time tweeting with dickheads, and you never look good in a digi-spat.

Never forget that there are real people behind those social handles. Be careful not to be sarcastic, rude, dismissive or short. Take newbies under your wing. Forgive minor slights. I have met scores of people in real life after first connecting on social media. Many have become clients. Some are now friends. Tread with care.

Social branding is a long game

The return on your time and generosity may seem like a lifetime in the coming. It's a journey. It's a way of life. Build it into your week. Dedicate 30 minutes a day to social branding. That is all you need. That, and great content… and patience.

Understand what social media can do

Social media avenues in conjunction with my blog, 'The Savage Truth', have helped me to build a global brand as an advisor and speaker in the recruitment industry. That is no exaggeration.

My blog, 'The Savage Truth', attracts over one million readers a year. I have garnered over 320,000 LinkedIn followers and 18,000 targeted connections in my niche. As I've said, in 2018, I was named one of only 342 LinkedIn Voices, those being the leading influencers on LinkedIn – out of 600 million members. My two Twitter feeds (@greg_savage and @SavageTruthBlog) have over 65,000 followers between them. I was named 'The most influential Australian Business Voice on Twitter' (Brand Data, 2016). 'The Savage Truth' Facebook page has 10,000 fans.

This niche social and digital footprint provides exceptional power to influence or to market.

I get clients from all over the world who learn of me via social media and contact me via social media. I receive between two and five inbound enquiries a week on average. Speaking events I do in Asia, South Africa, Ireland, Europe, Australia and NZ are now routinely filled via marketing to my engaged and targeted audience on social media.

None of that is because I am especially clever. In fact, I am not very clever at all. It's because I have worked hard to build a social profile in a niche.

Every recruiter can do that too – and must. Building a brand is hard work. However, it will pay bounteous dividends.

Social selling is the new cold-calling

So where does all the work on branding and building a social media profile lead us? It provides inbound enquiries, certainly, but also the opportunity for the individual recruiter to 'social sell'.

Social selling is using social media to create conversations. I see it as replacing the cold-call. It's a slow burn, it's sophisticated.

We are not used to selling like this in recruitment, but it's what is needed.

Social selling is not just posting material and hoping an ideal candidate or client 'responds' and rushes into our arms. It can happen that way, but life is not usually that co-operative, sadly. Social selling involves direct, proactive prospect interaction. We start to 'talk' to people we want to sell to.

However, there is no hard sell. We don't overtly sell our service on social media: we engage, and use it as a door-opener.

Start by providing value through meaningful content that is of interest to your target audience. This differentiates you, sets you up as believable and authentic, and paves the way for interaction.

People get shocked when I mention social selling, and I wonder why. It's a process whereby you actively, consciously, proactively engineer a way in to targeted engagement. Meaning you actually set out to spark a conversation, with a specific prospect! Why not? That is what we do when we make cold-calls, isn't it? In fact, those are much more intrusive. Social selling warms up the sales process early. You have pre-earned 'cred'.

Honing in on prospects

So, building your personal brand and social selling sounds good, but how does it work in the real world?

You build your credibility through ongoing content distribution over some time. Then you hone in by endorsing your target clients' 'social persona'. Here is how:

- Target your prospective client (or candidate) by following that person on Twitter, connecting on LinkedIn or 'liking' their (work) Facebook page. If your own social media platforms are compelling enough, a healthy percentage will reciprocate. Mostly, they follow you back (or accept your invitation to connect) after reviewing your profile. How about that? Your prospect is researching you!

- Track carefully what your prospect posts, and when they post something interesting or topical that is in your domain, share it. There is little more satisfying for a social broadcaster than to have their content or ideas re-tweeted or shared or liked. It's an endorsement, and they will more than likely click on your bio to find out *"Who is this smart person who recognises quality?"* Bingo! You are noticed!

- Sometimes that prospect will thank you for the share, comment or like. Imagine that? This 'impossible to contact' prospect is now *thanking you.* If that happens, you message them back, building on the original comment. For example, *"It's a pleasure, Dave. I agree, mobile technology will change the face of recruitment."* You could even point them to more material on the same topic, and so a conversation begins. Welcome to the highly clichéd nirvana of social media… *engagement!*

- Track down your prospect's blog, if they have one. Alternatively, their LinkedIn feed will do. Read it religiously. Find a good reason to make compelling comments on their blog or LinkedIn feed. You don't have to be sycophantic or agree with their point of view. Just push the debate forward. Bloggers love comments. Trust me, I know.

- If your client is quoted in the press or online or has an article published, spread it far and wide on your own social media channels. Even something as simple as a status update they make on LinkedIn can get the same treatment. They will know, and they will like it, and by extension, they will start to like you.

Imagine if you did all or even a few of the things I suggest above with a key prospect. How easy would it be to start an online conversation? How easily could you convert that conversation to a meeting, and eventually to business?

Candidates and clients behave like consumers. Recruitment has merged with marketing, as I covered in the previous chapter.

Every recruiter, every recruitment business, needs to act like a mini digital marketing company.

CHAPTER 15

Recruiting skills that make the difference

INFORMATION AND influence are what drives success in recruitment. Moreover, that is why our industry will never die – because the craft of managing the process still determines whether a candidate is offered and, crucially, accepts a job.

Successful recruitment is not all about sourcing. It is about matching, too. Then consummating the deal, usually by finessing the attitude of both client and candidate.

Discrimination in recruitment – not just good, but essential

Some recruiters take the view that as there is a talent shortage, every candidate needs equal help and focus.

That's a big mistake. You need to discriminate when it comes to talent selection. Not on the basis of creed, colour, ethnicity, sexuality or any other irrelevant, illegal or immoral prejudice. You need to discriminate on the basis of the answer to one golden question: *"Is this candidate placeable?"*

What qualifies a candidate as 'placeable' is whether, for these two questions, you can answer yes about them:

- If put in front of the right clients, is this candidate likely to be offered a job?

- If offered a job on reasonable market terms, is this candidate likely to accept it?

There it is – the definition of a placeable candidate. Seems obvious, huh?

Well, not so obvious if you see the bumbling efforts of most recruiters when it comes to deciding whom they spend their precious time on.

Common errors include working on the candidate with the most marketable skills (which may seem all well and good, but what use is that if his salary expectations are 25% above market?). Or working on a candidate who deep down has no real intention of leaving where they are but, in fact, has simply had a bad week and is now flirting with moving. After you have done all the work to find them a job, their current employer will easily woo them back with money or emotional blackmail, or both.

However, a great recruiter knows all this before they start trying to find someone a job.

Placeable candidates typically have all or most of these characteristics:

- They have skills and experience currently in demand.

- Their salary expectations are reasonable, and they present as an affordable option to a potential employer.

- They have legitimate and tested reasons for leaving where they are now – and you have dug down and unearthed their true motivators to leave, and you believe you can find them these things in a new role.

- As they are a desirable employee, there is the chance that their current employer may make them a counter-offer, but you have pre-empted this possibility.

- They interview well; they are likeable, personable and communicative.

- They buy into your 'rules of engagement' – your explanation of how you will work together – and during the process, they deliver on that commitment. For example, they return your calls and attend all interviews.

- They agree to allow you to handle their job search exclusively.

Remember this: finding someone a job is only half the battle. Getting them to accept it is the other.

So 'discriminate' to your heart's content. Work hard on candidates who will get a job offer if put in front of a client and will accept it once it comes.

Avoid making assumptions

Often the more experience we gain in recruitment, the more shortcuts we take… and in seeps a toxic mix of arrogance, complacency and ego.

Once you've found a placeable candidate, you mustn't relax and take your eye off the ball during the recruitment process. 'Reality' is a moveable feast. What was true today may no longer be so tomorrow. You have to test, confirm, re-test, reconfirm.

The biggest cause of placements going wrong is the recruiter making assumptions, assumptions that are flawed. This is the mother of all recruiting stuff-ups. As I became more successful, the guiltier I became of taking shortcuts and assuming what was in play.

I remember negotiating a long and convoluted deal where a senior auditor went through a process with one of the 'big five' consulting firms to lead its practice in Papua New Guinea. There were four interviews, psychometric tests and countless meetings with the team.

I thought I had handled the offer well. The candidate accepted the job. Wrapping up, he mentioned how he looked forward to telling his wife about the role.

"You mean, that you've accepted the job?" I asked.

His response hit me straight in the gut. *"No, I need to talk to her about moving to Papua New Guinea first."*

I had assumed that this senior exec would have discussed such a decision with his family. I had also assumed his wife was fully briefed and supported him. I was wrong, and so was he.

The next day he called to tell me the deal was off.

So, next time your 'dead cert' placement goes belly-up, resulting in tears all round, don't blame the candidate, the client or 'bad luck'. It's most certainly your fault – because you assumed something, and you were wrong.

Multi-listed, contingency recruitment is a fool's game

As my career evolved into accounting recruitment and then creative and marketing specialisations, the need to offer contingent fees (where payment is made when the job is filled) became imperative. And that's fine – if you take a qualified brief, have a client working with you as a partner, and are afforded the time to do a quality job.

This is not the case, however, when recruiting becomes a résumé race, often driven by clients.

We will not survive against machines and low-cost digital matching platforms if we waste 80% of our time on jobs we won't fill. In Australia, New Zealand and the UK, and probably everywhere else, most recruiters are filling one role out of five.

We are better off working on fewer, better qualified, exclusive job orders.

Multi-listing of job orders across multiple agencies, and recruiters accepting briefs on a contingent and in-competition basis, is dysfunctional.

All stakeholders lose when jobs are multi-listed, because:

- Clients get a service based on speed and nothing more. They do not get the full commitment from any recruiter, and they damage their employer brand.

- Candidates suffer the most because they do not get service or care from recruiters who are too busy chasing mythical job orders in competition with five others.

It's no wonder that candidates are increasingly transferring their job search energy to web-searching, social media and other tactics.

Yet, the reality is that if recruiters worked on all jobs exclusively, they would work on 20% of the number of orders but would fill 300% more! I have tested this in real life with Aquent where we only accepted exclusive briefs (see Chapter 8). And who would benefit the most? *Candidates!* Yes, candidates, who would no longer be treated like cattle and more like the valued partners they are.

For recruiters, multi-listed, contingency recruitment is a total nightmare, flying in the face of good process and good mental health. I am not joking. Do you know what recruiters in your business (and industry-wide) really mean when they say they are 'burnt out'? They mean they can't stomach rejection and failure anymore, which is inevitable when your business model sets you up to please only a tiny fraction of your customers.

It's a vicious cycle of discontent. Clients become increasingly irritated because they are dealing with recruiters who are encouraged to do a rushed job. Ironically, the fault lies partially with the client, who asks recruiters to compete on the same position, thereby dumbing down the process. Recruiters become disillusioned, desperate, burnt-out and take shortcuts, which continues the cycle. Worst of all, of course, candidates suffer.

It is a dysfunctional, counterproductive business model. You need to recognise this and work against it. As a skilful recruiter, you will find that if you take the plunge and go with your instinct of working on an exclusive-only basis, you will have more success, more fun, more money and more self-esteem.

Selling job order exclusivity

In order to secure exclusive job orders and bypass all the multi-listed job order pain, you need to first understand client psychology.

There are five primary reasons why clients multi-list job orders and expect recruiters to compete on the same order, with a 'winner take all' outcome for the agency that fills the role:

1. Clients operate under the erroneous belief that by pitting several agencies against each other, they somehow 'keep us

179

honest' and will get better service because we will compete more aggressively. This is not true. Good recruiters put in effort where clients are working in partnership and show commitment.

2. We are seen as résumé-flickers, which, while not true for most, leads clients to believe that the more recruiters they contact, the better candidates they will get. They *will* get more candidates, but probably not better candidates. One quality recruiter, with time to do a proper job, will unearth unique hidden talent.

3. Clients do not understand how we actually come up with a shortlist; they think we dip into a database and refer candidates on, not realising we need time to do quality work.

4. Clients fail to comprehend that dealing with many recruiters is time consuming, frustrating and costly. If they worked that out, they would see the benefit of getting one recruiter to do all the work.

5. The final reason is the most damning. Clients do it because most recruiters don't have the knowledge or the courage to push back and tell them why it is *not* in anyone's interests to multi-list job orders.

This gets to the heart of being a 'consultative' recruiter. Unless you want to be a transactional beast of burden, you must be entirely articulate in positioning why a client is doing themselves tremendous harm by getting recruiters to compete.

A great recruiter has the credibility and the confidence to secure the role on a retained basis or at least exclusively, so they can have the time to put a full range of appropriate strategies in place to find the right person.

Paying a contingent fee for a multi-listed job is like paying a Wild West bounty hunter from the olden days. If you pay recruiters like you pay cowboys, you might just get... cowboys. Clients need to understand that.

Why exclusivity is in your interest

The real secret to selling exclusivity to your client is to be able to articulate why it's in their interest. First, though, why is it in your interest?

The primary reason is that you will move from 80% failure to 80% success.

If you can switch from one out of four jobs being filled to three out of four jobs being filled – you will deliver an exponentially higher number of filled jobs and have more time to focus on what you do, and do it in a more consultative and partnered relationship fashion.

It also allows you to give a better service to candidates and ultimately make more money!

Why exclusivity is in the client's interest

As I talked about earlier, clients multi-list job orders in the belief that it is in their best interests. It's not.

Working exclusively with one highly skilled, quality recruiter is by far the better path. You, the recruiter, must be supremely adroit at articulating why.

There is a plethora of strong reasons, but these are the strongest:

- The client is getting the *recruiter's full commitment* to fill their vacant role. Let's not beat around the bush here. A client may think they get more effort from a recruiter when the role is in competition, but what really happens is a short burst of activity from the recruiter, and then interest wanes as we realise the client is not committed. Instead, we go and put our energy into clients who will work with us as partners.

- The *responsibility for success is now shifted to the recruiter.* If the job is given to one recruiter, retained or exclusive, we own the problem. The client can focus on whatever it is they do for a living.

- The client is taking the *focus off speed and on to quality.* Why would you want your crucial hiring decision based on who arrives first? Would you hire a brain surgeon because they could do the job fastest? A house painter? A hairdresser? Exclusivity means the recruiter has time to do thorough work.

- Exclusivity allows the recruiter *to bring all their resources to bear in the talent search.* They don't do just a quick database search; rather, a thorough, detailed talent search including networks, communities and social media.

- Working exclusively usually means there is *time for the recruiter to take a detailed job order.* The better the order, the better the match.

- The recruiter will be able to *fully qualify the talent* regarding start date and salary, once again saving the client much time and frustration.

- *The client will save time* by dealing with one competent recruiter. There won't be multiple agency briefings and numerous contacts to deal with.

- *The client's confidentiality is preserved* as the role is not being touted around town by five or six recruiters, each speaking to nine or ten candidates about the position.

- *The client's brand and image is improved* by using one recruiter because their job is not devalued in the eyes of talent, who will be suspicious if multiple recruiters represent the job.

Selling exclusivity

You must be prepared to look a client in the eye and say:

> *"Mr Client, when you give an order to four recruiters, you are effectively giving each recruiter 25% of your commitment. What makes you think that any one of those recruiters will provide you with more than 25% of their commitment in return?"*

And then:

> *"What you are doing, Mr Client, is inviting us to approach your crucial hiring decision on the basis of speed – instead of on the basis of who can do the best quality job."*

Then go on to ask the client for a 'window of opportunity' to handle the role exclusively, so that you can give the role 100% of your commitment and bring all your resources to bear to ensure the best quality outcome.

> *"Give the job to me exclusively, so I can have the time to put appropriate strategies in place to find the right person – which will, of course, include researching my database, working my talent communities, advertising, using my networks and searching the passive talent pool."*

Having these kinds of hard conversations in front of other, perhaps less experienced, members of your team is also a great real-time coaching opportunity.

Remember, working on multi-listed, contingent permanent job orders is a terrible business model. It is better for your recruiters to each work on six exclusive job orders – of which they will fill five – than to work on 20 orders in competition, of which they may fill three.

Triage your jobs

When I was working in executive search, all orders taken were retained. I was always confident that I had a real mandate from each client and therefore every job was important. However, in the rough and tumble world of Accountancy Personnel in London, and later when I worked as a manager in Sydney, things changed dramatically, and I learned a big lesson about how to get paid more often for the work that I did.

As I've already covered in this chapter, contingent multi-listed recruitment is a recipe for disaster. If you must take multi-listings, the only way to survive in that world is to understand that urgency is essential and to make sure that the jobs you are working on are fillable.

To this day, it amazes me how even experienced recruiters don't understand the concept of 'triaging' their jobs to sort out where the biggest priority lies. This is the biggest cause of burnout, failure and working hard for little return.

As an industry, we've got to work out how to get paid more often, and clearly, that's through retained and exclusive job orders. If we don't have our focus on the jobs where clients are committed to hiring and partnering with us, we cannot deliver.

Here is why. Job orders are *not* all created equal. I often find that a recruiter working on 12 open briefs will allocate one-twelfth of their time to each brief. That's a bad mistake.

You need to regularly and consistently 'triage' your job orders to ensure that at all times you are working on those with the highest priority.

So, which jobs deserve the highest priority? The most senior vacancy? The job paying the highest salary? The job with the highest potential fee? The job that came in most recently? No! No! And no, a thousand times!

The jobs that survive your triage cull do so because they meet all or most of a few key criteria:

- The job is well qualified.
- You know exactly what the client wants.
- The job is real and urgent.
- The hiring criteria are reasonable and achievable in today's market (i.e. the salary matches the skills required).
- The client is committed to hiring and has signed your terms of business and has internal approval to hire.
- The client is working with you as a partner; returning your calls, interviewing your talent and taking your advice.
- You have the job exclusively.
- The client is a long-term supporter whom you have worked with many times.

I believe in this so much that once, with Firebrand, we manipulated the ATS/CRM to ensure each recruiter had to go through this checklist as they entered a job order in the system. Then the system gave that job order a 'fill score'. If it didn't hit a certain number, the system didn't allow the recruiter to enter the job.

It certainly got us all thinking about qualified and fillable jobs and how we should spend our valuable time.

Only very few of your orders will tick all those boxes. These are your top priority, and they get the majority of your attention. Then you work down the list, triaging your jobs for priority. It's a movable feast. Changed circumstances might mean a job goes up the priority list, or down.

If you find there are a few jobs right at the end that get no attention – well, it's sad, but they just get sacrificed. Actually, it's not sad at all. Typically, they are unqualified orders from uncommitted clients. Good riddance, to be frank!

Fire these clients, now!

As I evolved as a recruiter, I learned that the most significant stress in recruitment is not sales, nor pressure, nor targets, nor offers turned down.

The biggest stress in recruitment is working with dickheads.

Not colleagues, although that can happen too, but irrational, uncooperative, unethical clients.

Here is the irony. As recruiters push ever harder to win the business, they become more superficial in their work, more transactional in their approach and less discerning about who they do business with. Why? Why work with clients who treat you like mud, and jerk you around consistently? It's crazy.

In an environment of chronic and sustained talent shortages, you need to head in the other direction.

You will not survive by spreading yourself so thinly. The superficial phone call, the multi-listed, non-exclusive job order, the mad rush to get résumés across on some crazy deadline. This is not a path you want to follow.

It's transactional. It's superficial. It's dangerous for your financial health. Moreover, it will smash your self-esteem.

The best business is often the hardest to win, but the most profitable once you have it. The future requires us to invest time, resources and brainpower in developing, nurturing and retaining long-term clients with fee-generation growth potential who will use our services regularly.

I get resistance to this from some recruiters. They say the transactional model is 'just the way the market is'. They acknowledge it's mud against the wall, but claim it's what clients want, and to win you need to throw more mud. If that is true, God save us all.

However, thankfully, it is not true. These recruiters have caved. They have capitulated to the transactional recruiting tsunami, and joined the shallow mob of hard-selling, résumé-pumping, cold-calling, candidate-burning, price-cutting recruiters, willing to play that dirty, cheap game.

I don't buy it. There *is* a market for quality recruiting. So, you need to be brave enough to fire those clients who won't work with you and give more time to the good clients who *do* want a partnership.

Who exactly should you fire as a client?

Let's start with the following:

- Clients who jerk you around with sketchy job specs, who demand the world from you and give nothing in return.

- Clients who pull jobs halfway through assignments or fail to return your calls and use three other agencies in competition with you.

- Inflexible clients, who take no advice and ignore your feedback.

- Clients who unfailingly try to negotiate fees – especially after you have gone to the ends of the earth to fill their job.

- Clients who see no value in service or quality, but only want to talk about price.

- Clients who show no respect for what you do or say, who abuse your guarantee and who, in the end, refuse to pay the bill.

You recognise your client here, don't you? (And I'm sure people in other industries also recognise their clients here.) You are smiling as you read this. Yet, we still work with these guys. Why? They absorb your time and they torpedo your self-esteem. They take your focus off where it should be – your targeted clients and prospects who can offer you long-term, sustainable, profitable business.

Frankly, it's like putting lipstick on a pig, working with these 'clients'; a pig is still a pig, with or without gloss. (No offence, piggy.)

Call a team meeting in your office today. Identify the culprits. Then fire these so-called clients – these renegades and buccaneers, users and abusers – and put your effort into those key prospects and clients whom you have identified as the sorts of employers you want to do business with.

Need to fire a deadbeat client? Here's how...

Before you sit the client down for a good firing, you must decide whether there are any circumstances where you *would* do business with this client again. Usually, that *is* the case. That being so, it's crucial to leave the communication door open for the relationship to be picked up again, if the circumstances are right.

Occasionally, where the client has been obnoxious or dishonest, you may decide never to do business with this client again (a liberating feeling, I promise!). In which case, you can kill the thing stone dead, there and then. However, still do it politely. Extra enemies are something none of us need.

My steps to firing a deadbeat client are:

1. If possible, physically sit down with your client, face to face. If that's not possible, then over the phone is the next best thing. Email? That never works. It always ends ugly. Don't go there.

2. Remember to use a collaborative tone of voice (avoid revealing any anger, bitterness, hate or frustration you really feel). Be polite. Be respectful.

3. Then, it's your time to explain to the client that you really do want to work with them, and you do want to help them acquire great talent; however, the status quo does not allow you to do that.

4. Next, go through the market conditions that prevail, the difficulties in finding talent, and go on to spell out everything you will do to assist this client to get what they need. Explain in detail your process and your quality commitments and everything else that makes up your service, and what you need to do to get the results the client wants.

   This might seem strange, as you are about to sever the relationship, but in fact what you are doing is laying the path for the client to be rehabilitated – either right now in this conversation (unlikely), or some time in the future when they realise they really do need your help (slightly more likely).

5. To follow, you shift the conversation to what the client needs to do to make the whole partnership work for their benefit.

   You see what you have done? *"I want to help you. This is what I can do to help you. However, this is what **you** need to do to help you."*

6. Then say, *"So, this is how we can get the result you want. Can you commit to working this way with me?"* (This is essentially saying, *"It's my way or the highway."* However, you are doing it nicely.)

7. If the answer to that question is a flat *"No"*, be upfront. *"Working the way we currently do, Mr Client, does not get the results you or I want. Of course, it is your choice how you work, so when you are ready to come back and work with me in a partnership model, in the way I have described today, I will be delighted to start working with you again."*

Bang! That client is fired. Yet the door is ever so slightly left open.

Making the most of client meetings

To build recruiter equity, sell exclusivity, position your business's brand and foster partnership working, it's still true that meeting your client in real life is often crucial.

When meeting with a prospect or client, ideally they should do 75% of the talking – because when the client is talking, you are selling. The chances are when you are talking, the client is at best silently critiquing you or most likely thinking about their dinner.

Remember – ask for the business

Every client meeting starts with high tension, particularly as the client or prospect usually feels they are about to be sold to. A great recruiter will diffuse that anxiety quickly and seamlessly by building rapport.

Building rapport early is critical. You don't want to present yourself as a 'stalker', but doing a bit of research will give you some idea where you and your prospect have common ground.

Start with broad, open-ended questioning and then slowly home in, to eventually get specific details about the client's hiring intentions. Resist the temptation to jump in early with your big 'sell'. Make sure the person you are meeting is the decision-maker, find their hot buttons and understand their history of hiring.

Once you have a clear picture, it's your turn to sell specific solutions based on the client's needs. Focus on your business's point of difference and what it is you and your team bring, and how you can solve the problem.

If the client asks questions, that's a great sign.

Possibly the biggest mistake at this point is to neglect to close. There is no point sitting through an hour-long meeting if you don't ask for the business.

The way to do this is to ask if there are any current vacancies. If they are forthcoming, then take the order. Job done! If not, then get a commitment to bring you in on the next vacancy.

So – always, ask for the business.

Also, whether you get work that day or not, don't leave without a follow-up time frame agreed and your terms of business understood and signed off on.

Six strategies to improve your client meetings – while you are in reception

Success in recruiting is all about doing a lot of small things... very well. Pretty much all recruiters follow the same process. We screen, we interview, we match, we meet clients, and we engineer scores of mini interactions which stitch the whole thing together.

Experience has taught me that getting the best outcome depends on making sure that you are just that little bit better than your competitors during each step of the process. Believe me, in this business you must strive to give yourself every tiny advantage you can. There are no second prizes in recruitment. You either fill the job, or you don't.

Let's take client visiting as an example. Do you make the very most of the opportunity it presents?

Consider the ten minutes you wait in reception for your client to greet you. Do you waste that time? Do you daydream, thinking about what to have for dinner that night? Or do you mindlessly read the magazine on the table in front of you?

Remember, success is about giving yourself any advantage you can. So what can you do during those ten minutes that will make a difference? Here are some small but effective tactics:

- *First, engage with the receptionist.* Have a chat and build rapport. If appropriate, ask a few questions. Maybe you learn that they are a temp. Could that be interesting to you? What other great information will they share as you chat for five minutes? Not only that, the receptionist can become your greatest ally. Make sure you get to know them, win them over, and next time you call you will be put straight through.

- *Pay attention.* Listen to the incoming calls. Listen to the conversations of staff members as they walk through the reception area. What can you learn about the company and its culture, its staff and their interaction? Can that help you during the client meeting itself? Could it assist you in making a cultural match? Can it help you sell the company to a potential candidate?

- *Read the visitors book.* Yes, I know, this is a little controversial – but I don't care. I want to know who has been visiting the company recently. And guess what? If the visitors book is full of other recruiters, that's good news. In all likelihood, that means there are jobs to be had at that company. Fish where the fish are.

- *Take what you can.* No, don't steal stuff – but yes, do pick up the newsletters, brochures and pamphlets. Information is power and the more you know about this company, its products, services and activities, the better. It can only help your credibility in the meeting about to start, right?

- *Read the walls.* Go on, look for mission statements displayed on the wall, look for awards, read the announcements, jot down the name of the employee of the month. There is so much to be learned. It will help you later.

- *Prepare your small talk.* No matter what type of meeting you are about to have, it is inevitable that it will start with a bit of small talk. Prepare yours. Please, make sure it's not inane waffle about the weather. A good, confident, intelligent start will set up a great meeting. Prepare a couple of comments or questions that are topical and show that you are 'on your game'. For example, as you walk with your client to his office, *"I was fascinated to read you are opening a new branch in North Sydney, Mr Client. How is that progressing?"* It's small talk, sure. However, it's smart small talk, because guess what? By the time you are sitting down… the meeting has started – and you are driving it.

Information is power. Winning in recruitment is a matter of inches. You just have to be that little bit better to take the main prize. Use every ounce of leverage you can to give yourself an advantage

Even when you're sitting in the reception.

CHAPTER 16

Negotiating fees and margins

AS YOU may have worked out from the first part of this book, when I was a young recruiter I had plenty of desire, but few of the smarts.

In commercial negotiations, I was desperate to secure every order. I had a raw competitive edge that lacked finesse. I *had* to secure the work. Moreover, if the client wanted to negotiate, I was always keen to 'do a deal'. However, it was dumb.

The percentage of orders we fill is on average pretty low in recruiting, so why muddy the waters further by working on orders that offer a lower return?

I did wise up though. Sure, occasionally I'd negotiate a fee to secure a particularly attractive piece of work. But price-hagglers usually become problem clients in a broader sense. Ever noticed that?

I was also clumsy with fee negotiations, often trying to barter with the client on the percentage or the dollar amount. That is a loser's game. You can't allow the discussion to focus on your percentage versus some other mystical 'lower percentage' that the client quotes as gospel. That's a fight you can never win.

Don't talk dollars, talk differentiation

This is the secret sauce when it comes to negotiating recruitment fees.

It's a fact of recruiting life that clients will push you to negotiate your fees. And with so many recruiters quick to drop fee percentages to secure the brief, it can be a hard discussion to deal with.

The starting point for successful fee negotiations is, strangely enough, to get the conversation off the fee percentage, and on to the question of what it is your fee *is actually for*. Bundled up in that conversation is your ability to sell your differentiator.

What have you *got* and what *do* you do that gives your client unique value?

Now, please understand, this strategy only works if you do in fact have meaningful differentiators. So, here is the bad news. If you do not have parts of your process or your abilities that offer unique or at least advantageous value – you won't be able to hold your fees when things hot up at the negotiating table.

However, if you have worked hard to create differentiators – and you must – that is where you want to focus.

At Aquent and Firebrand Talent Search, for example, we emphasised our niche focus, our unmatched access to creative, marketing and digital talent, our multiple branches in APAC and Europe, our specialist knowledge and understanding of client needs, our proprietary testing software which meant we knew candidates had the design skills they claimed to have. This was all wrapped up in a 110% money-back guarantee.

That was (and still is) a compelling argument. (I am sold, just writing the previous paragraph!)

It's also vital that the differentiators you nominate have relevance for the client and are centred in the advantage you bring regarding access to talent.

I remember going with a junior recruiter to visit a small design studio in Surry Hills in Sydney. The client had ten staff members, and the meeting went well initially until it came to our turn to sell how Aquent could help him.

Proudly, the recruiter with me started to talk about our global offices, bizarrely naming Barcelona and Amsterdam in particular. She was doing her best to showcase our capability, and she was proud of our global reach, but the relevance to this small client was zero, and I could see his eyes begin to glaze over.

What we needed to focus on at that moment was our unparalleled database of local UX designers, many of whom were available to start tomorrow and solve his workflow problems.

Don't talk fees, talk value

So, when a client does ask you to drop your fee, don't talk about your fee!

Go through your entire recruitment process, explaining all the things you do to secure the right person. Take your time. Start at the beginning and don't miss out anything. Talk about your screening, interviews and your talent generation strategies such as social media and networking.

Focus particularly on your ability to find candidates that other recruiters, and the client themselves, cannot. That's the sweet spot.

Talk about your database and the fact you have several offices (if you do) tapping into talent. Explain how you act as an advocate for the client, and how you will qualify each candidate concerning fit, salary and skills. When you drill down on this, you find we recruiters do a lot.

That's the point, so *tell your client.*

The biggest reason clients want to push down fees is that they don't perceive the value in what we do. Usually, they don't recognise the benefit because they don't know what we do to earn our fee. They don't know what we do because we, stupidly, don't tell them!

It's like looking at an iceberg. Only 10% of an iceberg is visible above the waterline. The rest, 90%, is out of sight. It's the same scenario with our work (as mentioned in Chapter 12) – 90% is out of sight, so the client does not factor it into his perception of 'value'.

Put the ball in the client's court

So, tell the client everything you are going to do to solve their staffing problem, chapter and verse. Then, and only then, ask the client why they feel a reduced fee is appropriate. This is important. Put the ball firmly into the client's court.

The client is asking for a discount. They should be squirming – not you. When it comes to fee discounts, you don't have to justify why not – they have to justify why. It's a shift in the dynamic, and it's very compelling indeed.

Sometimes the client pushes hard for a reduced fee. Don't feel pressurised. It's a purely commercial decision – and it's your decision to make. Is this client and this order so attractive it is worth taking a lower fee for?

Remember this before you discount next time. Don't think of the fee only as dollars gained or lost – think of the fee as what your service is worth. A discounted fee means a discounted 'you' – never forget that.

If you must compromise...

Sometimes you will feel it is worth a compromise to secure a particular opportunity. In these cases, remember one golden rule: never reduce your initially quoted fee without extracting a concession from the client.

In other words, you may say, *"My fee is 20%."* The client asks for a discount. You say, *"OK, 15%."* You have just signalled to the client that you never believed in your value proposition and your service in the first place. You will struggle with getting that client's respect ever again – and you will never get your fees back up.

So, if you reduce your fee, always ask for something in return – a retainer, exclusivity maybe, or for the client to give you multiple orders, or perhaps you may waive the guarantee.

Make sure the negotiation involves both sides giving a little. In this way, an equal partnership stays intact. So too does your self-esteem – and in our business, that is crucial.

Look for clients in pain

I am particularly fond of telling recruiters that a client in pain is an excellent thing. When a client is under pressure, they are more committed to getting an outcome, and therefore more likely to be committed to our process, and to us.

A client in pain is also unlikely to focus on the fee. They are looking for a solution.

So, what does this mean? Well, as you make your judgement on which clients to work with, look for these signs:

- Your client just had a key person resign.

- They are suffering from high turnover in the team.

- They just won a massive piece of work from one of their clients.

- They shared with you that they are under pressure to perform or deliver results.

- A direct competitor has just launched a new product or service, and you know your client is under pressure to compete.

- The client's high season is just about to start, and the pressure is on.

- It's salary review time, and you know your client's staff are underpaid and will be asking for raises.

- Your client has a massive personal workload with many deadlines, just at the time they're starting to hire.

- They have no HR support, maybe no admin support, and are clearly no expert in interviewing, recruiting, hiring or onboarding.

There are many more examples, but I think you get the picture. Look for a client under pressure, and you will find a client in pain.

Excellent! They need a solution – and you have it.

Don't be scared by the 'C' word

Sometimes in a fee negotiation, the client will utter the dreaded 'C' word. It's this use of the 'C' word that often scares recruiters, leading them to concede too early and by too much.

The 'C' word?

Competitors!

"But your competitors charge less!" says your client triumphantly.

I love it when clients use that word. If they do start to talk about competitors' low fees, your response is to ask: *"Can you tell me about a situation, Ms Client, where you were charged less than the fee I am suggesting today, where you got the level of service and the calibre of talent you want – on a regular basis?"*

True, this is a gamble. However, the fact that you are there, in the client's office, taking the order (or even on the phone taking the order), means that it is most unlikely the client is happy with their current supplier.

It amazes me when a client spends 20 minutes bagging another recruiter, telling me how hopeless they are, and then when I quote my fee, they say, *"Hey, but the other recruiter only charges 15%!"* Of course they do. They are no good! You just told me that.

That is the time to remind the client that a low fee, quoted by a supplier who does not deliver, is not a benchmark against which you will measure your fees – and nor should the client.

Be prepared to stand your ground on this with your client. Quoting a fee is easy and meaningless. Delivery at a price is what counts.

You need to say, *"I can deliver at this price."* Then make very sure you do.

Negotiating temp margins: focus on the outcome, not the rate

Some of the mark-ups on the temporary worker rate I see staffing companies offer in Australia, the UK and elsewhere are shocking. They suggest desperation bordering on hysteria.

The 'big secret' when it comes to negotiating with clients about temp bill rates is to shift the client's focus from the rate – to the total cost.

If you allow all the focus to remain only on the dollar value of the hourly rate, then you have very little negotiating leverage. If the client quotes another agency that will charge less, for the same job, and you argue about the hourly rate only, you have nowhere to go.

However, if you focus on the other part of what the client said, then you have plenty to discuss. I am referring of course to where the client says another agency will charge less *"for the same job"*. That's the weak spot to tackle in a client's argument. Will the client indeed get *"the same job"* done by the cheaper option?

"No!" is our response. In fact, it could cost the client plenty.

So, for example, let's say you advise a client that a mid-weight freelance web designer is going to cost $50 per hour. The client says, *"That's expensive – I can get a designer from your competitor for $45."* You see, the client focuses on the rate only (and tossed in the 'C' word to shake you up).

Most temp consultants cave in at this point. They reduce the bill rate to win the assignment. That teaches the client that our rate is negotiable, and it immediately reduces our margin. That is bad.

A more appropriate strategy is to focus the client on the comparative cost of the entire project. Get the focus off the hourly rate. How? Well, like this usually works…

"Ms Client, all our designers have been interviewed, screened and tested for both their skills and their attitudinal fit to do freelance work. In the case of the person I propose to provide you with for this role, she has worked for us many times before, and I have many glowing testimonials on the calibre of her work, her initiative and accuracy. Ms Client, the person I will provide you will come in, sit down and start being productive in the first hour. She will make minimal mistakes, need no supervision, and the quality of the outcome will make you very happy indeed. What's more, she will do this project within the two-week time frame you need. To get someone of this calibre we need to pay $50 per hour."

$50 × 8 hours × 10 days is a total cost to you of $4,000.

"If you take the cheaper option, Ms Client, you may well pay $45 per hour, but it is most unlikely that you will get the calibre of individual and the quality of work I can promise you here today."

"Indeed, your $45 an hour person is likely to take longer to do the job, absorb more of your time, and quite possibly make more mistakes."

In this case, $45 × 8 hours × 15 days is a total cost to you of $5,400.

"The so-called cheaper option, Ms Client, will ultimately cost you far more."

"It's quality work done at the best cost that I am offering you, and that's why I am suggesting my talent at $50 is in your best interests."

What day can she start?

That's the way to sell quality temps. Think about it. BMW does not compete on price with Hyundai. They are both cars with engines, seats, GPS and reverse parking cameras. However, people pay far more for a BMW because the quality and value is there.

It's the same with our temps. If your client wants an excellent freelance experience, and the client wants their problems solved quickly and accurately, the price may be a little higher, but the value will be measurably better.

'Temp-to-perm' fees – are we stark raving mad?

This is one thing our industry has all wrong. We give away our temps at discount rates. I have never understood this. I know the market is competitive. I appreciate a dollar is still a dollar. I am also aware that clients are screwing us with all their might.

A temp on your payroll is a precious asset. In talent-short times, I cannot fathom why anyone in our industry would give a substantial discount on the fee when a temporary employee turns permanent. (This is called a 'conversion fee' in some markets.)

It's just so illogical. A temp-to-perm fee is a once-off hit which is nice when it happens, but we seem to forget that in the process we have lost a tried, tested and hard to replace revenue earning asset – our temp worker.

I have heard all the arguments on this from clients, and they simply don't wash. Let's start with the classic, *"But you really should discount the permanent conversion fee because you have already earned so much margin on the temp."* What hogwash. The temp margin is for the temporary service rendered: finding, managing and insuring the temp. Also, paying them sometimes up to a month before the client pays us. The perm fee is for the acquisition of the permanent staff member. There is no leveraging one against the other.

We need to be clear with the client that it's far from a celebration for us when a temp converts to a permanent position. A perm fee is scant compensation for the lost revenue that the temp could have earned on future assignments.

Some clients will even try to use the 'hire purchase' argument. *"But can't you see,"* they say *"It's like me renting a TV and then buying it. It's always cheaper to buy a previously rented TV."* This sounds neat, but it is fallacious. A TV is a depreciating asset.

A human being, in a contract assignment where they are getting trained, absorbing the company culture and learning the systems, is an *appreciating* asset.

The perm fee should be *more*, not less.

There's one more thing…

Don't pro-rata perm fees for long-term contract assignments

Say your client wants a person for six months. That's a temp job. However, they want to pay a one-off fee and put the person on their payroll. That's OK. However, the client wants to pay a one-off perm fee, discounted because the job is not for a full year. Don't agree to that. That's dumb. You lose.

Keep the distinction between temporary/contract and permanent crisp and clear. (I know in some countries our hands are legally tied on this, but in many countries it's about negotiation.)

If it is a fixed-term assignment, it's a contract role, and therefore it's a timesheet hourly rate with our margins on top, or it's a fixed weekly or monthly rate. Don't for a minute think, *"Well, it's a six-month role so we will take our perm fee and divide it by two because it's half a year."*

Do the arithmetic!

A perm fee at 20% for a $75,000 placement is $15,000.

If a client wants to pay half the perm fee because it's a six-month gig, then you get $7,500.

However, the margin you will earn on a temp valued at $75,000 over six months, at a margin of 22%, is $12,500 (based on industry norms).

$7,500 vs $12,500… You can see why the client likes the idea!

Sure, if the client wants to pay a perm fee instead of a margin for a six-month gig, that's cool. However, it's the *full* perm fee they will need to pay.

That's fair and proper.

If you are not convinced, think about this. If you owned an investment property and rented it for five years to a lovely young couple, and then they wanted to buy it from you, would you give them a 25% discount off the sale price because of the rent they had previously paid? I don't think so. So why do you give your temps away cheap?

Believe me on this. We have nothing else to sell, apart from our service and our talent skills.

Don't give away the farm.

CHAPTER 17

Leadership is action

IF MANAGEMENT and leadership roles are on the cards for you as you move through your recruitment career (or any other career, for that matter), what is there for me to say in these areas that hasn't already been said?

Well, quite a lot it turns out, because our industry has some unique twists.

Driving growth in a recruitment business through exceptional leadership is something that few master. I am not even claiming I managed it. However, I did get far better at it as the years rolled by.

So, if you are a recruitment business owner or manager, or perhaps plan to be, this chapter and the next (on the Seven Cs of Savage Leadership) will be more than useful. Developing your leadership abilities is going to be crucial to your success as a manager.

Managing versus leading

You can be a manager without being a leader. Most of us are just that. You can also be a leader without the title of manager. You no doubt know people like that in your teams right now – and they can use that 'leadership power' either for good or evil.

The critical point is that merely managing the process won't be enough for you to build an exceptional business. Nor will it allow you to build an outstanding career in any industry.

And that's why this truth is so important: you don't get a great team without a great manager who is *also* a leader.

Is there a difference? Most definitely, yes. 'Manager' is the title you have on your business card. 'Leader' and leadership is about how you influence attitude and behaviour.

Roll that second sentence around in your mind, if you will.

Do you?

Do you *influence attitude and behaviour* in the people around you? For the positive, obviously. Do they *follow* your lead?

That is your role as a leader. That is what makes the difference. That is what defines you; influencing attitudes and influencing change, in pursuit of the corporate goals.

I think of this in pretty blunt terms, and so should you: managers have subordinates, leaders have followers.

This differentiation is more important than it might at first appear. I am not talking management buzzword psycho-babble.

If you are a 'manager', this differentiation affects you in the most profound and real way. It is critical, because developing your leadership abilities will be vital to your success in the role you have right now, and in your career going forward.

In the future, robots are going to do all the hackwork, all the process, all the measurement, and much more besides. However, artificial intelligence will *not* provide leadership nor decision-making. Nor will it foster collaboration or creativity.

Your leadership capability is so critical because *talent* is at the epicentre of competitive advantage, and will remain so for the foreseeable future.

Technology will take care of the drudgery, and most organisations will be able to afford the best technological systems to do this. So, technology fails to be the differentiator.

The differentiator is *people*. The best talent will always gravitate to the best leadership. That is a fact, based on my 40 years' experience in human capital. Creating an environment where people *want* to do things, rather than feel they *have* to, is the difference between great and mediocre.

However, here is the good news. Leadership can be learned, and it can be improved. It *has* to be improved.

Learning true leadership skills

It is true that many of us in recruitment leadership have been promoted into leadership positions because we were technically competent in our previous roles. We were good recruiters, good billing managers. I see that so often, and so do you. The best recruiter is made the manager of other recruiters. However, there is an entirely different skill-set required.

Promoting a top team member can often be a disaster (as I talked about in Chapter 11). In many cases, the reality is that the good recruiter eventually gets promoted beyond their level of competence – which is a scary thought.

Yet, why would that not happen? These people have no doubt had much training on the technical side of the job, and on process and policy. It's likely they have even had some 'management' training, too.

However, who taught them anything about leadership?

If you are lucky, you have learned to manage along the way, but who taught you about true leadership? What is it? What does a leader do? How does a leader behave?

You need to ask yourself this next question, and it might hurt.

"Why would anyone want to be led by me?"

It's a frightening question.

As a leader, you are inviting people to follow you. You cannot do anything in business without followers. We know it's all about the people.

Yet, in these 'empowered', millennial generation times, followers are hard to find, right? People don't follow blindly, and they don't merely do what they are told unless they believe. They question. They quibble. They think for themselves.

You must find ways to engage people and rouse their commitment to the company goals. Then you can evolve to leadership from management. A key component needed for that to work is for you to be the champion of change in the business. I believe that great leaders promote constant incremental disruption.

Leaders need to understand that people will not be impressed by their work history or their qualifications or their title or their awards. The leaders who people respect and will follow are those who care, and those who make a difference in people's lives.

That is the kind of leadership we should be focused on – our ability to impact our people and make a difference.

Don't get me wrong, I am not talking about 'caring' in some lovey-dovey, kumbaya-singing, hippie commune way. Trust me on that. There is no incense burning when I run my board meetings. I mean a leader who cares about the professional success and development of their staff.

Think of your history. Is there a person or two who made a difference to you, taught you things, mentored you, and influenced your values? A leader who showed faith when others didn't and inspired you through their actions? Do you find yourself thinking, *"What would (so-and-so) do?"*?

That is leadership, because their influence has lasted. Your managerial 'authority' lasts about as long as you are in the room. 'Influence', on the other hand, lasts forever.

Leadership is not about talking a good game. It's not about thumping the table like some deranged half-time footy coach. It's not about dreaming up an esoteric vision statement that no one believes in or acts on.

Leadership is action. It's what you do that counts. Not what you say, so much.

It's your behaviour that people will remember and emulate. It's your example that people will follow. Leadership is showing the way, not telling it. That is the case regardless of your industry or business type.

In the following chapter, I get into the nitty-gritty of strong leadership, outlining my Seven Cs of Savage Leadership.

Quality control as a leadership way of life

All of us struggle with quality control – in our leadership and personal job performance, and the performance of our team. It's a competitive world. It's fast. The demands on us are huge. Yet we constantly face criticism for falling standards.

What's more, as your team grows, the potential for a severe drop in quality is very real, and even likely. Yet it doesn't have to be so.

Develop the culture

Trying to keep quality standards up by threatening consultants or chastising them will only have a short-term effect. The goal is to create a culture of quality where people have pride in their output. I have found it very effective to involve staff in generating a list of standards that 'we as a team' want to stick to. People take ownership of quality standards that they have input into.

This need not be a complicated exercise. It should include such basic things as these examples (which you may want to word as your own):

- *"In our team, it is not acceptable to keep someone waiting in reception for longer than 10 minutes."*
- *"In our team, every client who lodges a temporary job has a call back within half an hour as to our progress on filling that job."*
- *"In our team, candidate phone calls are returned on the day we receive their call."*
- *"In our team, changes to client or candidate records are kept updated on the database the day that they happen."*

Once you have developed a set of expectations that everyone owns, this becomes *"The way we do things around here."* Hang them up on the wall. Display them in reception so visitors see them. Include them in offer letters for your own staff. Talk about these expectations often. Update them when required. Own them. Share them. Live them.

Once bred into the DNA of your team, it is very easy to hold up a mirror to a consultant who has not met these expectations and say, *"Hey, these are the team's values that you are not meeting."*

It's a powerful message and it provides self-sustaining momentum to quality control.

CHAPTER 18

The Seven Cs of Savage Leadership

TO PIN down what leadership is all about, I have developed what I call the 'The Seven Cs of Savage Leadership':

1. Clarity

2. Climate

3. Communication

4. Coaching

5. Courage

6. Creativity

7. Comprehension.

These seven aspects apply to leadership across all industries, not just recruitment. Steal at will. Go on, you should!

Clarity

Real leaders leave no room for confusion.

It's crucial you make sure everyone knows what you are trying to achieve in the business. That's actually a lot harder to maintain than you might think. You would be amazed at how vague and inconsistent with messaging most people are. That is a leadership issue.

Could every person in your business be brought into a room, individually, and tell me what your business vision is? What your company goal is? What the business plan is? What their priorities are? What 'good work' looks like?

Would everyone say the same thing?

Great leadership ensures clarity around roles, expectations, activities required and behaviours. Leaders spell out how these individual aspects and goals combine in the business to achieve the corporate goals.

I remember many years ago at Aquent, the management team were reviewing performance and one particular young man's name was raised. Long debate about his suitability for the role and his results ensued – and the discussion ended up with the possibility of him being managed out of the business.

Coincidentally, that night the team were out celebrating the good end-of-quarter results. I joined them, and ended up sitting next to the very consultant we had been discussing. In small talk, I asked him how things were going. His answer shocked me.

As he turned to me, his eyes were aglow, and he said, *"Things are going great, I'm doing so well and I couldn't be happier. I really see my career in recruitment."*

My heart sank, not for him, but for our poor leadership. We had not clearly communicated to him our expectations, including the performance level we expected of him.

So, the next Monday I gathered the management team together, the main topic to discuss being: are we communicating with great clarity on people's performance? It was obvious in this case we had a lot to do to give this individual a chance to step up. He was living under the illusion that things were great. That was poor leadership.

Climate

So, leaders provide clarity. However, that clarity has to exist in a particular climate to be able to take root and flourish. And, of course, it's always the leader who dictates the climate of a business.

I genuinely believe that a great deal hinges on the optimism or otherwise of the leader. When I hire leaders and potential leaders, I value that core trait.

I am a tragically optimistic person. Once a plan has been developed, or a strategy sensibly agreed, I rarely countenance the possibility of failure. It's not mindless enthusiasm, but a belief that we can do it.

I believe in PMA (positive mental attitude). Not being idiotically optimistic, like *"Hey guys, it's the second last day of the month, and we are on $75,000. Our target is $500,000, but heads down, we can still make it!"* Yet if the leader is sure it can be done, if the leader spells out that goals can be met, if the leader believes in the vision, repeats the message and acts on it, then – suddenly, miraculously – others do too, and those goals are met.

If, on the other hand, the leader expresses doubt, fear or panic, it's those negative thoughts that will filter through to the team.

Ask yourself. How do you rate on the PMA scale? What climate do you set in your office via both your verbal and non-verbal communication?

Remember: leaders are far more influential than they realise they are. When it comes to morale, mood and momentum, we have a significantly greater impact than we might typically appreciate. Are you providing the PMA leadership you should? Think about the words you use, the body language, the mood, even the tone of your messages.

When we look closely at the 'climate' created by leadership, there is one area I want to focus in on, even over and above PMA...

Communication

It is obvious, but much of what defines a good leader is their communication style: what you say, how you say it, when you say it. Also, importantly, what you don't say.

I have made mistakes in all of the 12 aspects of communication listed below, and I sum up my learnings for you in what I egotistically like to call 'The Savage 12 Communication Commandments'.

You can't ever over-communicate

You will never be accused of over-communicating. You are not going to have the exit interview where someone says, *"I was kept too informed, and you just shared too much important stuff with me. I have had enough of being looped in. I am leaving!"*

You *will*, though, hear the exact opposite of this as people resign because of poor communication.

Communicate early and often

Don't wait until people start to make up things because of a lack of information. Trust me, they will. Don't communicate only once and think people will 'get it'. They certainly won't. Repeat the message in different ways and at different times.

Tell them everything or tell them nothing

Revealing everything is not always possible. However, when it is possible, paint the full picture, anticipate follow-up questions and concerns, and address these early.

I have learned that telling people half the story is dangerous. They will fill in the gaps themselves and invent the missing information.

I remember a manager who, on discovering that the office lease was up in three months, raced straight out to tell the team, prefacing her news with the fateful phrase, *"Don't panic, but…"*. Of course, they all panicked and started imagining, and believing, bad scenarios such as that the company was going bust, which was far from the truth.

It would have been far better if she had kept that information to a trusted few, found new premises and then announced *"our exciting move to better offices"*.

Empathise before you communicate

This is critical. So many managers get this wrong.

For example, you are cutting the recruitment advertising budget. Don't just deliver that news as a fait accompli, bluntly, with no sense of understanding how it will impact the team. They will be

211

upset about the reduction in the advertising budget but resentful about your lack of empathy. Something like this is far more likely to soften the impact:

"I know that cutting the advertising budget is going to make it harder in some respects, and we are not happy about that. So, for a while, you will need to adjust. The fact is, it's not working, so we want to be smarter about how we spend the money and use it for more effective candidate sources."

Deliver on commitments

Not delivering on commitments is your most significant and most potentially damaging mistake. We are all guilty of over-promising and under-delivering. We use our 'authority' as 'the boss', as an excuse to let commitments slip. It's easy to do.

"Next week, Bob, I will make time to come on two client visits with you." Then it never happens. Plus, we make a thousand other statements of intent, big and small, that we don't follow through on. The point is, this damages your credibility and it erodes trust.

What I have learned is if people can't trust you to deliver on your small promises, they won't believe you on the big ones.

Use informal and formal channels

Formal communication channels, like email and newsletters and even staff briefings, tick the box in the sense that 'the information has been passed on'. However, has it been understood? Especially by the key people?

Target follow-ups, whether at the desk, over drinks, on the way back from client meetings. This is when you will get the questions that are not asked in public or in replies to group emails. This is where concerns are raised and can be handled at source. This is where you will be able to really cut through any confusion.

Celebrate wins – small and frequent

We are great at celebrating big milestones in recruitment: a record quarter, the annual 'big biller', superstar awards.

However, good leadership understands that success builds belief. Thus small and frequent celebrations are a superb way to reinforce behaviours and massage self-esteem.

Share the news of Sarah's biggest placement, Matt's first retained order, our biggest placement ever, a key new client won. People want to work with winners, and love to hear positive 'war stories'. They are happening every day. Communicate them.

Share confidential information regularly

Approach this activity with caution. It depends on company ownership, policy, and a range of other factors, so you have to make your own call on this, but I believe it builds trust and buy-in.

I was International CEO of Aquent for ten years, running all of their business outside America, and I stole a nice little tradition from my US colleagues. Every month, I would address the company – by which I mean *everyone*. We had 30 offices in 17 countries, so we used video, Skype, conference call, and even recorded it when I gained responsibility for Europe, which of course has irreconcilable time differences to Sydney.

I would often share the company results, operating profit against the budget, margins, client revenues, top biller fees. Yes, it's sensitive stuff, but mostly I find people will be mature and will value being brought into the inner circle.

It's a question of feeling respected and included and taking pride in, and responsibility for, the results. As I say, tread with care on this.

Where possible, speak, don't email

You are at your desk, and need to tell the team about a new initiative, a big success, maybe a change in policy. Perhaps you need to give some feedback to a consultant. So you bang out an email. Job done, right? Wrong.

It's infinitely better and more effective to communicate verbally. Research tells us that, and so does common sense. You can always follow up with an email if you just can't stand not sending one.

Plan and prepare for delivering tricky news

If you have something undesirable to communicate, prepare honest, carefully crafted answers.

Say, for example, that your company is going to have to close a branch office. Predict the questions you are likely to get or what people are likely to think.

Be careful of the language you use. For example, *"We have decided not to replace the consultant who left the perm desk because we see the perm market plateauing for a while, and we think the people we have now are fully capable of servicing our current client workload."*

That's a lot better than, *"We are not replacing her because the perm market is so bad and will probably tank even further soon, so we think it is dangerous to hire someone else because none of you will have enough to do."*

Tell the right people the right things

Here is the golden rule, and don't ever break it (even though we have all done so at some point or another).

Never ever, *never ever* speak to a recruiter about the deficiencies of another recruiter. Yet it's easy to do, isn't it?

Imagine you are at the lift. A member of the accounting temp team comes out. You congratulate him on the team's record month, remarking how everyone did so well. He says, *"Yes it was great, just Betty didn't hit her target."* And you, fatally, remark, *"Ah yes, Betty, sometimes I feel she doesn't put 100% effort in."*

There it is! Mild, you think? However, when it gets back to Betty, do you know what she hears? She hears, *"Greg says you are a lazy bitch!"* because that is the way humans work. Is Betty loving me for that remark (true or not)? I think not.

Deriding one staff member in front of another smashes your credibility and their trust, it destroys confidence in you and stunts engagement.

Do not do it.

Don't have 'communications favourites'

Don't ever share news or plans first with a selected few. It seems an obvious rule, but it's easy to do because it's likely you will have better relationships with some staff members than others.

I remember a cataclysmic error of this nature I made as a young manager/business owner.

Recruitment Solutions had a mixed touch football team. I was a member of the team, and so were about 12 other staff ranging from senior managers to admin. Predictably, there was lots of chat and banter and beers in the bar after the game. Understandably, but still stupidly, I let my guard down and several times discussed matters that were best kept to a later date and in a different forum.

Later, I learned that the perception was that those who were on the touch team were 'insiders' – privy to special information and special attention. It was divisive, and it created negativity that was totally unintended. That was my lesson learned. Don't have 'favourites'. It creates distrust and resentment.

So, there you have it. The Savage 12 Communication Commandments, ready to serve as your template for leadership through communication.

Remember though, as much as you can work on your communication style, it can become too 'finessed' or 'over-rehearsed'. Authenticity can't be faked. People see through spin and they will reject it and reject you.

Coaching

I trust you will remember me saying in the previous chapter (and in other chapters) that leadership is action. Nowhere is this illustrated more than in a leader's ability to develop, teach and inspire. Let me relay a real-life story, which showed me a lot about this.

Many years ago, I saw an example of such exceptional leadership that it has stuck with me for two decades or more. I was the director and owner of the company, but this behaviour came from the team leader of the permanent division. This manager had about eight staff, all recruiting for permanent roles.

A particularly difficult client was about to make an offer to one of our candidates, and then tried to negotiate the fee at that point of leverage (there is a special place in hell for this kind of client, by the way). The recruiter was struggling with this client, and so the matter was elevated to the manager.

If it had been passed to me at that time I would have likely asked to be left to deal with the client and had a private conversation with the door closed. However, this manager did exactly the opposite – she asked the team to gather around. The receptionist was to hold all calls, to allow her to call the client on speaker for all to hear. While it didn't go that well, it showed massive courage to let the team hear the call and coach them in real time.

Not only did they learn lots, but the manager's creditability with the team rose significantly – she was showing them that she was only asking them to do what she was prepared to do herself. It was also true that she was prepared to expose herself and embarrass or humiliate herself for the benefit of the team, and for that she earned huge kudos.

The manager who had a tricky fee negotiation didn't hide in a closed room to do it in private, she called the team around to listen in. Now that's leadership!

In Chapter 20 (People leverage) I go into a great deal of detail on coaching, and I encourage you to make sure you review those ideas. For now, though, I will limit myself to saying that a great leader leads by example, and through the constant raising of skills via coaching and teaching.

Understand that 'training' is good, but coaching is better. Not only does the good leader work hard at honing personal coaching skills, the good leader will ensure that the organisation has 'coaching' built into its DNA – thus ensuring that all junior managers also have that ability.

Coaching is best done in real time, as learning is most powerful in either real moments of exhilaration during success or despair at failure. It's in these moments that we are open to truly listen and learn.

Recognition of things done well will ensure these actions are repeated. Gentle correction of things that need to improve will raise standards and an understanding of what 'good' looks like.

The most important statement I can make to you about coaching and leadership is that coaching is not simply passing on skills. Coaching is retention. People stay where they feel they are invested in and where they can feel that their skills are improving.

Remember that the accurate measure of a great leader is the creation of more leaders, not more followers. Only true coaching, mentoring and investment will do that.

Courage

Courage. It seems like a strange word to use in the context of leadership and business, but I use it advisedly because leadership in recruitment is lonely and often very daunting.

Often the bravest thing we have to do in leading in business is to make unpopular decisions. Most commonly, these are letting people go and enforcing changes to process that you know are in the best interests of the business.

My experience is, even if the decision is unpopular at the time, if the leader explains the rationale clearly and is steadfast in his or her resolve, people will not only accept it, but will respect the direction taken. It's wishy-washy half-decisions, backing down and inconsistency that destroys morale and performance.

It also takes courage to uphold standards. Particularly where behaviour or ethics are at stake and bucking the trend risks conflict.

In the modern work world there is quite rightly a greater concern for the welfare of employees than there was in generations past. Some of this is legislated, and some of it is driven by a desire to attract and retain skilled people from younger generations who, it is perceived, have different values and expectations.

That may be the case, but it has led to a pathetic trend from many managers to try to 'bribe' staff by offering every conceivable benefit in an attempt to appease and to satisfy. How many latte machines, snooker tables and beanbags does it take to retain a millennial or a Gen Xer, would you say?

Now don't get me wrong, you need to be in tune with what's important to people, but frankly, I believe people want what they have always wanted: fairness, communication, learning, safety, respect and fair rewards. A great leader has the courage to do this important thing – real leaders give people what they need. Not what they want.

Often, too much talk of how to 'manage the generations' leads to skipping over some of the difficult things that need to be done when managing people. I reckon those things need to be done no matter whom you are dealing with.

One of the ways I define great leadership is that the leader actually cares. Bureaucrats do not make leaders. Administrators don't make leaders either. However, before we go any further on the subject of 'caring' for our people, here's a word of warning on this.

Unfortunately, there is too much hype nowadays about the idea that leaders must show concern for their teams. Apparently, you have to give a figurative cuddle of support to staff on the hour, or they will resign and go llama farming in Peru. Well, that's codswallop.

You cannot fake the fact that you care about the people in the business. There is nothing worse than a manager returning from the latest interpersonal skills training program with 'concern for others' beaming from every orifice. It's not real, and everyone knows it.

Real leaders don't need training programs to convince their staff they care. What's more, real leaders empathise with the people they lead. By this I mean the leader knows what a recruiter does, knows how hard it is, and knows the inevitable peaks and troughs.

Tough empathy

I have always found it key to any success I have had as a manager of recruiters that I worked a desk myself. I feel the recruiter's pain to this day. I have had shocking months, offers turned down and phones slammed in my ear. So, I do understand the bruises the job will give you. I also like everyone I work with on an inter-personal level. So, I really do care when someone is having a bad month or day.

However, sometimes the empathy you need to have is of the 'tough' kind. And this takes courage – and tough empathy (not my phrase, I don't think, but very much my ethos). Tough empathy: it's what I mentioned above, giving your consultants what they *need*, not what they want.

That means often telling people things they don't want to hear, or setting work practices and goals that, at first, they may not agree with or like at all. Yet, that's OK because tough empathy works, and tough empathy is about what's needed at a particular point in time, not what's preferred by the consulting team.

After all, the team may want something, or prefer something else, but they don't carry the ultimate responsibility for the business, do they? You do, though.

At its best, what tough empathy means is a balance between respect for the individual and the business imperative to achieve the task at hand.

So, it could mean sitting with a recruiter who is failing, but who you know can make it. It will mean putting that person on a rehabilitation plan. It will mean closely managing activities, impos-ing time management regimes, setting daily goals and providing intense coaching. It's confronting and scary for the consultant. It's frankly not that much fun for the leader either. Yes, it's tough. However, you are doing it because you care about their success and their future and, at a deep level, they will know that.

Do you see what I am saying here? The recruiter knows you are doing something difficult for you, and difficult for them, *because you care about what happens to them*. The power in that dynamic is almost immeasurable.

Erin Devlin is part-owner and MD of people2people Victoria. As I talked about in Chapter 9, I was instrumental in creating that entity by facilitating the purchase of Erin's business, rebranding it people2people Victoria, and then running it for three years as Chairman and shareholder. (When I say 'running it', Erin did all the actual work, you understand.)

Let's hear from Erin:

"I remember when I experienced my first real setback during the Devlin Alliance/people2people merger. I had been working 60+ hours a week growing the team diligently under Greg's mentorship, pouring all of my energy and focus into making it a success, when one of my favourite hires resigned.

It was a shock at the time and, as a newish manager in the business, it really knocked the wind out of my sails. I remember getting on the phone to Greg and to my surprise getting a little teary about it. Even though I knew Greg would support me through thick and thin, he knew just what I needed at that moment.

'ERIN!' he bellowed down the phone, 'Are you a WOMAN or are you a MOUSE?'

Shocked, I paused for a second, stopping my self-pity in its tracks. I took two very deep breaths and said, 'Greg – I'm a LION, I'm a bloody lion.'

'That's right,' he said.

And that was that.

Since that day, whenever I've had a setback I ask myself: 'Erin, are you a woman or a mouse?', then I dust myself off and get right on with it."

I don't remember this conversation, but rest assured I would have responded this way because I believed she needed to hear that. She may have *wanted* a shoulder to cry on, but she did not *need* 'comforting'. She did not need over-analysing. She needed to be reminded that this was a small road-bump that she could hurdle with ease, reminded who she was and what she was capable of.

Some people think that to be a great leader you have to be liked by everyone. That could not be more untrue. People in our industry, regardless of 'generation', are not looking for friends when they look to their boss. They are looking for direction, support, honesty and clarity.

Even though they may not know it at first, they may also be looking for the occasional dose of tough empathy too.

Creativity

The world is changing fast. Your staff are closer to the coalface than you. You need to engineer a DNA of self-disruption.

The irony is that, in many cases, it is the manager who is the barrier to disruption and creativity. Real leaders of the future are actually promoters of self-disruption – constantly asking *"Why do we do it this way?"* and not allowing the historical precedent to be a reason to resist innovation.

A big learning for me has been that innovation can be incremental. We don't always have to have a big epiphany or life-changing moment.

In recruitment it seems that even those leaders who are open to change are always looking for a massive disruption, yet in fact we can make small steps that can lead to significant change over time. The important thing is to have an attitude that allows you to slaughter sacred cows and encourage brave new thinking. Always frame this in the context of *"How does this help solve the client's problems, or improve the candidate experience?"*

Comprehension

And so we reach the final 'C' of leadership in the Savage lexicon.

I like to think I am a solid communicator, and it's true I can write a pithy paragraph and contrive a sound argument. I can communicate ideas from a stage, or in a one-on-one, as well as most, I suppose.

However, communicating is listening too, right? In fact, surely 'understanding' is the foundation of it all?

Too often in leadership we assume we understand. We don't really listen. Really listening means digging to understand the real opinion, the real concern, the real motivation. In this way, 'active listening' is a key business skill and a non-negotiable leadership trait. I need to work on this as much as anyone.

I am working on becoming a better listener and so should every leader.

How?

- Listen to understand, not to formulate an answer.

- Stop interrupting. (I am disgracefully guilty of this.)

- Be 'more present'. Don't allow your mind to wander. Focus and concentrate on the other person.

- Stop assuming you know what someone is going to say.

- Listen to 'the whole person'. In other words, be attuned to body language, tone and other non-verbal signals, so you really can understand.

- Approach a conversation with a more open mind, with more empathy.

- Be 'slower to understand'. Don't jump in with a solution too fast. Think more before you talk.

- Ask more and smarter questions, so you really do understand.

- Avoid becoming defensive when you sense criticism or a different point of view.

Leaders need to worry far less about 'being right', and far more about 'being right about what the other person thinks and feels'.

I need to remind myself every morning (and you might consider doing the same) that *nothing I say today is going to teach me anything*. Only by listening will I learn anything new.

I mentioned in Chapter 11 that Graham Whelan is the best recruiter I have ever known, and that part of this achievement is due to Graham being a great listener. When someone really listens to you, you feel respected, validated.

Every leader needs to be able to do that.

Improving every day

I have made many poor leadership decisions. I have not always displayed the kind of leadership traits I espouse here. In fact, I have let myself down often. Yet, I have improved.

Perhaps one of the most meaningful 'thank you' notes I received in my life came after I resigned from Recruitment Solutions. It was the day before I left, actually. Ross Clennett (with whom I worked at Temporary Solutions, developed from Recruitment Solutions, as described in Chapter 6) gave me a handwritten note. He wrote it on the flight from Adelaide to Sydney where he was to attend my farewell dinner.

It was much longer than I have shared below. This meant a great deal to me then, and probably more now, as I fully appreciate how much leadership is about impacting others.

Here's part of what Ross wrote:

"There are so many things to thank you for, it's hard to do them justice in a letter, but I will try. Thank you:

For having confidence in my abilities.

For having faith in my judgement.

For bollocking me when I deserved it.

For turning my failures into learning opportunities.

For turning my successes into reasons to celebrate.

And, most importantly, thank you for caring about me as a person, the most precious gift you can give anybody."

Ross has been forgiving on the 'bollocking' because I am sure I went overboard more than once. His success in business life is his alone, but a good leader can help. I was only learning to lead, but if I helped, that knowledge gives me so much joy.

Twenty years after he wrote that note, we remain close friends. He badgered me into writing this book. He has written the Afterword. I gave the speech at his wedding. I continue to learn to be a good leader.

Final leadership tips

I leave you with some final leadership thoughts.

A business is never going to outpace its leader

Your people are not going to overtake you. Your reason for existence is to set the pace in all things. Lead with energy, integrity, quality and optimism.

Your impact and responsibility are both massive.

People don't leave companies, they leave leaders

Here is a thought that may give you something to ponder. Next time someone resigns, don't write them off as a loser. Don't blame the market or their lack of focus. Look at yourself.

I believe people don't leave 'a company'. They leave an environment in which they are unhappy and don't feel supported. Or, at least, where they see a better environment elsewhere. That comes down to leadership.

Look to yourself – your leadership – and the company you have created. It's confronting to do so. It's scary. However, doing this could just be the beginning of a better business, which makes more money. A business where people have more fun and stay longer.

Take action

This is how it plays out.

Leadership is action.

Be brave. Take action.

CHAPTER 19

Recruiting recruiters

PART OF being a strong manager and leader in any industry is hiring the right people for your business. While we are professional recruiters, we are often weak at hiring our own staff. The reasons are many and varied, but include lack of planning, hiring in panic, lack of definition of what makes a great recruiter and, of course, poor induction and training.

It's also a lack of time and energy put into the process, which is crazy because we know success is all about the people. In the recruitment industry for sure, and probably elsewhere too, we are our own worst enemies when it comes to hiring. Many owners and managers don't give hiring the attention it deserves, and they pay the price.

At the time of writing this book, we have just had a record year for agency recruiters in Australia and New Zealand. Revenues are up, profits soaring. It's the same in most of the world.

Underlying these numbers, however, are three worrying trends (the following data comes from staffingindustrymetrics.com):

- The annual remuneration package for income producers in Australian recruitment companies is at an all-time high – $111,000 in 2018, up from $68,000 in 2004.

- Average operating cost per income producer (including salary and bonus) peaked at $220,000 in 2017; it was only $157,000 in 2004 and $189,000 in 2014.

- Critically, gross profit delivered per $1 of income producers' salary (a key metric) has dropped from over $3 in 2006 to a concerning $2.30 in 2018.

Costs up, productivity down! That is not sustainable.

So many owners of recruitment businesses are looking for a silver bullet when it comes to recruiter productivity – a quick fix. Yet, neither the smartest strategy nor the best technology will save you; the leverage point is still the people you hire and retain. Staff turnover remains catastrophically high: over 47% in Australia in 2018, according to Staffing Industry Metrics.

The 'recruiter' is still by far our most significant cost. The 'consultant' still absorbs most of our management time. Hiring people has never been harder.

The recruiter remains our key differentiator: everything still hinges on recruiter success. So, we need to up our hiring game and invest far more in induction and training. That is hardly earth-shattering fresh news. Trust me, though, that message has not sunk in universally.

So, we need to add a bit of science to the 'gut feel' and apply a lot more energy and resources to getting our people attraction, recruitment and retention right.

Recruiting resilience

When hiring recruiters, you need to start with a clear understanding of what it is you are recruiting for. Recruitment is one of the toughest gigs around. It takes a special breed of human to thrive in our industry.

Most people who become recruiters do not last… *because it's a frigging hard job!* The world is littered with ex-recruiters, burnt out, scarred and resentful about their all-too-short recruiting career.

Recruiting is uniquely harsh because it's the only job that I know where what you are selling can turn around and say *"No"*.

Think about it. I sell you my car. You agree to buy the car, I agree to sell the car. We agree on a price. The car does not then jump up and say, *"Hey, you know what, I am not going to go with this new guy."*

Don't laugh. That happens to recruiters every day. We do everything right. Take an excellent job spec. Impress our client. Recruit great talent. Make the match. Manage the process. Construct a fitting deal for all parties. Secure a great offer. Get everything agreed... and at the last minute, our 'product' – the candidate – says, *"Nah, I changed my mind, I will stay where I am."*

And that's it – all over, red rover, with no thanks from anyone. In fact, the client will often blame the recruiter! The candidate probably ghosts the recruiter. And there's no fee – doughnut.

Recruiting is a killer because, for us, it is 'all or nothing'. Sure, a tiny percentage of our work is retained, but mostly recruiting is the first prize or nothing. We do all the work, use vast amounts of time and expertise, and manage the process with skill and diligence. However, if our five great candidates get pipped by a late runner from another recruiter, or an internal candidate, then it is big fat zero for us.

That's tough, hard to take. Especially when it happens often – and it does. Recruiting grinds you down because you do so much work you don't get paid for. When you hear the words *"I am feeling burnt out"* from a recruiter, what they actually mean is *"I just can't stand doing so much work for so little return."*

Contingent recruiters are lucky to fill one job out of five they take, and place one candidate out of ten they meet. Also, combined with the 'all or nothing' fee model most work on, it means lots and lots of hours for which we don't get paid and, equally importantly, for which we see no tangible success.

Success, in the form of happy clients and happy talent, is the bedrock upon which our self-esteem is built. So once that crumbles, it is the beginning of the end. Lay on top of this the fact that many recruiters join organisations with little training, support or infrastructure to assist in their success.

So, when you assess a potential recruiter, you have to evaluate resilience and ability to bounce back. It's critical to your hiring decision.

This reminds me of a conversation I had with a recruitment company owner a few years ago. We were debating how robust agency recruitment is as an industry. He went on to say that the rigours of learning the recruitment business were excellent for 'building character'. Of course, he was half right.

There is no doubt that agency recruitment is an exceptionally tough business, with many disappointments and obstacles, and constant learning. It's also true that facing these challenges will burnish the resilience and determination you already have.

However, on one point I can't entirely agree with him. Succeeding in recruitment does not *build* character. No, it *reveals* it!

To succeed in a job like recruitment, over the long term, you have to have resilience, toughness, determination and the drive to achieve already built into your DNA. The rigours of our industry will reveal it (or not!) and no doubt refine it, but cannot build on something that was not already there.

This is not an esoteric discussion. This is crucial to understand as you go about deciding who to hire, invest in, and promote.

Recruitment rocks! Right?

This is where you, the hirer, need to step up. You have to love recruitment to sell the dream of being a great recruiter. You have to be passionate and articulate about sharing why this job can be the best there is.

Seriously, I love this industry. I think that comes across when I talk to potential hires. Yet, 80% of people who enter the recruitment industry fail in the first two years, leave and are never seen again.

Ironically, there is a fate worse than being among the 80% of recruiters who fail. Being an average, mediocre, plodding recruiter who *survives* is really purgatory – because this job is too hard and involves too many disappointments to not be great at it. You have to be a great recruiter to reap the rewards that make it all worthwhile. For the top 10%, the cream, recruiting is the coolest job in the world.

So, when you are hiring the best potential recruiters, you need to be honest about the obstacles they will face, but passionate about articulating why this job can be so great. Here's why recruiting is great.

Recruiting is a win/win/win

Unlike most commercial transactions, recruiting is not a win/lose scenario. If I sell you a car, I aim for the highest price and you push for the lowest. One of us will feel they 'won', the other will be a bit despondent that they 'lost'. However, in the perfect recruitment scenario, everybody wins: happy client, happy candidate, happy you.

This is not as trivial as it seems. There is something intensely rewarding about doing a job where everyone is grateful, everyone is excited about the outcome – and then you get paid as well.

You create great outcomes

Maybe the coolest thing about being a recruiter is that you make good things happen.

The candidate is not keen to go on an interview… but through *your* influencing skills they reluctantly go along, do fantastically well, love the job, and get hired!

The client doesn't see the potential in your top talent because they are blindsided by something they spotted in the résumé… but *you* persist, explaining that the person is better than the paper. The client relents, and your talent gets the job, gets promoted, and in time becomes your client!

For me, when I recruited, this was the real buzz – making things happen. Controlling the process. I would crack open a beer on Friday and reflect, *"That would not have happened if I had not seen the opportunity and influenced the outcome."* That was beyond cool.

That leads us to another reason why recruiting rocks.

What we do actually matters

I mean, it *really* matters. Recruiters get a horrific rap sometimes, and often it's deserved but, hey, at the end of the day, we find people jobs! That's a good thing, right? It's something to be proud of.

It makes an impact. We change people's lives. We solve companies' staffing issues. We help people further their career ambitions. Fantastic!

Our business is so measurable

Measurability is one of the beautiful things about our business. This does not suit everybody, I know, but in recruiting there is nowhere to hide, and I like that.

If you have the right temperament, you will thrive in this competitive environment, love the fact that you can measure yourself against your competitors and colleagues, and revel in the transparency of fee-tables and pay-by-results.

You can own your market

If you have longevity, if you maintain integrity, if you deliver service and outcomes that your customers want... you can elevate yourself to become a truly trusted advisor, and then recruitment becomes a beautiful thing. All your work is exclusive, all your candidates come via referrals and recommendations, and clients treat you with respect, seek your advice, and bring you 'into the tent'. You actually 'own' your patch and that is a wonderful place to be!

Yes, it's true. Recruiting rocks.

Always be recruiting – even if you are not hiring

So, you know recruiting is a great job, and you communicate this passion to people you hire. How do you find the best people to interview?

In the knowledge economy, and in an era of systemic skills shortages, reactive recruiting is not going to work. Owners and managers of recruitment agencies need to build recruitment activities into their daily agenda, whether they are hiring right now or not. Indeed, *anyone* seeking to hire 'hard to find' skills needs to get with the program.

If you only start your recruiting activities once a vacancy emerges, you will lose the talent battle. You will also doom your company to be a 'B' grade business, at best.

If you are serious about getting the best talent, you need to work at it *every day*. This means constantly interviewing. It means coffee and conversations with a wide range of potential employees. You will be honest and transparent at all times, of course. The message is, *"We don't have a vacancy now, but adding the best people to our business is our number-one priority, so we would be honoured to chat with you."*

Set yourself a goal to have '100 cups of coffee' with potential hires over the next 12 months. That is two meetings a week. Sure, it's an investment. However, think of the return!

All your staff must be given the same brief. The whole company should continuously be in recruitment mode for internal talent. If necessary, reward your team for finding good people whom you subsequently hire. Celebrate the efforts of those who attract talent your business. Build it into your cultural DNA.

Create a database of potential recruits and set notifications to make sure that you find a reason to keep in touch. Make those conversations frank. Address issues that will either attract them to your business or knock them out as a potential employee.

Then, when the day comes that an 'unexpected' vacancy occurs, you will be ready with four or five pre-qualified, pre-warmed top performers prepared to engage.

Only hire recruiters from this generation

There is only one group of recruiters who will thrive in a world where talent shortages get worse, clients build their own tools to recruit, and technology continues to disrupt. I will only ever hire recruiters from 'Generation C'.

'Generation C' has nothing to do with your age or your birth date. Recruitment belongs to the 'Connected' generation. It's *knowing* people that counts. It's also those people *knowing you*. It's them trusting you. The 'connected' generation is also the 'credible' generation.

Generation C know where skills can be found, and how to use their connections to open new doors.

A Generation C recruiter will be well connected, but they will also be great connectors. Building a digital brand is woven into their DNA. They love social media; they are likely to create content, and will develop a community of connections across a broad spectrum of platforms.

They see LinkedIn more as a branding platform than a sourcing platform, and they behave there accordingly: sharing insights, answering questions, provoking debate. Of course, they are smart to the irony that once you treat LinkedIn as a branding platform, it inevitably becomes your best sourcing platform. (Yes, read that again, and reflect, please.)

Generation C are excellent users of technology, primarily social media, to build a network, but they are also great connectors in real life – having hundreds of cups of coffee a year, thanking people, being generous with time and information, and connecting people without thought of immediate gain. They go to events and they send thank-you notes.

They use their 'neck-top' as much as they use their laptop!

The unique skill of Generation C, their super-power if you like, is that they *make people feel special*. What a refreshing change that is in a recruiting world that increasingly seems to value technological efficiency and automation over human connectivity. It's the ultimate differentiator.

Yes, Generation C understands that the future of recruitment is that beautiful sweet spot where brilliant use of technology merges with highly evolved human influencing skills. They're the recruiting generation who successfully marry art with science.

Hire more drinkers

Yes, you read that right. Hire more drinkers! Oh, wait, slight typo… I mean, you have to hire more DRINCERS. This is what DRINCERS look like:

- *Digital natives:* People who 'get' digital, are comfortable with social media, are great e-sourcers, can find people on the web and can build relationships online. It's nothing do with birth date. It's to do with attitude and preparedness to upskill. At 61, I am a digital native, albeit a 'born again' native.

- *Reach:* By 'reach', I mean a network. It's people who know people. People who are connected and known in a niche. (See the previous section on 'Generation C'.)

- *Influence:* This is probably the key competency. People with great listening skills, credibility, and persuasion, who are talented at sales, consulting, and advising. People who are able to manage the key 'moments of truth' in recruitment, when human influencing skills can affect the outcome for the greater good.

- *Nous:* This is an element that is hugely underestimated in recruitment, I have found – intelligence, that is. Everyone says recruitment is not 'rocket science'. True, but we are not building rockets, are we? It's not easy, either. In the modern era, clients and candidates just will not deal with dummies. I am talking about intellectual prowess, which earns credibility, but also emotional intelligence. Knowing when to shut up, when to speak, what to say, and what not to say.

- *Content:* Yes, the ability to write. Not emails so much, but that's a bonus. I mean blogs, tweets, status updates, and compelling profiles. Building your brand so that you differentiate and are perceived of as a thought leader in your niche. This leads to inbound enquiries.

- *Empathy:* I know, you may think this is a crazy word when talking about recruiters. However, the days of the arrogant, showy, pushy, superficial recruiter are over. You want great candidates to work with you? You have got to feel their pain and understand their hot buttons. That is the only way to build an offline brand and become a 'talent magnet'.

- *Robust:* It's a tough, relentless job, with many setbacks. Resilience to me does not mean stoic. I am all for a good cry, an expletive, a walk around the block, when things go wrong. Let it out. However, to me, 'robustness' in recruitment means bouncing back fast after disappointment, and not letting that offer turned down affect your next conversation with a candidate, client, or colleague. That is resilience.

- *Seducer:* Not in the traditional sense, obviously. I mean in the sense that seduction requires building trust and creating interest, and so it is with candidate acquisition. It involves credibility, engagement, and slowly building a pathway to working together.

So, there it is. Throw away your old job descriptions. Only hire drinkers.

Sorry, I mean DRINCERS!

Do the due diligence

Are you unconvinced about the need for more thoroughness and less gut feel when hiring? If so, consider these seven facts:

- **Fact 1:** Over the last 15 years, I have had more than 1,000 people report to me, directly or indirectly. Over my working life, who knows how high that number is?

- **Fact 2:** 90% of those people have been recruiters or recruiting managers.

- **Fact 3:** Just about the most significant issue owners and managers of recruitment companies bleat about is finding and retaining recruiters.

- **Fact 4:** Our industry has an appalling record of hiring, retaining, and getting productivity from its recruiters.

- **Fact 5:** A critical part of any hiring process is reference-checking candidates to assess cultural fit, check facts, and uncover hidden strengths and weaknesses. (I am aware that some countries have restrictive laws around this.)

- **Fact 6:** I am available for reference-checking on any person who ever worked for or with me. Moreover, I take it seriously, giving considered feedback. I will spend as long as it takes.

I am also easy to find and easy to contact. I will return your call or email if you leave a message saying you want to take a reference.

- **Fact 7:** In the last ten years, I have taken *three* such reference-check phone calls.

That's right, three.

Why does our industry make these critical decisions in such a cavalier way? Are we so desperate to hire anyone with any industry record that we don't care enough to check if they are any good? Are our processes so sloppy, even though the impact on us could be so catastrophic?

I think this situation is getting worse, as the core requirements of a great recruiter are changing as our environment changes.

A proper reference call! Well, maybe…

Hallelujah, a couple of years ago I did get such a call. It was from an Asian office of a global recruitment company. They were about to hire a senior manager who had reported to me for almost ten years.

They had been impeccably professional in setting up the call, asking permission of both the candidate and myself. A woman with a confident and very polished phone style called me on the dot.

I was delighted. A proper reference call!

She started asking fundamental questions about tenure and attendance, and then moved on to a series of questions about ability and skill.

When she took a breath, I jumped in and asked her three key questions:

"Tell me, what exactly is the role you are considering my ex-employee for? What are the key responsibilities you need him to excel at, and what measurable outcomes will he be accountable for?"

Once I knew those things, I could make my answers much more pertinent, accurate, and relevant.

She lost her poise on the phone completely. She stammered and stuttered. Then she said, *"To be perfectly honest, I don't really know what the role is at all. I am just going through our reference form."*

It turns out that the person doing the reference-checking had not met the candidate, seen the job spec, been briefed on the role, or been involved in the recruitment at all. She was following a process. It may have been what she did all day, every day.

I answered all of her questions as thoroughly as I could. She thanked me, and it was over.

Yet this was bad… Bad recruitment, bad management.

My guy was an experienced people-manager in recruitment. He had led teams successfully. However, he was also an excellent senior recruiter himself. What's more, his best skill was business development and, since parting with me, he had held a senior regional role in business development.

What job was he being assessed for now? She didn't know. I didn't know.

When they asked, *"Would you rehire him?"*, my answer would have been different depending on the role!

When they asked, *"Is he good with people?"*, did they mean as a manager? As a colleague? Or was it his customer relationships they were interested in?

That reference-check call, for all its superficial professionalism, was a wasted opportunity. Appropriately done, I could have given them excellent guidance on what his skills and weaknesses were, as they related to the job they needed him to do. I could have coached them on how to get the best out of him. I could have prevented them from making a bad mistake, too, if the job was not a good 'fit'.

However, I could do none of those things, because that reference check wasn't an opportunity to improve the hiring decision. It was box-ticking, form-lodging, a bureaucratic process.

I don't blame the reference-checker in this case. I do cast a withering eye at the management of this business: at the ethos of an organisation (a recruitment business, after all) that allows a very senior hire (I am talking AU$200k plus) to be made without really getting to the heart of his historical performance.

Unless I know the job that the candidate is being considered for, all I can give you is a generic character reference. If you want a real evaluation of 'fit', you have to tell me what you are looking for the candidate to achieve.

This is why, back in the day when I used 'rec to recs' (recruitment agencies for the recruitment industry) to find recruiters for my business, I used to shock them by always doing the final reference check myself. I know what to ask the referee – and, equally importantly, what to tell the referee first! Moreover, I want to hear the tone of the referee's voice… the moment of hesitation in answering… the nuance in their words. A great deal resides there!

I know there are different laws about reference-checking in various countries. However, think like this: the reference check is part of the assessment, not part of the compliance.

My simple hiring challenge for you

This is simple, but powerful. When the time comes to make your next hire, regardless of your business type, simply ask yourself one key question before you make an offer.

"Will this person raise our average?"

That's it.

Ask yourself and ask the other hiring managers involved. If we hire this person, will they raise the average across all our staff?

The average of what? The average of things that count: energy, ethics, skill, attitude, network, sales savvy, niceness. Whatever it is that is important to you and your business. Will this new hire raise the 'mean employee score'?

Of course, it's not empirical. There's no science here. However, you will *know* the answer as soon as you ask the question.

If you are hiring to 'fill a gap', if you are hiring on the basis that 'he is the best of a bad bunch', if you are hiring 'to give it go' or if you are hiring when deep down you know this is not a fit – or at least, it's a giant gamble – then asking this question will shine a light on the mistake you are about to make.

Why would you hire any other way? Are we adding people to dumb down our business? Do you really want to hire this person, just to make your business that little bit worse? I think not.

Only ever add a person if she or he 'raises the average'. In that way, every new person you bring on board makes your business better, not weaker.

Five signs your new recruiter is destined to fail

So, you made a great hire. Good job – but beware…

The most significant cost to every recruitment firm is salaries, and the primary destroyer of profits is underperforming or failed recruiters. That is a fact. When we make a terrible hire, often we are slow to put it right: we hold on to underperforming people for too long.

Now, please don't misunderstand me. I don't believe in 'hire and fire'. Investing in people is the key. However, even so, there are sometimes early signs you have made a wrong hire and it's not going to work:

1. *Slow learners.* Intelligence is a much-underestimated trait when it comes to recruiting. I always look for it when hiring. A newbie who is slow to learn, repeats mistakes and just does not 'get' things is a potential disaster. Proceed with caution.
2. *Unwilling learners.* 'Coachability' is a crucial recruiter requirement, in my opinion. Poor listeners, know-it-alls and

those who just can't focus on learning different ways in their new environment are likely to fail long term.

3. *Social misfits.* Seriously, sometimes on the first day I know I have made a bad hire – not because the new employee can't recruit, but because they can't fit in. This may manifest in inappropriate jokes, overfamiliarity, or being too loud or too quiet. Of course, you have to take into account new-starter nerves, and often people settle in over time. However, sometimes, you just *know…* this is wrong!

4. *Late and lazy.* I always see a red light flashing when the new recruiter starts coming in late in the first week, misses meetings or does not follow up on simple, basic tasks you have given them. If that's their 'honeymoon' effort, just wait till a few months down the track!

5. *Lack of courage.* It sounds strange talking about courage in a desk job. However, in fact, you do need to be brave in recruitment. Make that cold-call. Tell that candidate they are not right for a job they really covet. Negotiate a fee. Lead a client meeting with your new boss in the room. I have noticed that new recruiters show their 'courage colours' early. Don't throw a raw newbie into the deep end: that's not right and is unlikely to help. However, they do need to be given little tasks which involve doing tricky things. How they tackle those is a strong signal of their long-term success.

Please use these tips with care. Every new recruiter will show some of these faults, and I am not suggesting you let someone go if one or even all of these signs emerge – but it should set off alarms and trigger action. If you see one of these signs or more in a rookie, home in on it. Examine it. Test it. Counsel them on it. Doing nothing is the one thing you should *not* do.

Then, look for rapid improvement. If improvement is not forthcoming, you may have a serious issue.

The very best hiring plan... ever!

I get into trouble when I give this advice. It's so uncouth, so politically incorrect, so old-school. However, I continue to give it, because it's right.

It's your hiring and retention plan for the next 30 years. Use it from today onwards. Never waver from it. See your business thrive.

Here it is: *No dickheads. No passengers.*

That's it. Job done.

CHAPTER 20

People leverage

AS I mentioned in the previous chapter, it is ironic that the recruitment industry, which deals in human capital, is poor at hiring and possibly worse at developing its people. The last chapter focused on getting the hiring right, as a recruitment manager and leader. This chapter gives you some pointers on the development side.

It is not universally true that recruitment companies are poor at hiring and developing staff, of course, and I have noticed that those companies which continuously outperform the market always invest in people development and mentoring. Recruitment Solutions was a notable example, as was Morgan & Banks.

Oftentimes, I see a lot of investment into training on the wrong skills. Today's recruiter needs fresh development of the necessary skills to thrive in today's market. Examples include training on smart use of social media, personal branding, selling exclusivity, digital candidate searching, and improving relationship-building and influencing skills. This would be time well spent compared to time focused on writing better adverts or cold-calling skills.

The other thing I often see is a huge amount of investment in 'newbies' or in underperformers. In itself, this is a good thing. However, there is usually a corresponding lack of investment in transforming good performers into great recruiters. The increase in profitability if you can take your 'good' recruiters to 'great' is massive, and it plays into significant associated gains like staff retention. Yet many good operators, billing solidly, are considered 'done' and left to plateau, which is a missed opportunity.

If leaders do not coach or have the skills to mentor or develop staff, then the business is going to stagnate. The point is, a successful recruitment company will invest time, thought, and energy into developing an affordable, consistent, and efficiently delivered people-development program.

Training versus coaching

Your business's training and development program needs to be scalable, to use technology, and to be structured into many levels that take the recruiter through the complete lifecycle of their career. (I have supported online training platforms such as Recruitment Juice and SocialTalent for this very reason, and dozens of hours of my training content can be found on both.) Training and development should be compulsory, and it should always be measured for its effectiveness.

Developing people will become more critical than ever before. It's always been the case that staff salaries absorb about 60% to 70% of our total expenditure, so it's already clear that upskilling that asset gives you the most significant return.

Nowadays, the rapidly changing recruitment market and the impact of AI, machine learning, and automation mean that recruiters must evolve new skills to stay relevant. The recruiter value is in market knowledge, advice, ability to influence and consult, networks, brand, and problem-solving skills.

The perfect recruiter skill set that you want will not be easily hired. Remember, too, my consistent point that leadership is action. Setting an example, teaching not telling – that's how you build a learning company. It's the learning companies that have the edge in this era of unprecedented change in all areas of our lives.

So, while training is critical in any staffing business, it's actually coaching that has to be woven into the DNA of a great recruitment company. The subtle and varied skills of our industry are best learned 'on the job', and they are always best communicated with the help of a mentor or coach.

One important aspect of coaching that is often overlooked is that it has a huge impact on retention. In our industry, we have appalling staff turnover rates (almost 50% per annum in Australia, according to Staffing Industry Metrics), and we put it down to all sorts of reasons. In fact, the most significant impact you can have on retaining your team is to ensure your people feel that they are learning and growing, and that comes from coaching.

Coaching involves continuously raising the bar for all members of staff – no different rules for different people.

So, training is good, but coaching is better.

Coaching newbies: succeed, or fail fast

I get into the specifics of coaching later in this chapter, but first I want to cover one of the most tragic aspects of the lack of leadership in the development of people in recruitment companies: the high percentage of newbies who don't make it.

Sure, it's a robust industry, and part of the reason is that we are not very good at hiring the right people to take on the rigours of recruitment consulting (see the previous chapter for more on this). However, as I've already mentioned, it's also true that we are very poor at onboarding, inducting, and training people new to our industry.

I believe that many people who could have succeeded exit too early because of a lack of support, and many others who should have left early limp along for months, sometimes even years, before it's agreed that they are not right for recruitment consulting.

So, your mantra needs to be that they need to succeed, but if they are to fail, make sure they fail fast. For that to happen, you have to invest a lot of hard-core training in newbies from the very beginning. I see so many newbies allowed to sit around reading training manuals or sit in on interviews, but with no real measurement and rigour behind their skills development.

The way to do it is with little, measurable, bite-sized chunks of learning and constant assessment, review, role play, and checking (see the next section for more on these areas).

So, if you're asking your newbie to learn the terms of your business, give them a multiple-choice quiz – and if they don't get everything right, ask them to go back, relearn it, and take the quiz again until they do.

Or, if you're teaching them how to phone-screen candidates – you teach them, show them, then they roleplay it, and finally, you put them on the phones and give them feedback.

I believe that a newbie should come in every day with their heart beating just that little bit faster! We're not trying to throw them into the deep end and terrify them, but people do learn when they are on edge and have lots of nervous energy: they concentrate and want to succeed.

Another mistake I see with newbies is that companies give them gross profit goals for the first quarter. This is hugely misleading. One new recruit doesn't make a placement, and suddenly there's a question mark over them. Another recruit flukes a placement – which we know can happen, particularly in permanent recruitment – and everyone is raving about what a fast learner he or she is.

What you want to measure in the first quarter are very clear goals around three things – learning, activity, and behaviour (LAB):

- *Learning:* Are they quick to pick things up? Are they getting better each day? Even if it's slow, if there is progress, it's worth persevering.

- *Activity:* Are they hitting the modest activity goals you set them? For example, *"Here are 20 temps we have lost contact with. Can you call them all by tomorrow night and check their availability?"* Did they smash that, or was it three calls made in two days?

- *Behaviour:* This goes hand-in-hand with attitude. Did they come in on time? Are they concentrating? Do they show willing, fit in, make an effort?

Then, in quarter two, all newbies should have a gross profit target. However, if none or few of the LAB elements are in place and progressing, then put them into remedial mode – fast.

Recruiters only learn by being coached in 'real time'

Experience has shown me that people learn by doing things, seeing things done, and being coached in real time. Sure, classroom-style training has a place, but coaching is often more powerful as a practical learning method.

Let's home in on some coaching tactics that I have learned and used over the years, and from which I have seen fantastic outcomes in terms of professional development of the teams I have run.

Coaching recruiters with 'live feedback'

A good leader who wants to have an impact as a coach should actively look out for opportunities to catch their consultants in the act of doing something right.

If you want to see a behaviour repeated, reward it via recognition. So, for example, if you hear a consultant doing a great job of selling a temp rate to a candidate who was hoping for more, as soon as that recruiter puts down the phone, tell them that.

For example: *"I heard the way you handled that conversation, Bob. Great job! It's really crucial we keep our margins up on this temp desk, and that starts with paying our temps market rates, but no more. Well done."*

What's more, I think you should pass on this recognition publicly and immediately. It is wonderfully uplifting for the individual and will positively reinforce that behaviour. It also starts to create a team ethos and a culture that 'rubs off' on everyone in the team.

Of course, as a manager, you must also be on the lookout for practical situations to improve a consultant's skill and performance. This is the 'correction' component of effective coaching. This will mean keeping an ear out for conversations in which you feel the consultant has said the wrong thing, or could have said something differently or better.

The key here is not to be punitive or demeaning in words or tone. It's a real skill to position your feedback as constructive. Say you heard a consultant making a bit of a hash of handling a counter-offer. You may start with something like this:

245

"That was a tricky situation, Bob, and you handled it well, but I'm just thinking, when your candidate said he had been offered more money to stay, do you think it would have been good to take him back to his original reasons for considering a move…?"

Out of that question will then come an impromptu coaching session on handling these situations. It's immediate, it's powerful, and it's positive.

Always be prepared to speak to the consultant immediately after they have put the phone down or come out of the key meeting. The learning and retention by the consultant is far more powerful if you can relate a concept to a real and recent situation. This takes discipline and means that you often have to consciously listen out for situations and opportunities.

Live feedback is incredibly effective. It's real, because the consultant has just felt the euphoria of success or the pain of failure. You will never have a better time to really drive home behaviour.

Coaching recruiters by doing your job while teaching them their job

One of my significant learnings about effective coaching is that telling people how to do things is only fractionally as successful as showing them how it's done.

Neither is as good as having consultants actually try the task to perfect it.

Real-life situational coaching is best done on an individual basis and can involve quietly sitting down next to the consultant, listening to the way they make phone calls and providing feedback and guidance. Occasionally, it is vital to reverse the roles, and you can make the phone calls, allowing the consultant to evaluate the way you are approaching the task.

An excellent example of this type of coaching is where you have a consultant whose approach to selling a job to a candidate over the phone is lacklustre or generally poor. Instead of lecturing the consultant on how to sell the features of a job to a candidate, you pick up the phone. Call that consultant's candidate yourself, while the consultant is sitting there, and brief the candidate on the job.

It only takes a few minutes, and the learning is substantial. You also earn enormous credibility by actually doing the job 'live'.

I shared a message like this in my blog, 'The Savage Truth'. In response, came a comment from long-time employee, and long-time friend, Francesca Arcuri, who dragged out a story from way, way back that I had forgotten, but which apparently had an impact on her.

Here is what she had to say:

"I still remember once, Greg influenced probably the most stubborn of my candidates, who would not cross the bridge for a great job. Greg phoned him, turned him around and placed him within a week. I had egg on my face, but $$ in my pocket and a great lesson I've not forgotten since. Thanks again."

You are coaching, of course, but you are also being productive because you are executing a task that could well lead to revenue. You are doing the job while teaching the job. It's a beautiful thing.

Where possible, make your own recruitment consulting visible to the team, so they can learn from real situations as they occur. Like the example of a great leader I mentioned in Chapter 18, instead of locking yourself in a room when you have to make those difficult phone calls (e.g. a fee dispute or a counter offer), gather your team around you. Explain the issue, brainstorm with the group how best to tackle it, and then make the call right there, in the spotlight.

Yes, it is nerve-wracking. Yet the learning is intense, and so is the respect you garner by putting yourself out there. You will certainly never be accused of not 'walking the talk'. Leadership is action.

Real life – there's nothing like it when it comes to coaching recruiters to greatness.

Coaching recruiters by 'plugging-in' for fast learning

If you spend all your time training consultants in a one-on-one situation, your own productivity will suffer dramatically. A neat solution to this problem is to 'plug' new recruits into your own desk.

Assign one or even two new people to literally follow you around and listen to every conversation you have for an entire morning.

Let them listen to you taking job descriptions, let them come with you on client visits, let them sit in on interviews with you.

In this way, you expose new people to the full variety of consulting situations and they absorb your style and ethos – after all, they are getting it from the best consultant in the team (hopefully).

You can also 'plug' new recruits into other senior members of your team. One word of warning, though. If you do 'plug' consultants into yourself or others, it is essential to have regular debriefs to ensure that they understand what has been happening and they have the opportunity to ask questions. Three or four times a day, stop and ask them to tell you what they have heard and learned.

Then refine their perceptions and explain any dynamics that they may have missed. Maybe set them follow-up tasks. At the very least, it tells you where they need more input.

You can't limit your new hire training to this technique, but you can certainly liberally 'plug in' new recruits during their early weeks. It's much better than having them sit there and read a training manual.

Coaching recruiters by shutting up and letting them talk

Many managers I have worked with feel that if they are not doing the talking or showing the consultant how the job is done, they are not providing valuable input. This is not always true. From time to time, it is highly effective for the manager or coach to reverse roles, only providing feedback after the event.

For example, once you have developed a consultant up to a certain level of competence, or even with your more experienced people, take them on a client visit with you where *they lead* the discussion. Let them take the job, let them do the selling, and you play a secondary role.

You may be surprised how difficult this is to do. Many managers just cannot help themselves on a client meeting, they leap in to take control. I understand why, because I am the worst offender, but look at the bigger picture. When is the recruiter ever going to learn if you always take control? You are setting up that person for disaster because the first time they actually get to run a client meeting, they really will be on their own, i.e. you will not be there.

So, sure, be ready to leap in if the visit goes entirely off the rails, but otherwise, let the recruiter run it. Afterwards, in the cab back to the office or in a coffee shop, do a full, immediate debrief, pointing out missed opportunities or where things could have been handled differently.

The same role swapping should be applied to interviewing candidates. Your consultant interviews, while you observe and give feedback afterwards.

This is the most potent coaching you will ever do.

Remember also, technology or not, the difference between winners and losers in recruitment is still people, so people leverage is the front line of competitive advantage, and coaching is your weapon of mass development.

You have to win that arms race.

Do not allow a 'prima donna' to destroy your 'cred' and your team

Inevitably, within a group of recruiters, one, maybe two, will rise to the top. These 'big billers' either inherit a great desk or, less often, they build it themselves, and soon they are consistently out-billing everyone else.

Sadly, in many cases it seems with strong billers, the higher the fees they bring in, the bigger the 'pain in the butt' they are.

It's not always the case, and I have known many great recruiters who are humble and willing to share, but with many high billers it seems it is no longer possible for them to operate without making it perfectly clear to their colleagues that they are not entirely on the same consulting planet. I'm sure every industry has their own version of the prima donna employee.

Smugness sets in. Lack of co-operation on new initiatives becomes the norm. The big biller comes late to meetings because, *"I bill a lot, you know."* Administration is suddenly beneath them.

Ironically, as the prima donna gets more complacent and more arrogant, complaints from clients and candidates about the big biller start to rise.

And boy, if the prima donna gets a headhunting call from a competitor, the whole world knows about it in three seconds flat.

Now, this is a management challenge – and a coaching challenge. Over many years, I have noticed that managers of prima donnas fail miserably to address the problem because they allow themselves to be held to ransom by the big biller. They have an action-stunting fear that the fees will be lost if the prima donna is offended in some way and, heaven forbid, resigns! It seems many managers put up with a thousand varieties of bulldust from big billers because *"We can't afford to lose them."*

This is a massive mistake that a good manager must avoid at all costs. If you allow top performers who evolve into prima donnas to blackmail you because they 'bring in all the money', you are setting yourself up for a life of pure hell.

The first rule and the non-negotiable rule with these guys is this: do not allow different rules to develop for prima donnas because they are 'special'.

It is a slippery slope you are creating if the perception is that *"As long as my fees are good, I don't have to attend meetings on time or do my admin like everyone else."* Do not compromise the type of team you are trying to build, the culture you are creating, for the short-term benefit of one high-production consultant.

If you do this, the problem will multiply as the prima donna takes even greater liberties. You will lose respect from the rest of the team, and ultimately you will lose them.

The best strategy for dealing with prima donnas is to confront their behaviour head-on. The way to do this is to keep raising the bar. The psyche of a prima donna is based on a belief that they are 'the best'. Turn that label back on to them. If they are as good as they think and say they are, then they will want to achieve higher activity levels and standards than the rest of the team.

So, with a prima donna, you must explicitly tell them what they are consistently doing well. Compliment them and encourage repetition of that behaviour.

Also, very importantly, let them know what they need to do to be a truly excellent performer – what they must do more of and less of. So, for example, you might compliment your big biller on a quarter of excellent fee production. However, then go on to point out that 50% of the jobs they took in were lost to competitors (not an uncommon figure for contingent perm recruitment). Focus on this. If possible, compare it to other recruiters with better ratios.

Set the big biller a goal to reduce jobs lost and increase their fill rates. These guys are so used to praise and fawning from leadership, but all this praise actually stunts their development.

I have never met a recruiter in 40 years who could not improve, so focus on that. Detail areas for improvement. Bring them down to earth. Set goals which, while fair and business critical, you know they will struggle to meet. It gives the old prima donna a wonderful sense of perspective.

On behavioural and attitudinal matters, I recommend a zero-tolerance policy. After a few standard warnings and coaching on areas the big biller must improve in, it has to come down to this:

"Bill, your fees are excellent, and we value your contribution greatly, but one of the non-negotiable aspects of working in this team is that we all attend daily meetings on time. We have spoken about your lateness several times, and now I have to tell you that if you wish to stay on the team, you need to be there on time, every time."

Be prepared to follow up on that threat.

You see, big billers are important, but more important than their fees is equity in the team, co-operation and an environment of mutual respect.

Don't trade off the long-term harmony of your business for the short-term gain of the fees provided by a toxic big biller.

Fees do not beat ethos.

CHAPTER 21

Performance management

IT WAS one of the thousand cups of coffee I have with recruitment company owners every year. I love these meetings. This is where I learn and keep my finger on the pulse.

This particular guy wanted to talk about business development. The pipeline was drying up.

He was an old-school sort of guy (not old; he is at least 20 years younger than me), so he soon expressed his love for a good key performance indicator (KPI). I took no umbrage. I believe in measurement too. Moreover, I believe in smart, quality activity.

He was quick to tell me that his recruiters were tasked with hard-core, cold-calling targets. *"We demand that 100 cold-calls are made a day. Measure it closely, too,"* he beamed.

I asked, *"How is that working for you?"*

His reply was both predictable and shocking, and I quote verbatim: *"Pretty shit actually, but don't worry, I have a solution!"*

Now I leaned forward. This was good. He had some fresh ideas. I could learn something new.

"Yes," he said, as he sipped on his soy latte in the Westin Hotel coffee shop, *"we have upped the KPI to 150 calls a day!"* He leaned back and smiled broadly.

I could not help myself. I gave him both barrels.

It was something along the lines of, *"You have proved what does not work, so you ask your frazzled recruiters to do more of it? You grind them into the dust, destroy their morale, crush their self-esteem and waste their expensive time, on a tactic that is not working?"*

He was unperturbed. *"But Greg, for every 100 calls we make we get a lead. So, if they make 50 more, we may pick up another one."*

I am all for smart business development, and I love the use of the phone, but let's get smart about turning cold-calls into warm calls.

Let's use social media, and specifically social selling, to turn a closed door into a half-open one. There are a hundred ways a call can be finessed to create rapport, have a reason, offer value or follow up a previous engagement.

The *"Have you got any vacancies?"* call is past its use-by date. That is, if you ever get to speak to a prospect at all. Blind, untargeted, mindless cold-calling is, in reality, a race to see who can piss off the most prospects.

This reliance on cold-calling is actually just one indicator of the biggest issue with some recruitment leaders the world over: they have no innovation, no fresh ideas. They just keep on worshipping on the altar of tired, old tactics that were only marginal in a business world that has long gone.

It's ineffective, even damaging, these days. However, more importantly in the context of this chapter's focus, this approach also highlights the soul-destroying and destructive misuse of KPIs.

The recruiting secret that made me more money than any other

I left that meeting frustrated and annoyed. However, that guy wasn't all wrong. Focusing on activity is correct.

I believe – actually, I *know* – that activity is key to the ongoing success of any recruitment professional. It is also likely the key to success for professionals in many other industries.

It's not all about activity, but activity counts. You just *have* to do a certain amount of 'stuff' to get the results you want. Now, those activities might vary depending on your sector, your experience and the depth of your customer relationships, but they are likely to include all the usual suspects such as client meetings, follow-up calls, talent interviews, and candidate–client interviews (CCIs).

These days we need to add new activities: networking events, content creation, connections, engagement and talent community building as well as a well-evolved social networking component to our work.

The point is that I have never seen a successful recruiter who does not consistently churn out activities that drive the outcomes they seek. It comes with the territory.

However, it's not *all* about activity. Too much activity, of the wrong kind, and of inferior quality, will be counter-productive. Hundreds of low-quality, ill-thought-through cold-calls, for example, are not going to enhance your billings or your reputation. Nor will desperate cookie-cutter (i.e. identikit) InMails to source people on LinkedIn, or indiscriminate résumé spamming around town.

The second component of the success formula is quality. We need to do lots of activity to be successful, but it needs to be high-quality activity. By quality, I mean quality through every step of the process. Your job is made up of thousands of tiny interactions and your success is driven by the volume of those interactions (activity), but also, and crucially, by the *quality* of those interactions.

This is where a real recruiting professional will display their well-honed questioning, influencing, counselling, persuasion and negotiation skills. That is the quality I am referring to.

So, success is about *activity*, and success is about the *quality* of that activity. Yet, there is a third part to the equation – which most recruiters fail to spot. We have to do lots of activity – yes. We have to maintain high quality – yes. However, the other integral element is: we have to do that high-quality activity… *with the right people.*

If you do 15 client meetings a week, and the quality of those visits is superb, you can still fail if you are meeting with companies that have no need for your services, or if you meet people who are not decision-makers.

I know what you're thinking now. You are thinking, *"But this is so obvious."*

I know. Isn't it just? However, do you do it? And if you are a leader, do you run your business on this premise?

Sad to say, but I know you probably don't. Only a couple of months ago I ran a 'Secrets of the Successful Billing Manager' leadership masterclass in four cities around Australia and New Zealand, which was attended by over 600 recruiting managers. I asked them, *"How many of your companies have regular, weekly one-on-one meetings with consultants to monitor and set activity goals?"*

It was less than 40%.

So, we are not in fact measuring what we purportedly manage. The obvious might be really obvious to say, but it is not being done.

In 35 years of coaching recruiters and running teams of recruiting professionals, when I have seen someone go off track, or a team start to fail, I have always found the answer by applying this formula:

- Are we doing enough activity?

- Is that activity of the right quality?

- Are we doing it with the right people?

It has never let me down. The reason for the failure will be found in one or more of these areas. Also, the funny thing is that the explosion in technology impacting our sector makes applying this formula even more pertinent.

So, there it is – the holy grail of how to be great at this job. Success in recruitment is lots of activity, done well, with the right people.

Activity × Quality × Target market = Success = Fun and money!

Setting the right KPIs for your recruiters

If that's true, and my formula is correct (and it is), then what are the activities that we need recruiters to focus on? Also, what volume of activity will lead to success? What's reasonable to expect? And, how do we keep them on track?

Well, out of those questions were born the much maligned, even hated, agency recruitment KPIs.

It's easy to see why they are so disliked. So many recruiters are currently getting better and better at doing things they *should not be doing at all*. This situation is made worse by draconian, antiquated and overly onerous KPIs being forced on recruiters, who don't understand why.

Of course, we can't manage recruiter productivity and forecast potential results unless we measure activity. However, the key to working on the *right* activity, and getting recruiter buy-in to that activity, is 'backwards planning'.

Don't focus the recruiter on the outcome. Focus the recruiter on the activities that are proven to lead to success.

Goal-setting and KPIs is a science, not a whim.

Working backwards to get it right

Here is my classic 'backwards plan' – the primary starting point for making sure you are working on the right stuff. This plan is designed for permanent, contingent recruiters.

For a perm recruiter, tracking CCIs is the only metric that really matters, so let's put some science behind our daily goal.

The following table explains itself if you track through from the top. Essentially, you start with your gross profit (GP) quarterly goal and divide by average placement value.

1	Target quarterly billings	$120,000	Insert the GP required to hit quarterly goal
2	Average placement value	$6,000	Insert the average fee per placement
3	Placements required per quarter	20	Divide 1 by 2
4	Placements required per week	2	Bang! That's the weekly goal
5	Client interviews per placement	5	Insert the average CCI/ placement
6	Interviews per week to meet goal	10	This is the key KPI
7	CCI per day to meet goal	2	Easy to digest daily goal

In the example shown in the table above, this goal is 20 placements per quarter. Most recruiters don't even know that goal. Then you can work out you need two placements a week to hit your target. Work out your average interview to placement ratio (CCI/placement). Your ATS will tell you this (if you actually enter that data, of course). This figure tells you that you need to set up ten CCIs per week; alternatively, two a day.

Bang! You have a real, achievable, measurable daily goal, which is proven by science to lead to $120,000 in fees per quarter.

You can apply the concept in different ways. Here is a second backwards plan for a perm recruiter, the magic 'job order backwards' plan.

1	Target quarterly billings	$120,000	
2	Average placement value	$6,000	Insert the average fee per placement
3	Placements required per quarter	20	Divide 1 by 2
4	Average job order/ placement conversion	3	Jobs filled out of jobs taken
5	Job orders required per quarter	60	Multiply 3 by 4
6	Average job orders per week	5	Bang! Job order weekly goal

Again, it's simple. You want to bill $120,000 in a quarter? And each placement is worth $6,000, on average? So, you must make 20 placements in a quarter, right?

However, you only fill one job out of three that you take. Your ATS will tell you this. (Mind you, it's more likely to be one out of five, but let's not go there.) So that tells you, if you fill one out of three jobs, and you need to fill 20, you must take 60 jobs in a quarter. That's five new job orders per week.

It's science, not an opinion. Add rigour to your daily work effort. Set goals that are achievable, digestible, understandable and effective in driving results.

Then hit these daily goals and watch the money roll in.

The temp/contract backwards plan

This plan is very different.

You still start with the ultimate goal and work backwards. However, you target different metrics. Work with me as we smash through my example temp plan below.

1	Target quarterly temp billings	$250,000	Insert the temp GP required to hit profit goal
2	Average net margin per hour	$10	Insert the average net margin per hour
3	Required billed hours per quarter	25,000	Divide 1 by 2
4	Average assignment length	150 hours	Insert average assignment length
5	Filled assignments per quarter	167	Divide billed hours by assignment length
6	Number of consultants	3	Insert number of consultants
7	Quarterly 'filled orders' target per consultant	56	Divide 5 by 6
8	Weekly 'filled orders' target per consultant	5	Divide 7 by weeks in quarter
9	Daily consultant 'filled orders' target	1	Divide by 5

Candidate interview goals	Client visit goals

This plan is for a temp/contract team, because that is often how they are viewed in business, and often how they are paid – as a team. However, it can be very simply adjusted for each individual, by just taking out row 6 (number of consultants) and dropping in numbers for the target of one recruiter only.

So, let's go.

We start with target temp GP billings for the team (you may call it net temporary margin) (row 1, $250,000). Then insert the average net margin (after taxes, etc.) per hour and divide total GP margin by margin per hour. This immediately gives us a very cool number, one we should recite in our sleep – the number of temp hours your team need to invoice to hit the goal (row 3).

Next we drop in a funky little number, which is the average assignment length in hours. Get this from your ATS. It is the total hours billed for the previous year, divided by the number of assignments filled in the year. Bingo! The number is 150 in my example (row 4).

Why is this number important? Because now, when you divide the number of hours needed to bill (row 3) by average assignment length (row 4), it tells you that you must fill, as a team, 167 assignments per quarter.

Now, what a gorgeous, sexy, alluring number that is. Because it's science, and science cuts through the BS, and the science further tells us that, as we have three consultants on our temp desk, each of them must fill 56 assignments to reach the goal.

So, if you divide 56 orders (row 7) by 12 weeks in a quarter (one week is always lost due to sickness/holiday), you now know that each recruiter must fill five orders per week (or if you like, the team must fill 15 per week).

That's one order per day per recruiter, or three per day for the team – simple, achievable, measurable. Also, it's undeniable!

That, my recruiting friends, is a contract recruiter KPI to cherish, and genuinely fall in love with.

What a smart manager will do is drive fresh KPIs out of that 'filled order per week' number, creating backwards planning KPIs for candidate interviews, client visits, job orders taken, goals, etc. The perm backwards plan can serve as a model for that exercise.

Thus you have worked out how to define and justify the activities your team needs to achieve.

Now, implementation

In my experience, managers of recruitment teams adopt one of three approaches to KPIs. No doubt this is true of managers in many businesses. Two of these approaches are disastrous, and then, of course, there is the right way.

KPI disaster #1

In this company, there are no KPIs. Alternatively, if there are, they are never met, never managed and seldom talked about. In fact, the business operates as a bit of a freewheeling hippie commune. It has no goals, no structure. Unless your recruiters are peak level, self-sustained top performers, who operate as businesses to themselves (which can happen, but is exceedingly rare), this laissez-faire approach will fail – badly.

KPI disaster #2

The company and its recruiters are slaves to the metrics. The week's work becomes all about the KPI report. There is a whole range of KPIs that are measured, numbers are managed relentlessly, often the wrong activities are measured, and the inevitable result is resentful recruiters who feel stifled and bullied. They start to 'finesse' the reports, just to 'keep the boss happy'. Productivity drops, while staff turnover increases. You can't hire intelligent, motivated people and then treat them like robots.

Implementing KPIs the right way

So, what do we need to do?

As we know, activity is the key to success. Quality is just as essential, and so too is the targeting of those activities (with whom you do them). Thus, in my view, activity management is crucial to individual and business success. It's how you implement and manage the KPI regime that makes all the difference.

Here is what works best:

- The KPIs actually serve as a *'dashboard' for recruiters to run their own desk.* The recruiters use them to manage their time and to keep track of personal productivity, with the focus in the right place. KPIs are there to help the recruiter, not to satisfy management.

- To achieve this, it's critical that *the consultants help develop the KPIs in the first place.* It's done in collaboration, with the recruiter working out what they need to do to succeed. Of course, the manager massages and debates this until all parties are happy. However, if the recruiter is invested in the goals, they will achieve them.

- The consultant must understand *why activity leads to the desired results.* Managers often assume that their staff understand this. As covered in the previous section, take the time to work out a 'backwards plan', so the consultant truly 'gets' how activity, done well, flows on to results.

- *Only measure the four to six key metrics.* A massive spreadsheet of KPIs that the recruiter has to monitor is a distraction. Just measure those that are crucial for weekly time management. Also, those KPIs might be different for people doing different things or working in different markets within the team.

- *Relate activity to success,* and ultimately to the consultant's earning potential. Quality activity means placements, which means dollars, which means a bigger bonus for them.

- *Change the metrics measured* depending on the market and depending on the state of the consultant's desk. Got no jobs? Measure business development activities. Got no candidates? Measure candidate acquisition activities. Flex the KPI report for the outcome desired. It's a means to an end, not an end in itself.

- Make sure everyone understands that the *management of KPIs is vital.* A good manager will look not only at numbers, but also the quality, e.g. *"You interviewed ten candidates last week, but none of them have been referred to clients"* or *"Good to see you sent out 25 résumés to clients last month, but that has resulted in only four interviews."* Dig beyond numbers.

Nirvana is achieved when the recruiter takes ownership of the KPI report and understands how activity drives their business forward. They end up hitting the KPIs because they *want* to meet them, not because they are told to.

You want recruiters with high self-esteem, retaining a sense of autonomy and hitting their activity numbers because they believe in them and they see the link between activity, quality and success.

The missing link: accountability

The big difference between an average or poorly performing recruitment business and an overachieving business is tolerance of long-term, serial mediocrity. Recruiters who underperform are the principal reason for lack of profit and growth.

I don't blame the recruiters. I blame the management.

The key is consistent activity management, and performance management for under-achievers. It's not to fire people, but to mentor and guide them to greater success via ongoing coaching and activity management.

Call it what you will, but there is no other way.

Moreover, even if the desire is there, the will often isn't. The missing ingredient is accountability. So many companies have KPIs but they are not measured, or if they are, shortfalls are not acted on.

Accountability requires a culture of definition and understanding of what's acceptable and what 'good' looks like. It requires an ethos in the business of considering feedback as positive, not personal or punitive.

For this to be achieved, shortfalls in performance must be dealt with immediately and with clarity. With this in mind, the fact that 60% of Australian and New Zealand recruitment companies *do not* have weekly one-on-one consultant activity meetings is totally shocking. (See earlier in the chapter where I talked about my

'Secrets of the Successful Billing Manager' speaking tour.) How can they possibly be dealing with this crucial issue?

Accountability also means there are consequences for unacceptable behaviour misalignment and for performance and activity shortfall. Why have goals if when we miss them nothing is said and done?

Please understand, 'consequences' is not meant to be a threatening word. In most cases, it means gentle correction, guidance, mentoring or extra training. However, it can also mean more challenging conversations, questions, redress on shortfall and censure.

The point is: we don't just 'let it slide'. That is not 'managing performance'. That's watching it. Like a spectator at a rugby match – interested, informed, aware, but totally useless to the actual game afoot.

Meetings that add value to overall performance

Don't we recruiters love a good meeting? (We're not the only profession where this is the case!) Job meetings, status update meetings, talent updates, pipeline reporting, key account meetings, sales meetings, management meetings, debtor meetings, database meetings, finance meetings… The list is endless.

Yet, here is the thing – many of these meetings, I would argue most of them, are a total waste of time.

Here is what I have found works in making meetings more effective in the recruitment business, whether you are a junior team leader trying to herd a group of recruiters or the CEO determined to impose order and direction:

- Meetings are to *start on time*. The value of meetings is inherently dubious because they take us away from our customers. If you keep a group of ten of us waiting 15 minutes to start a meeting, that is 10 × 15 minutes = 150 minutes, or three wasted hours. These are hours that could have been spent servicing clients and talent and generating revenue. That's unforgivable. So if the meeting starts at 8am, it starts at 8am. Those who come late are clearly and publicly reminded of the meeting start time, and that we would appreciate them getting here on time, next time. We do not go back to brief latecomers on what has been discussed. They can find out later. Why should we waste more time for people who did get to the meeting on time? Those who arrive obscenely late are asked to come to the next meeting as they have missed this one.

- The underlying theme of every meeting is *"How does this meeting help our customers?"* Ask the question every 20 minutes. Hang a sign on the wall asking that question. Give everyone the right to ask that question if discussions go off track. If the meeting becomes too 'internal' or too waffling, simply call the meeting to an end. Yes, I'm serious. Meetings are not sacred.

- *Have a time limit* for every meeting, publicised beforehand. For example, *"This meeting starts at 9am and finishes at 10am, if not before."* Never allow it to go beyond the set time. This allows people to plan the rest of their morning efficiently, and it focuses the discussion wonderfully to ensure you get through the agenda swiftly, concentrating on the important stuff.

- *Have an agenda* and invite all attendees to contribute to the agenda beforehand. If the topic is not on the agenda, it does not get addressed. This approach is really effective in ensuring people prepare their thoughts and stops all those meeting 'hijackers' raising irrelevant topics on the fly as it occurs to them – which is very disruptive.

- *Contributions from attendees must be limited to discussions where decisions or strategies result.* This is important. There must be no waffle, no grandstanding, no post-mortems or war stories. So, the meeting convener says, *"How does this lead to us agreeing a strategy for XYZ?"* If it does not assist in that direction, move on.

- When chairing meetings, *move fast through the agenda*. Don't get bogged down on petty and small points. Make sure the meeting has a purpose and a result.

- *Delegate tasks coming out of the meeting to consultants or attendees.* You, the manager, shouldn't end up with 20 tasks. If someone has suggested sponsoring the local football team, and the group agrees, the person who raised the idea gets the job to research and cost it and come back to the next meeting with a proposal. This is a great tactic, and self-regulating, because it quickly results in people only raising items that they are passionate about. If it flies, they get to do the work!

- If possible, ensure *all attendees come to the meeting having done some preparation,* especially if they have nominated agenda items. Make sure they have to present the topic and sell their idea.

- In preparing for a meeting, *if you find there are few or no burning issues to discuss, cancel the meeting.* Meetings must result in definable outcomes and action steps, which are tabled and followed up at the next meeting. If there are no issues, then it's better to cancel the meeting and spend more time with customers.

For more insight into aligning meetings with performance, here are the three types of meetings I ran and still recommend, depending on the circumstances.

Daily meetings

These are consulting, operational meetings. The best time is first thing in the morning – 8am is a good time. They always start on time. Everyone in the team attends. There are no exceptions. The goal is to focus our efforts, swap information and set targets for the day. The temporary meeting, for example, will review vacant jobs, discuss finishers for recycling (temp assignments ending), decide on advertising. It is quick (15 minutes) and each person knows their priorities for the day by the end of the meeting.

Team meetings

I'd suggest running these maybe monthly. They must have a time limit and must be limited to discussions where decisions or strategies result. Let there be no waffle, no grandstanding, no post-mortems or war stories.

These meetings usually cover team results against target, new initiatives, trends, threats and opportunities, along with individual recognition. Move fast through the agenda. Don't get bogged down. As mentioned, if there is nothing real or important to put on the agenda, scrap the meeting.

Make sure the attendees have preparation to do. Have some attendees present short segments. Deliver learnings and case studies. Celebrate small victories.

Don't let anyone tell you that meetings are good for team building. Unless there is a problem to solve or an issue to address, they are not. You don't build teamwork in a meeting room – you build it on the coalface, while people are doing the job.

Consultant one-on-ones

Managing is getting things done through other people. In recruitment, we all know that working hard is not enough. A hard-working consultant without direction, goals and a plan will get frustrated, tired and eventually fail.

Your job is to keep them on track. The weekly 'one-on-one' is the best way I have found to do this. This meeting takes place with the consultant at a set time each week. It does not get cancelled. It could last an hour if there are issues to cover and it could last three minutes if everything is on track.

Typically, it lasts 15 to 20 minutes. It is not an opportunity for the consultant to go through every job and every candidate. Nor is it a time for you to lecture consultants on their shortcomings.

Your desired outcome of this meeting is simply that the consultant leaves the meeting with a clear idea of priorities and an understanding of your expectations for the week ahead. That is all.

In a typical one-on-one meeting the manager might cover the following:

- *"What's on your mind today?"* (The best start ever, in my opinion.)
- Briefly review the week (the good, the bad).
- Ask for the plan for the week ahead.
- Agree activity targets.
- Agree specific tasks to be achieved by next week.
- Congratulate and thank the consultant for work well done.
- Offer specific help.

As with all meetings, ensure you leave the work resulting from the meeting with the consultant. Agree deadlines. Remember to always record what has been agreed.

Standing room only

One final example: one of the best meetings I attended was a job meeting at 9am in our Tokyo office when I ran Aquent. The purpose was to cover open orders, highlight fresh new talent and set goals for the day. The meeting was held standing up! It was fantastic. Everyone stood there, delivered their news, shared their issues and, 15 minutes later, it was over and… on with the day!

CHAPTER 22

Directing the traffic

I AM on the board of 14 recruitment and HR tech businesses in eight cities in four countries, and I speak to owners and managers every single day. Most are looking for advice and are prepared to share their deepest fears and bravest plans. I am in the very fortunate position of being on the 'inside'.

The biggest weakness in recruitment industry leadership is the lack of a genuinely strategic approach to business management. This is not surprising, given that most recruitment businesses are small and run by people who might be great recruiters, and very street smart, but who are not given to thinking like a company director.

There is a pervasive reluctance to take a long-term view. Many in our industry are chronic short-term thinkers. *"Show me this month's numbers." "I want a return on every dollar, now."* I understand it. I was there, and I feel that pain. Yet, we need to build a recruitment business to compete in the way the world is going to be, not so much for how it is today or, even worse, how things were yesterday.

I find myself continually urging owners and directors not to be lulled into a sense of false security by past or even present success. The market is good right now. The industry is growing, and profits across the world are up. However, we must not be seduced by short-term profits. Build a business that is going to thrive in the environment to come. This chapter takes you through a few areas to focus on, starting with disruption.

You need to disrupt your business now

Disrupt, before someone else does it for you in an excruciating way.

We all have our set paradigms of the world, so it's hard to change from within. The best way is to engineer micro-internal change based on a plan for the future – that is, self-disrupt.

And, the best way to do that is to continually ask the question, *"Why do we do it this way?"*

You don't have to innovate with one big earth-shattering idea. Who really does that? Innovation can be incremental – making small steps of progress and improvement.

A powerful example of this is investing in technology, which many leaders are reluctant to do. Some are actually resisting automating parts of their business because the 'good old ways are better'. No! This is the type of disruption I speak of. Automate the transactional and the drudgery. Then get your recruiters to excel at the part of the job which requires human interventions and influencing skills.

Believe me, it's 100% a leadership issue because complacency leads to lethargy.

In smaller companies, the blockage to disruption happens way before the strategic stage. In some cases, the owner and founder is just not suited to leading the business at all, and the company is severely hampered when the owner stays in a role which, as it has evolved, is no longer suitable for them.

This has damaged, even derailed, many businesses. For example, the founder insists on remaining in the 'general management' role, when in reality they are a very poor people manager and can contribute much more as a rainmaker or an account manager, or in a strategic role.

Alternatively, perhaps the owner insists on billing heavily and feels their worth is only proven if they out-bill their team, when what the business needs from them is direction or senior business development or people management, or some deep attention to strategy.

This is a common state of affairs: the high-billing owner who unwittingly puts a cap on the growth and value of the business by trying to remain the recruiting rock star. Owners staying in the wrong job have cost companies millions of dollars in value, and it happens everywhere.

It is very hard to fix this without outside help. Many people do not even see that they are the blockage, but often the best way to grow is to stand aside. You can still be the owner, always be a director and still pull many strings – but focus on what you are good at, and if the ship needs a new captain, grow or hire that captain.

I was instrumental in engineering exactly this as an advisor to an eight-person recruiting business in Sydney, quite recently. It just could not grow beyond that point. One of the most challenging conversations I ever had was to tell that owner he was the problem. He was a great recruiter, a superb client guy and a God-awful people manager. He hated managing.

However, his view was that 'he was the boss'. In his mind, it was cast as his lot that he had to manage everyone. I persuaded him otherwise, we gave him a resourcer and he hired a professional manager to lead the team. His billings doubled and the company grew to 20 people. He has never been happier.

Credit is due to this owner for recognising his strengths and weaknesses, and acting accordingly. In a way, stepping aside was an example of disruption – and excellent leadership – by him.

You must know your cost of seat to improve productivity

Staffing Industry Metrics, respected analysts for the Australian and New Zealand recruitment industry, tells us that consultant productivity is at an all-time low. Yet, sales are going up for many Australian and NZ recruiters. So, into sight looms the dreaded prospect of 'profitless revenue growth'.

Individual recruiters are billing less as a percentage of their salary and oncosts than ever before. In fact, from a ratio of almost three times GP to salary cost in the five years from 2003 to 2007, we have seen that ratio declining for the last four years, reaching an all-time low of 2.2 in the 2016 financial year and bumping along to 2.3 in 2018.

Yet, even now, I often hear owners and managers of recruitment businesses say things like, *"Oh, she is not my best recruiter, but I only pay her $80,000 a year, and she is billing $120,000 a year, so she is covering her cost, and more."*

This attitude is wrong – very wrong. Let's examine the *real* cost of a recruiter to your business:

- **Base salary.**

- **Direct oncosts:** These vary from country to country, but include statutory pensions, superannuation, payroll tax, insurances, etc. In Australia, this is comfortably 15% of salary, and maybe more.

- **Additional employee benefits:** These could include obvious thing like a car provided, but other costs can slip under the radar, such as car parking, membership fees, etc. Include these in the cost of the individual if they are *direct benefits to the employee* that would disappear if the employee disappeared.

- **Cost of seat:** This is the biggie – the cost that most managers don't truly factor in. I define cost of seat (COS) as: the average cost of each recruiter, not including recruiter salary.

This is how you work it out. Go to your P&L. Take a period of a year, preferably. Go to the total expense line of the business, or for a branch or business unit. Subtract the total consultant salaries and bonuses from that number. *Leave in* the salaries of the manager and the admin staff, as these are there to support the recruiter.

Once you have that number, divide it by the number of consultants in the team. That number represents the cost to you for each consultant to put their delicate derrière in your seat *before* you have paid their salary.

So, here is my shocking prediction. That number will be between $80,000 and $100,000. (It's normally closer to $100,000 in Australia; £50,000 in the UK.) This is per consultant, before you take into account their salary.

Now, let's add up the cost of a consultant on a basic salary of $80,000 per annum:

Salary	$80,000
Oncosts (15% of salary)	$12,000
Benefits	$2,000
COS	$100,000
Total cost (before the business makes a single dollar):	**$194,000**

From this we know that if this person bills anything less than $194,000, they cost the employer money. That's why we want every recruiter to bill three times his or her base salary. Typically it works like this:

- One third for the consultant salary

- One third to cover COS

- One third for return to the business.

The sad fact is that many recruitment companies are happily paying the first two thirds, and never seeing the final third.

The critical business imperative across our industry is to improve consultant productivity. To do that, you need to hire the right skills, train, coach, mentor and provide all the modern tools your recruiters need to thrive.

Carrying long-term mediocre recruiters is like running a sheltered workshop. Of course, running your business as a 'not for profit charity' to help enrich your mediocre consultants, while you mortgage your house, is fine, if that is *really* what you want to do. However, if you are going to be giving your hard-earned money away while you carry all the business risk, wouldn't it be better if you give the money to Save the Children or Cancer Research?

Take your time, now… have a think.

In recruitment, everybody sells, baby!

In Australia, New Zealand and the UK, over 80% of recruitment companies have fewer than ten staff. Of the 19,408 staffing firms in the United States, almost 85% have less than $5 million in revenue, and in fact, 11,000 of them have less than $1 million in revenue (US figures from *Breaking Through*, by Mike Cleland and Barry Asin, Charted Path, 2018). So what I am going to tell you now most likely applies to your business, and indeed I think it applies to much bigger organisations too.

In recruitment, everybody sells – and I mean everybody.

With productivity declining, the last thing you want is 'administration managers' poring over spreadsheets, number-crunching, tweaking budgets, checking KPIs all day, planning, strategising, reviewing, assessing and (God help us!) calling meetings.

Of course, most of those things *are* essential. However, they do not constitute a full-time job, except perhaps in the largest of organisations, and even then I doubt it. Why else is it that these roles get cut the moment the market dips? They provide the least value, and everyone knows it.

The actual 'selling' will vary… but everybody sells, the CEO included. When I say 'sell', do not automatically think of cold-calling or the relentless 'hard sell'. The selling is often likely to be sophisticated, and sometimes digital, but the point is that everybody bills, or directly engages in activity that leads to billing.

The team leader, supervising one or two people, must hold a full personal dollar budget. The manager, running a team of up to eight consultants, will still bill, but will increasingly farm work out to consultants in support. However, that billing manager still sells, even if they are handling just a couple of jobs. The placements dwindle, but they still rain-make, account manage, see clients, and front networking events. So, as the team grows, their billing drops, *but selling does not.*

In the GFC (2009), and other recessions before it, balancing this took care of itself, because recruitment companies cut out middle management and everyone went back on the desk. My advice to you is: do not allow non-billing managers to emerge as things improve.

There are only three things that recruitment managers should focus on. They should spend 80% of their time:

- **selling** (that could be billing, rainmaking or account management)

- **coaching** recruiters to greater success

- **performance management**, ensuring no long-term mediocrity.

If you have a CFO, they should see clients, especially those with multiple temps on site. We want to be paid on time. So should your HR manager. Why not? They need to be as connected as possible to the ultimate customer, surely? Admin staff should be brought into sales meetings and rewarded for sales growth. Your senior management should have sales responsibilities, which might include a goal for client meetings or running key accounts.

In my last corporate role, I was CEO of Firebrand, a company with ten offices in eight countries, I did my share of selling. In fact, I did 100 client visits in 2012, and I also sold via my ambassadorial role, speaking at conferences and events where clients and candidates were among the audience, and creating PR and branding opportunities.

It's a skill to handle both selling and leading people. It's not easy to find people who can manage both. But whoever told you it was going to be easy to run a great recruitment company that makes lots of money and provides real careers?

It's difficult. However, it can be done – and it *must* be done unless you want a fat layer around your middle. I am not talking about your physique. (How could I? Look at me.) I am talking about your business; bogged down by overpaid middle management who do not really impact profitability, except inasmuch as they reduce it.

Remember: everybody sells, baby!

Revenue is vanity. Profit is sanity. Cash is reality.

I speak to a lot of business owners and managers. As mentioned earlier, I am on the board of 14 recruitment and HR tech businesses. I have what feels like a million cups of coffee with recruitment business owners every year. Some are green, some very experienced. I find that many simply do not understand the actual financial position of their business. You might be shocked to hear it.

Some just don't ensure accurate, timely financial reporting. I mean, with no P&L for months! Many others clearly do not understand the numbers put in front of them. Yes, really. Even the difference between 'revenue' and 'gross profit' eludes many. Plenty of others get lots of information but focus on entirely the wrong data when they *do* look at it.

I am not being demeaning here. It took me years to fully grasp financial management, and I am only mildly proficient now. I know also that many people who rise to management roles have little or no financial training.

However, if you manage or run a business – any business – you need to understand the numbers. It's more than just being able to read a P&L. You must not allow yourself to get seduced by numbers you see on a spreadsheet either.

Remember, it's not numbers, percentages or ratios you put in the bank – it is dollars.

Thus I find myself cautioning disbelieving owners – who are celebrating a massive temporary PSA win, for example – that they need to reject the contract.

"But it's worth nearly a million dollars!" they cry. *"We have to do it!"*

No, you don't actually. In fact, you must not take it on at margins and payment terms that will cripple you.

"But this will grow our sales by 25%!" they wail. *"And what we lose on margin, we will make up on volume."*

Oh dear, oh dear, oh dear. What a seductive but fallacious argument. If you are losing money on a transaction, greater volumes of that transaction just mean you will lose *more* money, *more* quickly. I have seen it countless times. Usually, the cash flow implications will do the damage before the shitty margins get you.

Precision Resourcing is an excellent medium-sized IT recruitment business in Sydney. I have been an advisor on its board for almost five years.

When I joined there was a big problem. The business was growing – fast. Yay! It was also going backwards in profit as fast as it was growing. It was a classic scenario. So we dug deep and the problem began to emerge.

For a number of years, the contracting business was running on an average GP percentage margin of 17.6%. A large PSA with the NSW government was making up 26% of the business at that time. Precision was excited by the prospects for growth at the NSW government. It was a classic 'revenue over profit' blind spot.

Precision pitched and won a new contract with the NSW government, and was appointed to a new NSW government panel (using a set of terms called the 0007 scheme).

This was a classic high-volume, low-margin deal, and quite swiftly the average percentage margin across contract/temp significantly decreased. Within 12 months, the margin across all the NSW government business was 8.3% and made up 53% of the total contracting business. We were getting bigger – and poorer.

I remember very well the board meeting where we addressed this problem, and I am sure the directors of Precision do too. My advice was simple. *"You are going to fire the NSW government."*

There was shock… horror… tears. (OK, there were no tears.)

However, we worked through it. We couldn't make money at 8.3%. We were placing great candidates at tiny margins, for whom our corporate clients would pay full fee. Our highly paid consultants were spending their time on business that was in fact losing us more money every time we made a placement – and then we were paying them commission to do it.

So, the decision was taken to no longer fill vacancies within the NSW government 0007 panel.

The government was shocked. We held firm. They kept phoning. We kept explaining, *"Happy to supply, but not at that rate."* The consultants were jumpy and needed constant reassurance and coaching. The directors were a bit nervous too, to be honest.

Current contractors slowly finished up, and the consultants focused on high value business. Margins bottomed, then started to climb.

Today, the NSW government makes up less than 3% of the Precision contracting business, and the average percentage margin has increased back to pre-panel levels. Precision sales turnover has decreased, but profit has soared. The bank balance is healthy. We have given up the overdraft. We no longer factor our debts. Risk is minimised.

I take my hat off to the directors of Precision for recognising the problem once it was pointed out, but especially for having the courage to act on the solution. The business is immeasurably healthier for it.

This is not the only example I could relate. Increasingly, I find myself interrupting a self-satisfied board meeting where we are studying a gorgeous set of P&Ls, which show juicy profits. Then I go and spoil it all by asking for a balance sheet, a debtors aging report and a cash flow report. What a buzzkill!

Smiles fade as we realise the 'massive profit' we have made this year does not correlate with our almost empty bank account and massive list of creditors we need to pay (often, in such cases, owing money to the government – an institution not known for patience or forgiveness in any country where I have worked).

Why the mismatch? Because we are not collecting our debts in a timely way, or sometimes we have not accounted for GST, BAS, group tax, superannuation or some other statutory payment, which subsequently looms like a massive iceberg that many a recruitment Titanic has failed to see.

Cash is reality

No matter what industry your business is in, look at revenue, profit and cash like this.

Revenue is only the bluntest of instruments when it comes to measuring business health. All revenue is not equal. We have to look at both margin and the cost of generating that revenue.

So, while obviously it's important to grow customers and sales, chasing revenue at the expense of all else is vanity and a potentially fatal blunder. I know companies with $50 million in sales, which at the same time carry $5 million in debt and make annual profits of $100k. I also know businesses with total revenue of $10 million that are debt free, have $2 million in the bank and make almost $2 million EBIT per annum. Which owner do you think sleeps better?

Profit is a far more reliable indicator of business robustness, but profit on a P&L can be misleading too. A rigorous P&L will give you a snapshot of your business performance over a set period of time, and it will tell you whether your business model is working. However, 'profit', on a P&L, is still a mirage. It's a fairy tale. It's not real – yet. You can't pay next week's wages with a set of financial statements, no matter what those statements say.

You need cash. Cash is the love of your life. Wad is God. It's your one true friend, the one you can trust. Not everyone agrees, by the way. I have been lectured by countless 'high-flyers', much cleverer than me, who tell me debt is good, using other people's money is smart and cash in the bank is lazy money. Most of them are bankrupt now.

Cash is reality. Make sure every 'deal' you plan to do, every new strategy, every new hire, is only ever agreed once you know the cash implications.

Most business meetings focus on revenue and paper profit. Yes, these are important, but always ask these three questions:

- How much cash do we have in the bank?
- Who are our debtors and what are our liabilities?
- What is the cash flow projection of this initiative?

Cash is (almost) like oxygen. OK, it's not what we live for, but if it runs out, you are sure as hell going to notice.

Revenue is vanity. Profit is sanity. Cash is reality.

CHAPTER 23

Planning for exit

MOST RECRUITMENT businesses are lifestyle businesses – by which I mean the owners create a job for themselves but fail to build an asset that has a saleable value.

Often they started the business because they were good recruiters. Yet, it turns out that they lack the management and leadership ability to plan and implement a growth strategy – to make the business sustainable without their daily input.

As I've mentioned in other chapters in this book, 80% of recruitment companies worldwide have fewer than ten staff, and a very high percentage of those have fewer than five. Very few recruitment agency owners build a business with a commercial value.

During my career, I have started and helped build at least five businesses that were ultimately sold at many times the initial investment value. In the case of Recruitment Solutions, as I talked about in Chapter 6, the start-up capital of less than $120,000 was converted into $24 million on IPO ten years later and was worth twice that a few years later still. (Relax, I was just one of several shareholders! As I also noted in Chapter 6, listing did come with some downsides.)

people2people was an excellent personal investment too, made even tastier by the fact that I was non-executive and did very little of the real work.

I have also started a business, which I worked exceptionally hard at, and which realised a minimal personal return (well, zero to be precise), and I have invested in a couple that plodded along with no great success.

On the buyer side, I have tasted success as well as having had my fingers burnt. At Recruitments Solutions, we made several acquisitions, none of which changed our world in any meaningful way, although this did enable us to enter the Perth market with success. As International CEO at Aquent, I negotiated at least ten acquisitions that I can remember (geographically as far apart as Australia, India and the UK), some quite sizeable, and a couple of which were categorically a mistake... my mistake.

At people2people, I have been heavily involved in negotiating several deals that have paid off very nicely for all parties, including very successful entries into the Brisbane and Melbourne markets.

Today I continue to invest, cautiously and in a small way mostly, in recruitment and HR tech businesses. The only business I ever invested in that was not in recruitment or HR went under. The lesson there perhaps is to invest in what you know and understand.

Another business, Livehire, has gone to IPO, raising over $50 million, but is still in start-up mode, losing money, with a great deal to prove and it's still very high risk. However, I am hopeful it will fly. The company is solving a problem that needs addressing in recruitment – turning a reactive, repetitive, inefficient process into a proactive, quicker, less painful process.

Why I invested in Consult Recruitment

A few years ago I invested in Consult Recruitment, a specialist New Zealand accounting and finance recruiter based in Auckland. Why did I part with a big chunk of my hard-earned? And why did I believe at the time that my money would be multiplied many times over in the years to come?

You could consider my response below as my checklist of reasons why recruitment businesses will thrive in the new era. It is undoubtedly my template to review when considering getting involved in a business investment.

This is why I invested in Consult Recruitment:

- *I understood the business.* I had been on the board for three years. I knew all its secrets. I was an 'insider'. There would be no surprises later on.

- *I like the people.* Typically, when I invest in recruitment businesses, I join the board or maybe act as an advisor. We are going on a journey together. In the case of Consult, the owners are genuine people. They are honest. They share my work ethic, and my views of recruitment and service and quality. We laugh at the same things (except rugby results). It may seem simple or even trite but, believe me, when you are going into business together, it's like entering a marriage. There will be ups and downs, disagreements and challenges. You have to be able to work together, to trust each other, to think of the long term.

- *The leaders are brave.* They are prepared to take the risk. Not only with money, but also risking pride, ego and the status quo. That's big. It's inertia, complacency and fear that cripple so many owners of recruitment businesses. The Consult team are prepared to tackle things they have never done before. Indeed, they know that they must.

- *They take advice.* (Not only mine, but definitely mine; not blindly, but with thought and consideration.) I like that they know there is much that they do not know and are open to new ways of thinking. Then, that they act on that. This mindset of constant internal disruption is key to future success.

- *They follow through.* If we agree it needs to be done, mostly it gets done. It's so common in business for big plans to be made, massive visions laid out, broad goals set... and then nothing actually ever gets done. This is not so at Consult.

- *They are digital.* They are not digital natives necessarily, but digital converts, believers in social, online marketing and talent communities. Have a look at their blog, Twitter, Facebook, Instagram, LinkedIn. They 'get' that the future of recruitment is marketing, especially to candidates (as I discussed in Chapter 13).

- *They love temp and contract.* They live and breathe it. They started their business with a temp desk. It's high-margin, juicy stuff too. 65% of total GP is made up of temporary and contract net margin. This I love because it's a beautiful thing to behold. It will maximise profit in good times and protect us from disaster in the bad.

- *They turn away crappy business.* Low margin? Jerk of a client? Forget it. Consult believes in their value and that flows through to client relationships and, happily, to higher margins – and profits. Despite doubling revenue every two years for the past six years, Consult retains an EBIT margin (operating profit as a percentage of sales) of over 10%. This is how it needs to be. Transactional commoditised recruiters will be replaced by algorithms. True consultants who know how to bring unique talent to the hiring table will not. That's why I invested in Consult.

- *They invest.* They invest in digital, in technology, in marketing, in people, in learning. Have a look at their 'What's my worth?' idea (refer whatsmyworth.co.nz), which is much smarter than it looks, generating client visits and streams of inbound inquiries. They also invest in great offices – funky, fresh and comfortable. They genuinely want to be the best place to work in New Zealand.

- *They develop their staff.* They have made investments in outside training vendors, for a start, but they are also building a training methodology and library. Most of their team are hired from outside recruitment. So, development is the Consult ethos, and I think that is smart.

- *They build relationships.* They love technology, but they get in front of clients and candidates at every opportunity. The guys at Consult are at one with me in the belief that the future of recruitment is the best use of cutting-edge technology, blended with the most sophisticated of human influencing skills.

So, I took a meaningful stake in Consult in June 2016, and just prior to this book going to publication, I can announce that we have negotiated for Consult Recruitment to be acquired by asset management company EFU Investment Ltd. The deal creates a significant growth opportunity for Consult Recruitment. The terms of the deal are confidential, but I can assure you the value was at the premium end of the scale for a business this size, and all three founding owners will stay on in the business in senior, challenging, well-rewarded roles. At the same time, they have realised the value of their asset.

For me, it was a very good investment, but much more than that. I felt the indescribable joy of helping keen young entrepreneurs realise their dream and secure their financial futures, plus we created dozens of jobs along the way.

Oh, and they asked me to stay on as Chairman on the newly restructured board. All board meetings have been timed to coincide with rugby and cricket international matches featuring Australia, in Auckland... naturally.

Plan, plan, plan

If you are planning to sell your business at some stage, then you need to do precisely that: plan.

Just 'working hard' and expecting the rewards to flow is naive and improbable. You have to construct an asset that will be attractive to an outside buyer. What *you* think your business is, and what it might be worth, is not relevant. It's how it's viewed by a buyer, and what value they are prepared to ascribe to it that is important. Also, they will almost always calculate that value on the basis that you and the other owners will no longer be there because, inevitably, in time, you won't.

Look ahead early

One of the most impactful days of my business life was when the three owners of Recruitment Solutions had a two-day 'retreat' in the Hunter Valley, outside Sydney. We were doing well, making serious profits and having fun. We had a facilitator to manage the discussion, and the point of the session was to discuss the future and see where we all wanted to go.

I was the youngest of the three owners – in one case by 12 years. What an eye-opener that two days was! I was only in my thirties, firing on all cylinders, ready to take on the world. However, each shareholder had different aspirations, different timelines, a different vision for themselves and for the business.

We worked it all out, but I have seen that dynamic several times since. So, shareholders need to meet regularly to assess where they are at, and what each person's exit aspirations are. That's an ever-evolving dynamic, let me assure you.

Be 'ready to sell'

You also need to consider how long you want to work at building the business until you do sell. You can always recalibrate that. However, you should have a time frame, three or five years, and you should agree what amount you would sell for. That gives you an EBIT number to aim at.

Make sure everyone understands deal structures. Say you want to sell in five years – that's cool. Remember, though, in most cases if you sell in five years you will still be on a two- or three-year earn-out post-sale date. So, that will be eight years till you are on that beach in the Caribbean.

The best advice is not to 'prepare to sell', because that is a mindset that might lead to poor short-term decisions; rather, make sure your business is 'ready to sell'. By that, I mean everything is in order, both financially and in terms of structure and management. You will need a clearly defined strategy and evidence of implementing that strategy successfully. This is what a buyer will look for.

Focus on sustainability

Most of us know that a recruitment company sale price is usually calculated via a multiple of historical profit (for the previous 12 months or perhaps an average of the past two or three years). However, what the buyer is *really* buying is the certainty of future profits.

So, your goal is to build a business that can point to its sustainability. That sustainability will include these factors, at the very least:

- *60% to 70% of GP from contract and temporary revenue.* I have this conversation with business owners all the time. The allure of perm seems so compelling that they can't see the risk. Of course, in good times perm revenue is highly profitable, and it seems like a tap that will never run dry… except it will. The most profitable and sustainable businesses will have a 60:40 or 70:30 temp GP: perm GP mix. That's also a business that will be most resilient in a downturn, whereas perm revenue can dry up overnight and stay weak for years to follow. Strong temp business is what saved both Recruitment Solutions and people2people in severe downturns. It's also what made them so profitable in the good times.

- *Several substantial 'foundation' clients* who provide regular, quality, ongoing work, but no single client providing in excess of 10% of GP.

- *Evidence of deep client relationships*, with longevity and multiple contact points, both on the client side and within your own company.

- *Evidence of a diverse client base*, not all exposed to the same risk – this is essential. Niche might be good, but beware being 'over-niched' because that could be considered risky. So, healthy diversification, even if it's within a discipline or industry sector, will be seen as more resilient.

In addition, the business will need a sustainable structure and critical mass. One or two consultants in a division is not sustainable.

A resignation or two and you are no longer in that business. It happens time and time again. The company or division must have multiple revenue earners for it to be considered 'in a market'.

The buyer will look closely at *consultant billing history*, and if they are smart (and increasingly they are), they will examine who actually manages the client relationship, not only who transacts. They will evaluate staff churn and will assess if the business is 'retail' or 'transactional' in nature rather than consultative and based on trust and deep relationships.

Evidence of a brand that is more than the sum total of your consultant networks will be favourably viewed, as will the sophisticated use of marketing technology along with your database.

Margins will be examined, and PSAs (PSLs) will be seen as valuable only if they are really 'preferred' and if they are actually profitable. 'Ego' PSAs, which have been signed because they add revenue, not profit, may decrease your value (because all they have done is add risk, absorb resources, restrict opportunity cost and choke cash flow).

Consultant productivity will be picked over in detail, and the succession plan via a second tier of management will be absolutely critical to the value you create.

Management needs to be proven to have the ability to execute institutionalised activity management with the team. In other words, the ability to extract productivity and develop consistent billers in an almost 'factory-like' manner.

Don't get me wrong, I do not mean running a boot camp, but the buyer will not want to see two or three high performers surrounded by many mediocre contributors. They want to buy a business that can hire, train, develop and keep high-performing consultants.

Performance history will count as well. Consistent revenue and profit growth will give the buyer confidence and add to your appeal.

Remember, if you have been paying yourself a below-market salary, the operating profit will be 'normalised', which means a market salary for you and the other owners will be added into the operating profit calculation before the EBIT multiple is applied.

Process and systems will be considered. Having a documented, adhered-to process in all things will add value. The buyer will be looking for 'systemisation' across the business. They don't want to hear that *"Betty knows how to use the database. We leave it to her,"* or *"Jim is our training guy. He does all that."*

You need documented and proven training processes – and the same for salary and performance reviews. Your ATS and CRM must be modern, up to date and used by everybody. It will synchronise with automated marketing and candidate engagement. Your operating processes will be detailed and documented and practised by everyone. Your financial data will be consistent and accurate. All your contracts must be signed by clients and suppliers, up to date, and every client will have signed your terms of business.

The buyer will want to see a historical budgeting and planning regime. They will also want to see realistic budgets going forward and evidence of the ability to meet them.

The post-sale pain

I will be brutally frank. I think most recruitment acquisitions lead to disappointment for all parties. I have no data to support that, just experience, but if not most, then many.

Mostly, it's down to misalignment between the principal parties. Even the concept of an earn-out is intrinsically flawed. Earn-outs are designed to ensure buyer and seller interests are aligned, but how can they be? The seller is pushing for short-term profits, possibly at the expense of the longer-term health of the business. The buyer wants profits now but is more interested in investing for the future. There is so much pain in that conflict alone.

Cultural mismatch post-sale is common, for vendor and buyer at management level for sure, but often for staff as well who see shifting expectations in activity, performance, dress code, ethics and ethos.

Much pain is felt when systems are integrated or changed. Business can be lost and data compromised.

The change of the seller's brand can almost cause riots but does most certainly lead to loss of business, sagging morale and staff walkouts.

Having said that, a carefully planned exit based on mutual trust, a fair price and an equitable earn-out, with sincerity and transparency on both sides, can lead to excellent outcomes for all parties. When two businesses merge successfully, and one and one make three, it can be a beautiful thing, with cost savings, career opportunities, cross-selling and much more besides.

Certainly, if you are going to work on your recruitment business for 10 or 20 years or more, make sure you build an asset that has a value, which can be realised and will give you choices, fund your next step or, indeed, your retirement. Closing the door on your final day, and walking away with just your memories, might be a very bitter pill to swallow otherwise.

The summing up

TOP OF mind for many companies that I work with is technological change and the future of recruitment. This is true for all companies, regardless of the industry they are in. Playing Nostradamus is dangerous, but it's clear to me that plenty of the HR tech whiz kids who plan to disrupt our industry are way off track.

Mostly, the HR tech guys do not understand where the *value* in recruitment is. Almost always their model is to connect the job seeker to the employer and thereby cut out the middle man (recruiter).

The false premise that this thinking is entirely based on is the belief that it's matching candidate profiles to vacant job descriptions that will crack open the golden recruiting egg. The HR tech boys and girls can get pretty excited about that because, indeed, algorithms can make that match.

Don't get me wrong, technology will change the face of recruitment, and wipe out many 'dinosaur' recruitment agencies that do not adapt and evolve. Indeed, some HR tech businesses are building sophisticated talent communities, and developing predictive analytics to address the real issues our industry faces – most of which I raise in this book.

What we need is technology that improves recruitment by humanising it more, not less. Don't try to 'change' recruitment by dumbing it down even further.

The question needed with every piece of HR tech ever dreamt up is this: *"Does this technology improve the candidate experience, or not?"* That is not a question HR tech types typically even dream of asking, let alone addressing. They are treating talent like an online commodity. It's not. It's people.

I am very confident about our industry. I am investing in recruitment companies and recruitment tech. Our industry is on the cusp of significant change, but it will not die any time soon. And recruiter jobs won't disappear altogether, but the role of the recruiter is under threat, and it will most definitely change because of artificial intelligence (AI) and machine learning.

So recruiters have to consider where they remain of value. What do you need to be good at to beat the machine?

It's critical to understand that you won't beat a computer at what the machine does well. Let the technology take from recruiters what technology does better than humans. This is critical to understand, because it shows us where we must excel.

Right now, there is a great deal that machines can and will do better:

- *Sourcing.* Talent identification will become easier and easier – finding people, I mean. Everyone is online, and most people are more online than ever before. Privacy is disappearing as a concept.

  The search tools these days are becoming more and more powerful, with greater levels of sophistication. Soon, an algorithm will do the job that sourcers thought was such an arcane art. AI will be programmed to find skill-sets across digital databases – and it will do it better than people can.

- *Screening.* Smart technology can easily and quickly assess candidate résumé suitability against the job description and will also parse résumés into a database automatically. There will no longer be a need for human screening at the first contact. This might be a good thing because most recruiters do not read résumés in full. They make gut decisions about résumés, don't review social profiles and certainly do not talk to every candidate. Robots may well do the screening job better. They'll be faster, for sure, but better as well.

- *Logistics* (like arranging interviews and organising reference-checking calls). Fully functioning chatbots already do this, saving the recruiter vast chunks of clerical time.

- *Matching.* Plenty of tools exist already to match databases of candidates against opportunities. They do it faster and in many cases more accurately than recruiters can. This will only continue to become more sophisticated and more accurate.

- *Chatbots.* These will soon be pervasive, and are becoming increasingly sophisticated. You see them online everywhere already. people2people have recently installed Pete the chatbot on their website, which is speeding up the pre-screening process.

  Chatbots can ask predetermined questions to screen out a candidate, answer candidates' questions or update a candidate about where they are in the hiring process.

  Recent research suggests that chatbots are *improving* the candidate experience and generating a higher percentage of candidates who follow through on the application.

So all that leaves the elephant in the room, the huge question that must be addressed.

AI is going to handle sourcing, screening, matching, logistics and even early assessment. If automation is going to do such significant parts of the recruiter's jobs, what is left for recruiters to do?

Will you have a job? Consider the following. This is what I believe.

Any task that takes no time to think about will be automated. Where potential answers can be predicted and predefined an algorithm can be written, and through machine learning a computer will predict outcomes with scary accuracy.

Yet, where it takes thought and planning and opinion, it is much harder for AI to replicate. Where there are shades of grey, nuance and influencing possible, AI is currently useless.

Tasks like screening and matching are the very easiest parts of the recruitment process.

These are the hard parts:

• Identifying candidates who are not looking, but who will fit a hard-to-find skill set.

• Approaching, enticing, seducing and bringing those candidates to the hiring table.

• Managing the hiring process, advising both parties, overcoming obstacles, negotiating terms, finessing the brief, handling the counter-offer, assisting with onboarding.

A brilliant example of what I am saying is what most recruiters call 'sourcing'.

Finding someone can be done by an algorithm. If you key in 'Melbourne, UX designer', a machine will scour LinkedIn, Twitter, Facebook and a thousand other digital storage houses and find those people.

Well actually, no, it won't find people, it will find profiles. And that's the point. Machines can find profiles. People are harder to reach. Approaching that person takes skill and finesse. It's a tailored, sophisticated, bespoke outreach, which takes thought, planning and market knowledge. It's a seduction. It's a sell.

How is AI going to do that?

This is how we must face a future that will soon be hard upon us. AI, and technology generally, frees you up to do much better at that which only you are able to do. The part of recruitment that is left for recruiters to do is the human part.

This is absolutely critical to grasp and act on. You need to be very good at that part of recruitment which machines cannot do, because that is the sweet spot.

Ironically, this means that the real value of a recruiter will now be in their selling skills. That is the part of your job that will be left once the machines march in.

Now, as I've discussed at various points throughout this book, when I use the word 'selling' I need you to understand sales in a different way. I don't mean cold-calling, handing out business cards at an event or spamming candidates around town.

I use 'selling' to mean influencing, persuading, advising, consulting, networking and building reputation and brand.

Yes, it is selling in a much more modern, holistic and consultative way.

This will mean two fundamental truths:

- The recruiter can act as a real strategy *advisor* to clients, credible enough to act as a talent consultant. They will be a sharer of knowledge, an influencer of tactics and creator of outcomes. This will be true of both agency and in-house recruiters.

- Also, the agency recruiter will shift to *acting as an agent* for the best talent, which is a much bigger statement than it first sounds, because it involves trust and exclusivity.

So, be smart about AI and technology. Give away your grunt work; don't hold on to it in a desperate attempt to hold on to your job. That will, ironically, speed up your demise.

Your value is in your knowledge, your advice, your consulting, your networks, your brand, your influencing and your problem-solving skills.

Embrace the technology; automate as much as you can, so you have the time to add value where it counts. That will be your competitive advantage.

Final thoughts

It's pretty clear that as far as my career is concerned, I am closer to the finish line than I am to the start.

It's been an exhilarating ride. Hard work always, dark days occasionally, but overwhelmingly fun and rewarding. I have met the greatest of people, learned every day, had the most amazing experiences and seen the world.

I am so grateful to my parents for ensuring I had an education that put me closer to the front of the line than the back. That was good fortune.

I am grateful to those who gave me opportunities in the early days.

Thank you to my business partners, who trusted me, and who helped me start great businesses.

My sincere thanks to all those recruiters who worked with me over many years, and to my leadership cohort, too many to mention, who have burned the midnight oil with me in the pursuit of excellence and success, shared so many achievements and some failure, and in so many cases shown loyalty and friendship that has lasted decades.

Thanks to the many industry colleagues I have met, learned from and laughed with. Many of my 'competitors' are now good friends.

To my consulting clients, the companies whose boards I advise, and the thousands and thousands of people who have attended my presentations and masterclasses all over the world, I am so grateful for your faith in me.

Thanks to the RCSA in Australia, the REC in the UK, and staffing associations and conference organisers around the world who have helped me bring my ideas to recruiters in so many places.

Thank you also to my sizeable online following, who inspire me to keep producing content and sharing ideas.

And, of course, thank you to my wife who has kept the home fires burning, supported my many ventures, tolerated my drama and provided the voice of reason over so many years.

The recruitment industry is much maligned and often written off. For me, it's been my life. And, by any measure, it's been a good life.

My overwhelming emotion as I near the end of my career is simply… gratitude.

Afterword

BETWEEN 1991 and 1998 I sat less than ten metres from Greg's office at Recruitment Solutions. For almost all that time, Greg was either my direct, or indirect, boss. I observed and experienced first-hand Greg's leadership as he describes it in this book.

Greg demanded a lot but invested more; he invested plenty in people who delivered what they were accountable for, who wanted to be better and were willing to do the hard work to get there. Greg then inspired, cajoled and extracted an even higher level of performance from me and like-minded others. Often, it was a level of performance I didn't know I was capable of.

Greg's impact on my life has, and continues to be, significant and long-lasting. Greg's impact on the life of the whole Australian recruitment industry has also been significant and long-lasting.

In September 2015, when I conducted a survey to discover the most influential people in the history of the Australian recruitment industry, I asked each voter to consider whether the nominee meets the following criteria:

1. **Built business(es):** Either as an owner or as an employee (or both), has built one (or more) successful recruitment business.

2. **Built people:** Significantly contributed to the development of other leaders within the recruitment industry.

3. **Built the industry:** Significantly contributed to the development of the Australian recruitment industry as a substantial and credible sector in its own right.

4. **Built the future:** Been responsible for innovation within the Australian recruitment industry.

Greg was voted equal first, along with Geoff Morgan and Andrew Banks, and V. John Plummer.

This book contains some, but not all, of the evidence for why Greg's peers ranked him at the very pinnacle of recruitment industry leaders. There are many things Greg has done, and keeps doing, that don't make headlines or are even known to people other than those directly involved.

Recently, a fledging Melbourne recruitment agency owner in his mid-twenties enquired about the possibility of Greg coaching or mentoring him. As he doesn't provide this type service, Greg referred the owner elsewhere. The owner thanked Greg for his prompt response and asked Greg whether he might be available for a coffee when he was next in town. Although it would have been perfectly reasonable for Greg to either decline or make a vague promise about the possibility of a future meeting, that's not what happened. During a subsequent trip to Melbourne, Greg made time to meet the ambitious owner and freely shared his wisdom for the price of a cup of coffee.

It's gestures like this that say just as much about Greg's character and his commitment to our industry and the individuals within it, as anything Greg has shared in this book.

As one of the instigators of this book, I am very happy that my high expectations of the finished product have been exceeded. I'm even happier that Greg's legacy and wisdom has been captured at this moment in time.

I'm confident that when recruiters read *The Savage Truth's* 30th anniversary edition, in 2049, they will see that that the drivers of success in agency recruitment, whether as a recruiter, leader or owner, have changed little from those that have underpinned Greg's lifetime of accomplishment in the global recruitment industry, as documented in this book.

Ross Clennett
Melbourne
August 2019

Acknowledgements

A 40-YEAR career breeds plenty of debts.

Thank you to all my colleagues, co-workers, clients, candidates, competitors and collaborators, as well as the vast global community of recruiters who have attended my events or engaged with me on social. You are all part of the rich tapestry that has made up a fabulous, fun-filled four decades.

I was reluctant to write this book. *"Who would care?"*, I mused. *"Too much work!"*, I surmised.

Lesley Williams of Major Street Publishing was a tireless seducer, brushing away my initial protestations and coaxing me to start the book, providing precious advice, then helping me turn it into something I am proud of.

Ross Clennett harassed me for years to write 'my story', even telling me I had an obligation to the industry to write the book because my career *"covered so much of the history of recruitment"*. He provided many anecdotes and reminders of the Recruitment Solutions era, and collected many more from the Savage alumni, many of which are included in the final text.

Lesley Horsburgh, too proposed the book on several occasions, gave excellent advice, transcribed many of the chapters and helped me believe it was a project worth finishing.

I thank you all for the faith and assistance you have given. Without you, there would be no *Savage Truth* book.

I met my wife, Bronwyn, at a recruitment company, so I guess the industry gave me even more than I have acknowledged in the book.

To Bronwyn, thank you for your unstinting support and encouragement, as well as your patience with my moods, rants, risk-taking, regular absence and long hours. You made our house a loving home and kept our family on the path we set, and I am forever grateful.

Index

value 195
Victoria 116-118, 127, 219

Wall Street 51
wasted emotion 152-153
Waxman, Dennis 28

Western Australia 118
Westin Hotel 253
Whelan, Graham 39-40, 49,
51, 68, 73, 144, 149-151,
154, 222